Beyond Just War

Also by David K. Chan

MORAL PSYCHOLOGY TODAY
Essays on Values, Rational Choice and the Will (*editor*)

Beyond Just War
A Virtue Ethics Approach

David K. Chan
University of Wisconsin – Stevens Point, USA

With a Foreword by
Claudia Card

First published 2012 by
PALGRAVE MACMILLAN

Palgrave Macmillan in the UK is an imprint of Macmillan Publishers Limited,
registered in England, company number 785998, of Houndmills, Basingstoke,
Hampshire RG21 6XS.

Palgrave Macmillan in the US is a division of St Martin's Press LLC,
175 Fifth Avenue, New York, NY 10010.

Palgrave Macmillan is the global academic imprint of the above companies
and has companies and representatives throughout the world.

Palgrave® and Macmillan® are registered trademarks in the United States,
the United Kingdom, Europe and other countries.

ISBN: 978–1–137–26340–7

This book is printed on paper suitable for recycling and made from fully
managed and sustained forest sources. Logging, pulping and manufacturing
processes are expected to conform to the environmental regulations of the
country of origin.

A catalogue record for this book is available from the British Library.

A catalog record for this book is available from the Library of Congress.

10 9 8 7 6 5 4 3 2 1
21 20 19 18 17 16 15 14 13 12

In Memory of
The Daughter of a Soldier,
The Mother of a Philosopher
(1926–2011)

Contents

Foreword

Torture is an expedient and an evil. The much-discussed ticking-bomb scenario presents torturing a suspect as better than the alternatives for dealing under the stresses of time constraints with a powerful and dangerous enemy. But ticking-bomb torture is itself a dangerous idea. Those who are willing to entertain that idea should ask, eventually, the critical question: is a nation, or a regime, that can be defended only at the cost of torturing its enemies (or torturing those who might have critical information about its enemies) worth the defense? What kind of nation, or regime, would be saved by such means?

Likewise, war can be an expedient. David K. Chan notes that the horrors of war multiply most of those of torture and that these horrors are predictably visited largely on noncombatants who are defenseless and not dangerous. And so he asks and pursues the same kind of critical questions about war: is a nation, or a regime, that can only be defended at the cost of war against those perceived to be its enemies worth that morally costly defense? He concludes that most of the wars we know of that have been fought throughout history have not been worth their moral costs.

War is an evil. The ethical subject of this book, war, is a social institution. Chan's arguments are addressed to leaders and to all of those who might elect them, follow them, or influence them. His focus, then, is not individuals who may have to make decisions about whether to enlist or how to respond to a draft once the decision has been made that there will be a war. Rather, it is the ethics of decision-making of leaders regarding such matters as whether to make war, how to conduct it, when to end it. Like other social institutions, war is governed by principles that have evolved through centuries. Many are the product of international treaties and conventions, collectively known as International Humanitarian Law (IHL). And yet, it is reasonably foreseeable that even wars conducted in accord with the relevant provisions of IHL will produce massive intolerable harms to persons who are defenseless and not dangerous.

To take very seriously that war is an evil is to reject the idea that war can be just if only the right rules are observed. This book takes very seriously that war is an evil. Accordingly, it rejects the project of just war theory. That project has been to articulate a set of principles specifying the conditions under which justice can be preserved despite massive violations of the biblical injunction against killing. Chan argues that there is no way to preserve justice in war. In lieu of either just war theory or pacifism, he offers a new paradigm for thinking about the ethics of war.

The problem with the old paradigms is not simply that of complications introduced by the "new wars." Mary Kaldor calls "new wars" forms of combat that have become common since the Cold War and that blur distinctions between war as previously understood and such things as organized crime and large-scale violations of human rights (*New and Old Wars*, 1999). In the new wars, it is often not clear who is a combatant, and weaponry has so evolved that it is no longer clear how to apply the principle of discrimination that proscribes direct targeting of noncombatants. These issues do suggest a need for new paradigms. But in the present volume, Chan argues that neither just war theory nor pacifism provided a good ethics even for the *old* wars for which their norms were intended.

The new paradigm presented here for the ethics of war is the philosophy of co-existence that stands intermediate between just war theory and pacifism. That war is an evil does not imply that co-existence is always a better option. As we know today from the experience of the Second World War, co-existence is not always even a possible option. Some evils, such as genocide, are enough worse than the reasonably predictable evils of war that a virtuous person might choose to go to war to prevent, halt, or contain those worse evils. Choosing rightly is not always choosing what is *just*. Right choice need not always require preserving justice. What is rightly chosen in the real world depends on available alternatives, which do not always include options that preserve justice. Yet, when justice is not realizable at a given time and place, it may still be possible to contain and alleviate injustice and to move toward a future in which relationships of justice do become possible.

War can be rightly chosen when its alternatives are even worse. Even when it is rightly chosen, there is much to regret. Instead of thinking of the choice to go to war as constrained by principles that define conditions under which war is just, we do better to think of the choice to go to war as a choice to try to contain evils, prevent some of the worst ones, and try to pave the way for post-conflict relations in which real justice might become possible. While eschewing John Rawls's use of the language of "just war" and his preference for principles, Chan's virtue ethics approach comes close to the spirit of Rawls's vision of how a

Society of Peoples should think and feel about justice in the context of war (*The Law of Peoples*, 1999).

Special highlights of Professor Chan's book include its historical review of just war theory, its arguments by analogy with how humans have learned to co-exist with predatory animals and with how societies have learned to co-exist with criminal elements in their midst, and its discussions of the difficult, timely, and controversial issues of humanitarian intervention, terrorism, and weapons of mass destruction.

Were today's leaders, globally, to take seriously the questions and the arguments of this book, the world might make significant progress toward bringing about a "realistic utopia," to borrow Rawls's term, in which war becomes obsolete, or nearly so.

Claudia Card
Emma Goldman Professor of Philosophy
Madison, Wisconsin

Preface and Acknowledgments

It will not surprise readers that the origins of this book can be traced back to September 11, 2001, the day of the Al-Qaeda terrorist attacks carried out against targets in the United States. I did not, however, start writing this book until the autumn of 2008 when I began a sabbatical. Not that the events of 9/11 did not have an immediate effect on how I pursued my academic pursuits. Just three weeks before the attacks, I had arrived in the United States from Singapore to take up a position at the University of Wisconsin at Stevens Point. Having lived for five years in the Bay Area in California when I was a graduate student, I had grown to love the ideals and character of the American nation. Now after 9/11, I could see the country changing in ways that dismayed me.

My philosophical interests are in moral psychology and virtue ethics. I plan eventually to finish a book on virtue ethics and I had assumed that the application of virtue ethics to applied ethics was something I would do only after I completed working out my account of virtue ethics. This is where 9/11 changed things for me. As the United States went to war in Afghanistan and Iraq, I began to be dissatisfied with how philosophers approached the ethics of war. I did not feel I should withhold writing on the ethics of war until I had done a book on ethical theory. As the years passed, I became more involved in various forums on the ethics of war that led me to formulate the ideas needed to approach the subject from a virtue ethics approach. Recognizing the urgency and importance of contributing to debates on the wars that America was fighting, I started writing this book.

The first person to thank for getting me to work on the ethics of war is Andy Fiala, who invited me to contribute to public discussions at Green Bay, Wisconsin, on the anniversaries of 9/11. This eventually led to my first paper on the subject published in the journal of the *Society for Philosophy in the Contemporary World*, which Andy edited. The annual meetings of the society also provided me with a circle of like-minded thinkers with whom I could sound out ideas. I also engaged in discussions with speakers that I invited to group sessions on the ethics of killing in war that were held at the APA Central Division Meetings between 2008 and 2010. Andy also read the complete draft of this book and provided me with many comments and suggestions to which, in making my revisions to the earlier version of this book, I probably have not done full justice due to my haste to get the book out.

Another philosopher who had a no less important role in the genesis of this book is Claudia Card, whom I first met at the Institute for Research in the Humanities at University of Wisconsin – Madison. During a Research Fellowship at the institute, I sat in on Claudia's graduate seminar on evil, which included much discussion of war. I have since engaged in many conversations with Claudia and her work on evil has obviously influenced my thinking. Claudia also commented on chapters as they were written and read the entire manuscript. I am grateful as well to the Institute in Madison for giving me an Honorary Fellowship during my sabbatical in 2008–9, which enabled me to make use of the Memorial Library at the Madison campus.

I would also like to acknowledge Dr Jude Chua of the Peace Studies Committee at the United Nations Association of Singapore for the two invitations to give talks as a Visiting Scholar, and Paul Woodruff and Joseph Orosco who, along with Claudia and Andy, wrote letters in support of grant applications. Here in Stevens Point, Wisconsin, my colleagues at the university have been very supportive of my scholarly work, enabling me to take my sabbatical and to set aside time between teaching to work on my book and go to conferences. My students in ethics of war classes have shared in the process of reviewing and exploring much of the standard philosophical literature on war. Most importantly of all, my wife Agnes and son Lucas have made sacrifices to provide me with time, space, and a conducive environment to do a lot of my writing at home.

Many parts of this book were first written in versions that I presented as conference papers. Two papers are due to appear in 2012 with material that overlap with this book. "The Ethics of War and Law Enforcement in Defending against Terrorism" in *Social Philosophy Today* contains material used in a section of Chapter 7. "Just War, Noncombatant Immunity, and the Concept of Supreme Emergency" in *Journal of Military Ethics* contains material used in Chapter 8.

Finally, I must thank Priyanka Gibbons and the editorial staff of Palgrave Macmillan. Many publishers have books on the ethics of war on their backlists, but Priyanka appreciated the originality of my approach. She and Palgrave have also facilitated the speedy publication of this book, which fulfills my desire to contribute to the urgent need for new ideas to rethink what America and other countries are doing in using military force. From hereon, if this book is going to make some difference to what leaders think and do about war, it is now in the hands of you, the reader!

Introduction: The State of Ethics of War

There has been a resurgence of interest in the ethics of war at the beginning of the twenty-first century. The obvious reason for this is that the September 11, 2001, Al-Qaeda terrorist attacks on the World Trade Center in New York City and the Pentagon Building in Washington, D.C., were followed by the declaration of a "Global War on Terror (GWOT)" by the United States administration of President George W. Bush. The GWOT began with the overthrow of the Taliban regime in Afghanistan where Al-Qaeda was based. Under the Bush Doctrine that was officially formulated in 2002,[1] the United States invaded Iraq, a country halfway around the globe that had not attacked America. In neither case were the leaders of the countries attacked directly responsible for the terrorist acts carried out by a non-state terrorist organization led by Osama bin Laden and based in the remote mountains on the Afghan border with Pakistan. Critics of the GWOT have argued that the distraction of the Iraq occupation, and the resentment among Muslims who saw the war as an attack on Islam, had reinforced bin Laden's claim to legitimacy as a defender of the Muslim world against Western aggression and afforded him time to regroup and plan further attacks on Western targets.[2]

What have philosophers contributed in their writings in response to the cataclysmic events of war and terrorism in the early twenty-first century? Like thinkers about war in the course of Western civilization, most of their books and articles have drawn on the long tradition of "just war theory." One debate that philosophers contributed to was that of whether the just war doctrine could be rightly used to justify wars such as the American invasion of Iraq in 2003 to depose Saddam Hussein from power. For those who concluded that the invasion did not satisfy the requirements for just war, but who nevertheless thought that it was necessary for the United States to fight terrorism, the question

1

was whether there was a need to revise the just war doctrine, or whether different rules were needed in recognition of how wars against non-state terrorist groups were not the conventional wars that traditional just war thinkers had in mind. Thus, they had to decide whether to broaden and reinterpret the just war doctrine to apply to the "new wars" or to devise another set of rules for wars that fall outside the scope of the traditional doctrine.[3]

For other thinkers, failure to satisfy the traditional requirements for just war meant that the U.S. invasion of Iraq was morally illegitimate. Those who believed this belong to one of two groups. The first group consists of those who think that the U.S. invasion was unlike other wars in being *unjustified*. There are just wars, such as the first Gulf War that took place in 1991 after Iraq under Saddam Hussein invaded Kuwait, but not this one. The second group consists of pacifists who think that no actual war in the past, present, or future (given the nature of states, armies, and armaments) could satisfy the requirements of just war theory. In this view, unlike the first view, the invasion of Iraq was not a special case, but was typical of all wars. The only way to satisfy the requirements of just war is not to go to war.

Remarkably, none of the positions listed above involves the rejection of just war theory. The just war theory either applies to all wars, or wars until recent times. It may be satisfied by most wars, some wars, or no wars. If just war theory seems unsatisfactory because it faces philosophical or practical challenges, then the response is to revise the theory to overcome the difficulties. There can be debate about how much change can be made to the doctrine. Traditionalists would insist that the early versions devised by Augustine and his contemporaries should be preserved.[4] Revisionists, of whom there are many, are those who try to develop versions that have more universalistic (in particular, secular) appeal, and more general application. Nevertheless, the doctrine continues to stand as the most durable paradigm in history for the moral evaluation of war.

No one person can settle the question of when it is time for a paradigm shift. Nor can any one person bring into effect a changeover to a new paradigm. But despite the fact that there continues to be a lot of new writing about the ethics of war within the just war tradition, there are some signs of unhappiness with the current state of philosophical reflection on war. First, there are those pacifists who do not wish to rest their objections to war solely or mainly on the (disputed) empirical claim that no actual or possible war satisfies the conditions for just war. The danger is not just that they cannot rule out a future war in which the conditions are satisfied, but also that accepting the idea that war can be just by satisfying a set of conditions contributes to the persistence of an illusion that some wars are just, even when they are not. The just war doctrine lends itself to myth-making about war and makes it possible for politicians to disguise and sell their unjustified wars as just wars.[5] If one thinks that wars are by their very nature morally wrong, then why rest one's case on a theory of how wars could be justified?

Second, there are two statements in recent publications that question the fruitfulness of continuing to debate the morality of war in just war terms. In 2003, an editorial in the British journal *Philosophy* lamented the lack of fresh philosophical perspectives on the issue of the Iraq war, beyond the standard rehashing of a just war doctrine "developed in the context of wars fought with medieval weapons and by comparatively small professional armies."[6] In addition, it has been noted that philosophers working in the just war tradition have often deprived themselves of opportunities to meaningfully contribute to public debate and to influence the course of human history with their ideas. In his acclaimed book, *Humanity*, which documents the many terrible events especially in wartime that took place during the twentieth century, Jonathan Glover describes a "general failure of philosophy ... to make a serious impact on the thinking of the wider community," and complains of philosophers who "bear some responsibility for a climate conducive to the evasive thought which contributed to Hiroshima."[7] It seems to me that to continue to debate wars in the twenty-first century along the same lines as in previous centuries would tend to leave philosophers trapped as before in impotency instead of harnessing the power of philosophical ideas to make the world better.

As a moral philosopher, I am motivated to respond to the GWOT and the many horrors of other wars in human history, as well as to the complaints against philosophy summarized in the previous paragraph, by contributing towards a paradigm shift in thinking about the ethics of war. In other words, I do not see the just war theory, in the various forms that it has taken, as worth salvaging (although I shall still be obliged to take it seriously as a rival theory). However, it does not seem to me that outlawing war or declaring all wars to be immoral, as many pacifists who have abandoned just war theory may espouse, would be helpful as a contribution to philosophical discourse about war, given that pacifists are then left vulnerable to being portrayed as naïve idealists who fail to understand the complexities of dealing with real and dire threats to the existence and security of human societies. The age-old question with which the just war doctrine has been grappling is that of when, if ever, can civilized human beings legitimately use organized (and state-sanctioned) military force against other humans to achieve political objectives. I shall try to show that the just war doctrine throughout its two thousand years of development has made it too easy to say "yes" to going to war and to killing in war. But to say "no" to the use of military force in every case amounts to the failure to appreciate the exceptionally grave and dangerous evil of certain threats, such as that posed by the Nazis in the 1930s. Moral illegitimacy comes not because a leader chose to go to war against such enemies as Hitler's Germany, but in thinking that we are often in a comparable position in going to war against some other adversary or in thinking that there are few limits to what we do in wars against Hitler-like enemies.

Rejecting the tradition of just war theory is a negative exercise that I will carry out in the early chapters of this book. But the default alternative for moralists is not necessarily pacifism. Presenting another alternative approach to the ethics of war is the positive (and longer) part of the book. The reader is asked to choose between the just war paradigm and the one that I shall propose to take its place. I do not presume to think that I will be providing "knock-down" arguments against the just war theory here that those who work in the tradition cannot somehow find a response to. But there is something I can say right now about why I am convinced that a shift in paradigm or a revolution in thinking about the ethics of war is needed (and long overdue).

In my view, the just war theory has taken on the characteristics of Ptolemaic cosmology prior to the Copernican revolution. The earlier view of the cosmos as consisting of sun, planets and stars orbiting around the earth at its center was once a well-established theory among astronomers. As more careful and precise observations of the positions of heavenly bodies showed inconsistencies with the Ptolemaic model, epicycles were introduced into the orbits to make the theory fit the data. With great ingenuity, any observation could be accommodated by the Ptolemaic system. However, the need to add epicycles made the system unwieldy, and when Copernicus proposed an alternative model that placed the earth and other planets in orbit around the sun, the Ptolemaic model became much less convincing. As I will explain later, the just war theory has undergone a number of changes throughout its long history, with additions to the requirements of just war that I take to be analogical to the addition of epicycles. Faced with changes in how wars were fought, how states and armies were organized, and how philosophers thought about ethics and the role of religion, the theory had to be adjusted to avoid serious conflicts with changing moral perceptions about what could or ought to be done in war.[8] There is no a priori reason why the theory could not be refined further when it is challenged again, and this is what just war theorists have been doing in their recent writings about the GWOT and the American invasion of Iraq. As long as there is no competing moral theory of war, there is not enough pressure to change the paradigm. As I said, those pacifists who disallow all wars do not present a compelling and realistic moral alternative to just war theory. Hence, the challenge of finding and presenting such an alternative, which is the challenge I take up in this book.

The GWOT presents problems for just war theory on many fronts, such as how to account for the need for states to take preemptive or preventive action and for the need to strike at an enemy that is difficult to identify and to locate. One of the ways proposed by just war theorists to deal with situations where it is necessary to disregard rules of just war is to make room for exceptions. War should be a last resort, except where waiting for the enemy to strike first or attempting to negotiate leaves one's nation far too vulnerable and at risk of catastrophic defeat. Troops should not target civilians, except when the costs of not targeting them is too high for one's side, bearing in mind what military defeat or a longer war would entail. A recent version of just war theory provides for a supreme emergency exemption to the rules of *jus in bello* (justice in the conduct of war).[9] So perhaps the just war theory should allow for preventive war and for attacks on enemy civilians when enemy soldiers wear civilian clothing and hide in crowded urban centers. But there is a different lesson we can draw. The fact that just war theory has difficulties with the GWOT should make us notice that there have been many other difficulties in the past history of the doctrine that have been dealt with by using "epicycles." Instead of adding another epicycle or two, we should now ask whether the just war theory has become an unwieldy patchwork system, the moral authority of which has diminished over the years as it adapted again and again to changing times and in response to new challenges.

Another question about paradigm change that is relevant here is whether the problem that is dealt with by adjusting a theory is a peripheral issue or one that touches the core of the theory. Comparable experience with paradigm shifts in other areas shows that it is difficult to answer this question in a definitive way. When observations predicted by Newton's Laws of Motion were slightly off the mark at very high speeds (approaching the speed of light) or at sub-atomic levels, did they constitute a fundamental challenge to Newtonian physics? As long as we are interested in everyday objects traveling at perceptible speeds, these experimental observations seem to be of peripheral interest. But from the perspective of physicists and astronomers, what happens to sub-atomic particles and to objects across the universe is more fundamental, and laws that apply only to things at the surface of the earth are of little consequence in the larger scheme of physics. The recognition that the problems impact the heart of Newtonian science set the stage for the transition to the new paradigm provided by Einstein's physics.

Do those adjustments to just war theory that are needed to adapt it to a policy of nuclear deterrence or to fight the GWOT have only peripheral importance? It seems to me that a change in the rule against killing civilians and other changes that enable states to go to war long before there is any threat of aggression and to threaten to annihilate the people on the enemy's side indiscriminately using nuclear weapons cannot be considered to be adjustments at the fringe of the theory. It is after all the business of ethicists to be concerned with right and wrong actions, and there can be no ethical issue more important than the killing of innocent people. The main moral problem in war has always been that war involves deliberate killing on a large scale. Too much willingness to make exceptions or to broaden the causes that justify war reflects a failure by philosophers to take the central ethical questions about war seriously enough. Thus, the repeated need to change the theory to, for instance, allow for the killing of innocent people does reflect a fundamental challenge to just war theory that strikes at its core.

Such problems for the just war theory set the stage for a new ethics of war that will be presented, explained and applied in this book. I begin in Chapter 1 with the main accounts of just war that have been proposed by past moral theologians and philosophers in the tradition of just war theory. My discussion will show how theories in the tradition have not remained the same and clarify how we arrived at the modern formulations of the theory as they are reflected in international law. In Chapter 2, I discuss what I think is seriously wrong with theories in the just war tradition. I do this by focusing on the central principles of just war theory that are found in almost every version. In my view, there is something theoretically untenable about the concept of just war and the idea that war and the killings in war can somehow be justified by satisfying a set of conditions. Chapter 3 begins the path that leads to a new ethics of war. I explain what is involved in making the shift from a rights-based ethics to the approach taken by virtue ethics. In Chapter 4, I discuss the nature of war and how war is one of the worst intrinsic evils in the experience of humankind. This chapter draws attention to facts about war that are not taken seriously enough by just war theorists.

But the evil nature of war also poses a challenge to the new ethics of war, the philosophy of co-existence, which I will present in Chapter 5. My new ethics of war is located in between just war theory that I consider too permissive and pacifism that rules out all wars, even when the threat is posed by a Hitler-like enemy. I, therefore, must show that there are ways to co-exist with enemies that threaten us without going to war against them, but also that there are some enemies such as the Nazis who are so evil that a virtuous leader who chooses to go to war against them is making the correct moral choice despite the evil nature of war itself. In Chapter 6, I consider and respond to a number of theoretical challenges to the philosophy of co-existence. In Chapter 7, I examine the practical implications of the philosophy of co-existence for current issues in the ethics of war, namely those of humanitarian intervention, the war against terrorism, the problems posed by the spread of weapons of mass destruction, the Bush Doctrine of preventive war, and the killing of Osama bin Laden in a military raid across borders. In the context of this book, this chapter is particularly important in showing how the philosophy of co-existence can be applied to provide useful practical recommendations on urgent and important policy matters that are quite different from the proposals of just war theorists. Finally, in Chapter 8, I conclude my book by making use of the just war theory's concept of supreme emergency to explain the differences between just war theory, pacifism, and the philosophy of co-existence.

1

The Moral Problem of War

Anyone who has read anything about the ethics of war will have come across references to and discussion of just war theory.[1] This is a long tradition of religious, philosophical, and legal thinking that began in the ancient Western world concerning the justification(s) for the use of force by a state or leader against another state or leader. It has become convenient for ethicists, jurists, and political leaders today to simply appeal to the tenets of the just war doctrine as the basis for either justifying or criticizing particular wars. The language of just war was evoked at the beginning of the twenty-first century in the debate about the doctrine of preventive war that was the basis for the American invasion of Iraq in 2003. It is fair to say that many of those who appeal to or reject the principles of just war do not fully appreciate the historical evolution of the just war doctrine and the many divergent viewpoints that have been included in the tradition. It is the purpose of this chapter to flesh out the important details of just war theory as succinctly as possible and to track the differences between the main versions of the theory, before I embark on a critique of the theory in the next chapter. For even someone who wants to bring a fresh approach to the ethics of war cannot ignore what has been written by just war theorists who have been so influential in the course of the last two millennia.

In the beginning

As can be discerned from any history book, war has been an enduring part of human history. It is impossible to document life in earlier times without mentioning the wars that had taken place and how the lives of people had been affected by war. To have an ethics of war is to have thinkers who recognize that, however natural or frequent war seems to be, there is a moral problem about killing people and causing suffering on a large scale in a deliberate manner. For unlike natural disasters, the harms that result from war are due to human choices. Almost every society has prohibitions against murder, although they differ about the exceptions to the prohibition under which intentional killing may be permissible. What is it about war that would make killing in war count as an exception to such a widely shared prohibition?

It is interesting that philosophers living at the height of Roman military power laid out the precursors to just war theory. Roman Stoics inherited from ancient Greek philosophy the idea of a common humanity and the importance of controlling passions with reason. In Stoic thinking, it is not enough to justify war that the Romans had the ability to wage war and triumph over their enemies, and that going to war was politically expedient and brought glory to military and political leaders. Cicero, the Roman orator and statesman, wrote that force should be resorted to only in cases where discussion is not possible.[2] Before a formal declaration of war can be legitimately made, there must be a grievance against the other side, which one has attempted to address without success by submitting a demand for satisfaction. In going to war, the goal is to live in peace unharmed. Thus, it is sufficient to end the war when the offender has been brought to repent of his wrongdoing and to make reparation.[3] In the course of fighting, Cicero observed that duties are owed even to those who have wronged one's side. Those who have not acted in a bloodthirsty and barbaric way should be spared, and consideration (including citizenship) should be given to the conquered people. Moreover, Cicero frowned on the use of guile and treachery to win a war.

We see here in Cicero's writings a distinction between justice in going to war (*jus ad bellum*) and justice in the conduct of war (*jus in bello*) that has ever since been a standard distinction in writings on just war. This is a natural distinction to make, since the decision to start a war is made by the political leader, but the actions undertaken in the course of fighting are mainly determined by soldiers on the battlefield, including their military commanders. The Roman state and economy were highly militarized and success in battle was the key to high office for young aristocrats. War booty, new territories, and the supply of slaves were the pillars of the Roman economy. So Romans had plenty to gain from engaging in war. But Cicero and his fellow Roman Stoic, Seneca, suggested that there had to be a just cause for war and the only legitimate reasons were when the state had been attacked or had suffered a serious offense from outsiders, or when the state had pledged to aid its allies. Their recognition of the humanity of Rome's enemies and rivals led them to call for voluntary restraint by the state in its use of force. Seneca, who was tutor to the Emperor Nero, further appealed to the importance of the virtue of mercy in terms of both its calming influence on one's soul as well as the political expediency of winning over one's enemy.[4]

The Romans believed that their military success was a reflection of the justice of their campaigns, and that their empire was a reward for their civilized way of fighting.[5] In fact, their success was more a matter of their military prowess and discipline, and their military leaders paid mere lip service to the rules of war. In particular, Julius Caesar engaged in aggression and expansionism in the name of self-defense.[6] It is no surprise that the guise of civility and morality came off once the Roman Empire began to teeter. Moreover, the increasing use of mercenaries in Roman armies meant that the fighting was done by soldiers who did not share in the belief in Rome's moral superiority. But as Roman power receded, the ideas of just war came to be incorporated and developed by another institution that would outlast the Romans: the Christian Church.

Christianity and just war

The relationship between the Church and just war theory was a complicated one to begin with. The early Church tended to be pacifist, in following Christ's teaching in the Gospels to turn the other cheek and his rebuke of Peter at the time of Christ's arrest: "Those who live by the sword shall perish by the sword." The early Christians encountered soldiers in the form of violent persecution by Roman authorities. As conversion spread beyond Jews, and Roman converts included soldiers, a dilemma presented itself to leaders of the Church: Can a Christian remain a Roman soldier? One of the Church Fathers, Tertullian, wrote *The Soldier's Chaplet* around AD 210, in which he asked, "Will a Christian, taught to turn the other cheek when struck unjustly, guard prisoners in chains, and administer torture and capital punishment?" Moreover, soldiers had to submit to the Emperor's authority and take vows before Roman gods, violating the Christian commandment to place no other before the Christian God.

When the Roman Empire was Christianized after the accession of Constantine to the throne of Emperor in AD 324, pacifism had already for some time been giving way to a more permissive view of Christians in military service. Since around AD 170, many references to Christian soldiers had been documented.[7] Some Christian writers sanctioned military service that served police functions. Clearly, upholding the *Pax Romana* against brigands served the interest of peace in the empire and the protection of Christians in their missionary work. Rome and Christianity were beginning to merge in opposition to the barbarian and the pagan. Thus, the end of the pacifist period in the early Church did not take place overnight but at the culmination of a long process in which Christianity slowly entered into the mainstream of Roman life. It then had to adopt some of the roles of the state, in particular the defense of civilization and of the conditions under which the religion could flourish. Ironically, this took place at a time when the Roman Empire was facing growing threats from outside and declining from within. The Church had to develop an ethics of war not only to provide a theological basis for Christian soldiering but also to defend itself against charges of weakening Rome, leveled by pagans who blamed Christian pacifism for the defeats by barbarians.

The formulation of the Christian view of just war began with St. Ambrose, who provided a sketch that was fleshed out by St. Augustine. Ambrose drew examples from the Old Testament to make the case for Christians serving in the military. The only people who should avoid such service were monks and priests. Augustine followed Ambrose in using the Old Testament to establish that killing ordered by God was not murder. He made distinctions between the outward act and the inward disposition, and between private actions and those carried out on public authority. In his view, any hostile act could be justified if it was motivated by charity or love.[8] This meant that a private person could not be permitted to use violence or kill in self-defense, as his motivation would be fear or hatred, whereas public officials acting from duty would be justified in killings that were done without hatred or other sinful passions. In addition, Augustine saw rulers as representing the authority of God, which meant that orders to kill should be obeyed and could be obeyed without bearing the guilt of murder.

Augustine's code of war was similar to Cicero's in making the restoration of peace the object of war. However, his view of just cause was colored by Christian theological assumptions. There need not be an injury inflicted or an attack by another party. Given that the earthly city is corrupt, perfect peace is attainable only in the heavenly city. Thus, Augustine justified war for the purpose both of punishing sin and of vindicating justice. Not only can the killing of sinners be compatible with Christian charity, but it may well be required or expected by God. For one shows less love for an enemy if one allows the enemy to live in sin without punishment. There is, thus, no distinction between defensive and offensive war in Augustine's just war theory. "The peace of the unjust, compared to the peace of the just, is not worthy even of the name of peace."[9] Any violation of Christian doctrine can be considered an injustice that warrants unlimited violent punishment.

Augustine's view of just conduct in war was similarly permissive. As long as the actions are done with the right inner disposition, coercive activities by public officials of the state are permissible. As examples, Augustine mentioned torture employed by a judge to determine guilt, and religious persecution carried out to expunge the evil of heretics. Thus, in a war fought to punish a sinful city, the only limits to acts of war are that they be sanctioned by proper authority and carried out without hatred. As long as a Christian killed without rancor and on public authority, he did not violate the law of charity but obeyed it in wreaking retributive justice, itself an aspect of charity.[10]

The innovations in Augustine's just war theory turned the earlier versions of the theory on its head. Cicero writing at the height of Roman power saw morality as setting restraints on what the armies of Rome should do. Some uses of that power are disallowed even if there were material benefits to be gained and success was attainable. In contrast, Augustine writing at a time of the empire in decline, in response to the pacifist tendencies of the Church, sought to justify the use of armed force in a way that could be reconciled with Christian doctrine. There was also a difference between them due to the theological underpinnings of Augustine's thinking. In Christianity, there is a God who could sanction killing as punishment for sin. This absolved Christians who fought in wars with proper sovereign authority and with the right intention of charity not hatred. This also required Christians to act against enemies for their sins, even when these enemies have not attacked them. Christians would be at fault for breaching a perfect peace, but there was only an unjust peace in the co-existence between Rome and the barbarians and pagans across the border.

The transition in just war thinking that began with Augustine would have far-reaching effects on medieval thinkers all the way to Aquinas. The eight centuries between these two thinkers saw changes in just war theory due to events in history that affected the position of the Church and the kinds of war that occurred. The fall of the Roman Empire at the hands of barbarian invaders meant that the Church became the unifying force and custodian of civilization in Europe. One problem for just war theory was the absence of a single sovereign authority that could provide the legitimacy for going to war that had previously been conferred by God through the Roman Emperor. Instead, the former empire was now divided into many small barbarian kingdoms and tribes. Many of these were ruled by Christians, and the pagan rulers were slowly being converted. But unlike Roman Christians, the barbarians often practiced a militarized Christianity. Another problem facing the Augustinian code of just war was the number of clergy who took up arms. And because the wars took place in a period of shifting and unclear boundaries, the cause for going to war was not so much to repel invasions as to protect and recover property taken in raids from neighboring groups.

One idea that became influential in the Church derived from a spurious work by Augustine, the *Gravi de pugna*, that provided assurance to Christians that God would take their side and grant them victory in a just battle.[11] The Church began to embrace the opinion that wars serving religious ends were justified. However, the authority to wage war still rested with kings who had legitimate political authority. The solution was to promote the idea that the just king not only defended his kingdom but also defended the Church by waging war on the impious, heretics, pagans, and infidels. The alliance between the pope and Christian kings was cemented in the concept of a Holy Roman Emperor. The link established between Christianity and the state laid the groundwork for the authority invoked by the Church to launch the Crusades at the end of the eleventh century.

The development of just war theory in the Middle Ages followed three strands. There were medieval Romanists who sought to develop Roman law into a form of jurisprudence for semi-autonomous city-states in Italy and elsewhere. These efforts proceeded without any attempt to accommodate Christian doctrine. Secondly, there was canon law, which reached a watershed around 1140 in the *Decretum* of Gratian, who compiled a massive textbook that collected and organized canon law collections and ecclesiastical legislation and opinions that had accrued over the previous centuries. The *Decretum* and the decretals that commented on it became the subject of study for canon lawyers after that. In the *Decretum*'s Causa 23, Gratian provided a treatment of the Christian theology of war that followed Augustine in focusing on the inner disposition of those who wage war and on the need to punish sinners.[12]

Thirdly, and most relevant for our purposes, there were the medieval theologians whose work on just war theory went beyond the narrower confines of canon law to develop general principles of morality for a Christian ethics. It is the work of moral theologians familiar with philosophy that paved the way for Aquinas's theory of just war. The moral theologians drew on the Bible, Augustine, and Aristotle as authorities. One thing they took seriously was the possibility that war at God's command may still be sinful. Thus, they were more suspicious of military service than Augustine. Could a soldier exercise his office without sin? Could he redeem himself by acts of penance, or is it necessary that he not return to military service? In considering such questions, the moral theologians sought ways to retain the possibility of justified military service and warfare. However, they recognized that obedience to authority did not absolve a soldier completely from moral responsibility for his actions when they were wrong.

Discussion of just war before Thomas Aquinas had followed the canonists in emphasizing just cause, right intention, and authority. Aquinas's synthesis of Aristotelian philosophy with the Augustinian tenets of Church theology gave rise to his view of just war that, while not departing much from traditional doctrines based on Scripture, was buttressed using philosophical ideas. In Aristotle's ethics and political theory, humans were defined as essentially political or social animals that require a peaceful and virtuous community to flourish. This imposed a duty on kings to defend the common good of the community against its enemies. Although Augustine's view that peace was the goal of war was preserved in Aquinas's account, in making defense of the common good the justification for war, a distinction had to be made between the actions of public officials and of private acts of self-defense. Only an official acting from princely authority could intentionally kill with the motive of promoting the common good, whereas private acts of killing could not be carried out with a right intention. Thus, authority had first place among the three requirements for just war. The second requirement was just cause, which referred to the enemy's guilt for some fault or sin, rendering him deserving of punishment. The third requirement of right intention meant that the purpose of war was to correct injustices and secure a return to peace, and not to settle private quarrels. Aquinas's formula in effect limited the scope of just war to military engagements between sovereign princes and leaders of states acting in defense of the good of their communities.

In discussing the conduct of war, Aquinas addressed the question of killing of innocents in wars fought to punish the guilty. Through the Peace of God, medieval canonists limited those subject to attack in war, exempting clerics, women, children, and other noncombatants (and their property) from hostilities. Aquinas could justify killing in defense of the common good by public officials. He could also justify acts necessary for self-defense, including killing when the defender's intention is to save his life, not to kill the attacker.[13] With regard to the killing of the guilty, Aquinas drew from theology the idea that even sinners had a nature endowed by God, and he made a distinction between the sinner and the sin. Thus, it is not justified to use more violence than necessary to right an injustice and punish the sin. Killing a just person, on the other hand, would be grievously wrong in acting in opposition to charity and justice and in depriving the community of a greater good. Yet Aquinas also held that by God's decree, both the sinful and the righteous may die and as such, "he who at God's command kills an innocent man does not sin" (*ST* II-II, q. 64, art. 6, ad. 1). Thus, although he raises the relevant questions, it is difficult to attribute a clear doctrine of noncombatant immunity to Aquinas.[14] The principles of proportionality and noncombatant immunity would become the central tenets of *jus in bello*. But in many respects, Aquinas did not challenge traditional practices of war such as pillaging and plunder (so long as the motivation was justice and not greed), and the enslavement of prisoners. The effect of his account of just war was to enable war to be seen as a natural function of political authority justified by appeal to the good of the community, thus completing the Augustinian reconciliation of war with Christian charity.

The medieval articulation of just war theory that sought to overcome moral objections to Christian soldiering was now complete in the Church. Later Catholic theologians basically drew on Aquinas in writings about just war, such as Cajetan's commentary on the *Summa Theologica*. In Cajetan's account, the Augustinian source of just war theory is also apparent in the legitimizing of offensive war for punishing those who have done wrong. Thus, Cajetan's work illustrates the influence of the tradition of just war thinking in the Catholic Church.

Just war and the reformation

When the Protestant churches split from the Roman Catholic Church in the sixteenth century, religious violence broke out in Germany, England, the Netherlands, and France. Rulers in Europe chose their allegiance and imposed their religious beliefs on their subjects, while the Catholic Church sought to suppress and eradicate the Protestant reformers. The wars that had been fought against Muslims on the borders and outside of Europe, especially the series of Crusades, were not considered to be subject to the restrictions of a just war doctrine, supposedly applying only to war between Christian armies. But what about war between Christians who were Catholic and those who were not?

Since the Catholic Church had developed the just war doctrine, what were the views of the new Protestant churches?

Luther's view provides a starting point. In many ways, he followed Augustine in developing his theory of the just war. However, he rejected the idea that the Church was justified to instigate religious war. The Church belonged to the Kingdom of God, while the state belonged to the kingdom of the world in which civil affairs were administered. The latter world was a fallen world with the state ruling over material things. It was in this world that civil authorities fought wars to maintain justice and to repel invasions. The Church, however, belonged to the world of spiritual concerns. Civil authority was an instrument of God to protect Christians, but the magistrate punished and killed sorrowfully with love not hatred. As a last resort, soldiers could be legitimately ordered to fight with the goal of peace in necessary wars. Resistance to Muslim invaders could be justified not as a war against infidels but as a defense of territory.

As had been the case in just war theory since Augustine, sovereign authority was very important for Luther. Thus, Luther condemned the Peasant Revolt (1524–26) that was ironically inspired by his own criticisms of the political status quo. He saw it rather as an act of rebellion to engage in revolution against God's ordained magistrate on earth. This view did present him with a problem of justifying defending Protestant states against the Holy Roman Emperor, who was seeking to eradicate the Protestant faith to reinstate Catholic authority. After Luther's death, some Lutherans adapted his doctrine to justify war by Protestant states against the Emperor by distinguishing between lower and higher magistrates, giving even the lower magistrates the authority to restrain or resist higher magistrates as a check against violations by the latter. The larger problem here is that the new Protestant churches were now facing an issue that the Catholic Church had similarly faced in earlier Roman times: How could armed violence be justified now that there was a Christian state that had to be defended?

In the theocratic state that the Radical Reformers sought, defense of the state and defense of the faith merged. As a result, some Reformed Churches moved in the direction of reinstating religiously motivated Crusades to defend their faith against Catholic enemies, dissolving the moral distinction between the worldly and the spiritual kingdoms that Luther had believed in. The view that fighting for religious beliefs was a form of just war was soon put into practice by Zwingli and by Calvin. Calvin held that the state was ordained by God to support the true religion. With Calvinist Geneva constantly threatened by surrounding

Catholic powers, the honor of God was at stake. Meanwhile in England, Oliver Cromwell led a Puritan revolution against a Catholic monarch, who was executed. This was a war against a sovereign authority by his subjects. But Cromwell was not bothered by disputes about the justice of his fight. If the war is fought for God, it did not matter what the prince or the people thought. It is ironical that even among the anti-Catholic radicals, the thinking on the morality of war had now gone full circle back to the Augustinian view that God's command made a war just.

Just war and the law of nations

How did an ethics of war developed by moral theologians for Christian Europe apply to non-Christians? It is one thing to subject non-Christians living under the rule of Christian monarchs and princes to the moral doctrines of the Church. It is quite another to apply these doctrines to non-believers who live beyond Christendom. In the Crusades, the rules for war that applied between Christian kingdoms did not extend to war between Christian and Muslim armies. The retaking of the Holy Lands at the urging of the pope could be considered a just war with authority, cause, and right intention. But the Crusaders did not fight according to the rules that governed war in Europe. Prisoners were executed after they surrendered and atrocities were committed against women and children. Homes and property were pillaged and religious places desecrated. Either the Christian armies did not think that the rules of war developed for war between Christians applied when they were fighting infidels, or they believed that there were no innocents among non-believers and all had to be punished for their sinful beliefs and lives. The conviction among Christians that they were fulfilling God's will and that they were getting divine help (in line with the pseudo-Augustinian *Gravi de pugna*) made the moral questions moot.

When the New World was discovered and Spanish armies started their conquest of the Americas, moral questions about the right of Christians to wage war on infidels could not be ignored. For unlike the Holy Land, which was once under Roman rule, the Spanish were forcibly taking new lands from the people who lived there. What had these people done that would justify the savage war of conquest waged against them? Of course, the conquistadors and their royal sponsors had no doubts about what they were doing, enriching themselves with gold and slaves for private gain and the glory of Spain. It was the Spanish Dominican priest Francisco de Vitoria who pointed out in his *De Indis* [On the American Indians] that neither Spanish civil law nor ecclesiastical law had any legitimacy over non-Christian nations. In the relationship between Spain and the conquered peoples of the Americas, there had to be a law of war derived from unwritten divine (hence universal) laws which were either revealed or known through conscience.

In working out the details of what is lawful in war in his *De iure belli* [On the Law of War], Vitoria hewed closely to the traditional just war doctrine. Sovereign authority and just cause were necessary conditions for just war. However, Vitoria denied that difference in religion, or the extension of empire, or the personal glory of the prince were just causes. War was justified in self-defense, to recover what is taken, to punish a wrong, and to secure peace. Deliberate killing of the innocent, when there is no cause, was forbidden by natural law. For the unintended killing of the innocent to be permitted, it must be absolutely necessary for the purpose of war. Vitoria, like Aquinas, considered permissible the seizing of property and the enslavement of non-Christian enemies, but he objected to the killing of innocent hostages. He, however, allowed for the retributive killing of the guilty after victory in war on the ground that security for the future cannot be had unless the enemy was restrained by fear of punishment. Yet he held that war must not be fought to ruin people and that the least degree of misfortune compatible with justice should be inflicted on the offending state. In other words, Vitoria believed that war may be necessary and lawful but should be conducted with moderation. Although it is necessary to punish the guilty, the punishment inflicted should not exceed the degree of the offense.

Despite working within the theological tradition, Vitoria provided insights into war as an issue of international relations, setting the stage for the development of a law of nations to govern the conduct of war between states that were not necessarily Christian. Some views were from priests like Vitoria, while other views were from the legal profession. His work influenced the Spanish Jesuit Luis de Molina, whose contribution to just war thinking was to reject the idea held by Vitoria of war as a form of punishment for the guilt of the adversary. Offensive war could be undertaken for a sufficiently grave material injury such as the seizure of territory, without presuming wrongdoing by the offending party. As Vitoria had acknowledged, a belligerent may have an erroneous belief in the rightness of what he is doing, due to factors beyond his control. Molina thus broke with the just war tradition found in accounts such as Cajetan's, setting the stage for modern views that limited the purpose of war.

Francisco Suarez was another Jesuit priest from the same period who taught in Rome and Salamanca and had very similar views to Vitoria.

His writings contained one of the most systematic treatments of just war. He reiterated a distinction Aquinas had made between the sinner and the sin, and argued that Christians were permitted, even obliged, to participate in war. War may not only be justified, but may even be required in defense of the state. A declaration of war is justified, even if it is aggressive, to repair losses to the injured party and to punish the offender (a point of difference with Molina). To account for the authority of a prince to wage war as punishment, Suarez worked out a concept of "vindicative justice," whereby one commonwealth comes to have jurisdiction over another due to the latter's being at fault. Offenses that are causes for war include seizure of property, denial of common rights such as transit, and grave injury to the reputation and honor of the prince or his subjects. Greed and ambition, on the other hand, are not legitimate causes for war. In addition, the injustice that is avenged by war must be both grave enough and not reparable in any other way. One alternative to war he suggested was arbitration. Thus, Suarez alluded to the condition of war as a last resort, which would play a larger role in later versions of just war theory.[15] Another condition he contributed to the doctrine was the idea that offensive war should only be undertaken where there is a reasonable expectation of success. Suarez also specified proportionality as a condition of *jus in bello*, which requires that force should not be more than what is in keeping with the aim of a just war. And he held that princes had obligations not to harm innocents, except as a side-effect in a way that satisfies the principle of double effect. This principle that had originated from Aquinas was now clearly a part of just war theory as it evolved into its modern version.

Alberico Gentili was an Italian Protestant lawyer, judge, and professor at Oxford who saw war itself as good when aimed at peace, and just when used as an instrument of justice. He likened war as a contest between two sovereigns, with a legal process between two litigants. Thus, both sides in war should conduct themselves in accordance to the same code of honor. Gentili's most unique contribution in the development of just war theory was his concept of "expedient defense," or preventive war. War is justified not just when attacked, or when the enemy is making preparations to attack, but also when one *fears* an attack. Gentili saw preventive war as lawful, more expedient, and more honorable. It is lawful to anticipate a wrong. It is more to one's advantage to meet the enemy halfway than to wait for an attack, especially since the sovereign has no higher authority to protect him, and the weaker party has a natural privilege of anticipating its defense. It would be disgraceful for one to prefer the remedy of an ill instead of anticipating it: "We kill a snake as soon as we see one."[16]

As international law developed in the age of empire-building during which there were frequent sources of friction between European powers due to the growth of maritime commerce, the Dutch jurist Hugo Grotius in the first half of the seventeenth century compiled the most comprehensive account of secular just war theory as had yet been written. His monumental work, *On the Law of War and Peace*, was both a founding treatise of the fledgling discipline of international law as well as a summation of the just war tradition. Divided into three books and preceded by a *Prolegomena* [Preface], the text dealt first with the authority to wage war, then with the grounds for fighting a war, and finally with the actions that are permissible in war. Grotius defended a common law of nations against political realists, such as Machiavelli. To him, the law of war and peace rested on a philosophical foundation in human nature and society. The law signified what was just in human society and it is comprised of objective rules of conduct that attributed rights to persons. Grotius the jurist, thus, continued to think within the natural law tradition of the moral theologians. However, he also distinguished a part of the law of war and peace called volitional law that was dependent on legislation by human or divine will.

A just cause for war was important if one were not to act as a brigand. The three justifiable causes were defense of self or property, recovery of property or debts, and punishment of wrongdoing. To have the right to slay an assailant in self-defense required that the danger be immediate and imminent and no other way of escape was open. Grotius did not think a war could be just on both sides. There was no legal equality between just and unjust belligerents, and only the side with a just cause may exercise the rights of just war.[17] A war that was unjust from the point of view of "internal justice" (justice in conformity with natural law) was unjust even when undertaken in a lawful way from the point of view of "external justice" (bilateral justice based on tacit agreement). Grotius set out separate accounts of conduct for unlawful and lawful wars in terms of what internal justice required. The just belligerent is permitted to do what is necessary to correct the injustice, but he may not do more. There are limits to acts of vengeance and punishment by those fighting in a lawful war, and duties are owed even to those who have done injury. No one can justly be killed intentionally, except as a just penalty or in case there was no other way to protect one's life and property. Slaves and conscripts in the ranks of the enemy could not be justly killed if they were without hostile intent.[18]

The laws of war and the rights of states to carry out military action were further articulated after Grotius by jurists and thinkers such as Samuel von Pufendorf and Christian von Wolff. Writing after the Westphalian system of nation-states that emerged in 1648 had conferred on European sovereigns the right to raise and maintain their own state armies, Pufendorf was optimistic about the possibility that peace and security between states could be preserved on the basis of rules of war that rested on natural law. Such rules were willed by God and had moral content. The state functioned to preserve sociability and peacefulness among its citizens and in relations with other states. Moral limits on the conduct of individuals foster virtues that keep them human. The virtues of the state and its institutions endow them with moral legitimacy. States, unlike individuals, have the right to punish wrongdoers and to use armed force against other states. Although Pufendorf took the opposite view to philosopher Thomas Hobbes in thinking that peace is the natural state of humans,[19] he did not set moral limits to actions carried out in war should war become necessary. Instead of rules of *jus in bello* based on morality, he merely provided prudential reasons, such as a concern to avoid retaliation, for states to limit their violence and brutality.

Unlike Pufendorf (and more like Grotius), Wolff did not think that a just belligerent had unlimited rights to act against an unjust adversary. He formulated a principle of *military necessity* that measured what was permissible in terms of what was required to achieve the goal of putting an end to the armed threat from the enemy. He also insisted on civilian immunity from direct military attack. Wolff differed from Grotius in holding that as each side in war had to decide on the justice of its actions, they each had equal rights in the use of force and should conform to the same set of rules. Thus, neither side could be justified in acting with unrestricted brutality in the belief that it possessed a just cause for war. Wolff's idea of rules of war that governed the conduct of war between sovereign states separated from its moral basis in natural law constituted an important contribution to the development of modern conceptions of international law.

Like Wolff, the Swiss jurist and diplomat Emer de Vattel advanced the idea of rules of war that were reciprocally binding on all states, regardless of whether they were fighting with just cause. In discussing the rights and duties of sovereign states, Vattel conceived of nations as entities whose conduct constituted an autonomous sphere with its own regulating norms. A state could not be judged for going to war without justification, as each was free to choose what would suit its interests. However, there was public accountability for violations of the laws of war. In articulating the norms that governed the behavior of states at war, Vattel had, in effect, provided the basis for the codification of international law that eventually culminated in the Hague and Geneva Conventions.

Pacifist, moralist, and realist responses to just war theory

While the law of nations was slowly taking shape, it was being subjected to criticisms from two opposite sides. Some moralists did not see the law of nations as restrictive enough, while political realists were skeptical of the application of morality to war. Such criticisms can be understood as reiterations of the reactions in Renaissance Europe to the Christian just war theory in the late fifteenth and early sixteenth centuries. In line with humanist ideals of the time, pacifists and utopians had hoped for a world where rulers renounced their militaristic ambitions to expand their territories or to seek glory in war. Some who denounced war pointed out that the kings of Europe were not sincere in their claims of justice, as they did not aim at peace and did not explore the possibility of reconciling their differences. Erasmus of Rotterdam, a renowned pacifist of the period, foreshadowed the just war pacifism of today in endorsing the just war theory but rejecting the wars in the Europe in which he lived as incompatible with the requirements for a just war. He did not accept wars to reclaim territory as just because lands had changed hands many times in history. Erasmus also believed that the shared brotherhood of Christians and the teachings in the Gospels should have priority over the appeals of nationalism and the political ambitions of princes. He believed that the concept of princes having a right to wage wars for just causes opened the door to abuse. He rejected the frequent use of the Old Testament by theologians to legitimize war because Christ's message of peace and charity was being overlooked. Although he studied the ancient classics, he thought that scholastic philosophy had subverted biblical teachings, as seen in the use by Aquinas of Aristotelian ideas in articulating the just war doctrine.

During the Renaissance period, the realist challenge to the idea of just war came by way of the development of the art of statecraft, with Erasmus's contemporary in Italy and author of *The Prince*, Niccolo Machiavelli, being the foremost theorist of the amoral use of power. To him, politics was a chess game and soldiers and civilians were mere pawns. Morality should not impede the prince in the exercise of his power to do what was necessary to achieve his goals. The ruler should be guided by prudence and be prepared to act ruthlessly to maintain the security of the state. A good ruler is one who should recognize and be willing to seize opportunities to increase his power. War should be dictated by the state's interest, not justice. The necessity of war, as determined by the logic of power, replaced the moral necessity that was Augustine's justification for war. A clear statement of where morality stood with Machiavelli can be found in his *Discourses on the First Decade of Livy*:

> For when the safety of one's country wholly depends on the decision to be taken, no attention should be paid either to justice or injustice... On the contrary, every other consideration being set aside, that alternative should be wholeheartedly adopted which will save the life and preserve the freedom of one's country. (Bk III, ch. 4)

Like the earlier just war doctrine of the Church, the secular account of just war articulated in the form of the law of nations was subjected to criticism in the eighteenth century by moralists and philosophers. Vattel, the Swiss jurist and diplomat, who as mentioned earlier had formulated the idea of reciprocally binding rules of war for all states, also wrote about the duties that nations owe to other nations. He compared these duties with the mutual duties of men toward one another required by universal justice, which go beyond the observance of strict justice. Nations should not just help to preserve other states but contribute to their advancement. This did not conflict with statecraft, as a sovereign was promoting the safety of his own nation by putting into force the spirit of mutual assistance. However, no nation has the right to force others to accept its help, as it is the right of free and independent nations to decide whether to ask for help. Nor does a nation have the right to demand help from another nation. A nation that refuses to help without good reason violates charity but does no injury. Hence, there is no cause for war. Furthermore, nations are not required to share what could be used against them in time of war. It would violate prudence to increase the strength of an enemy.

The Enlightenment in Europe led to a mood of pacifism among Christian leaders and philosophers. Many plans to eliminate war were proposed, going beyond the more restrictive rules proposed by Vattel and extending to the idea of a federation of states or a cosmopolitan world order. The Project for Perpetual Peace began as a scheme of the Abbe de Saint-Pierre, formulated between the years 1712 and 1733.

It was discussed and critiqued by the philosopher Jean Jacques Rousseau, who questioned the assumption that the princes of Europe would be willing to form a confederation that would abolish armies. Rousseau and Saint-Pierre were both concerned with how the civil order within a state could be transferred to the Hobbesian state of nature that existed between states. Rousseau disagreed with Saint-Pierre's assumption that sovereigns could be persuaded by reason and not be motivated by their own interests. He felt that the only way to federate was by force, but this undermined the aim of eliminating war. Thus, while supporting the ideal of peace, Rousseau was skeptical about the means to achieve such a peace.

The philosopher who worked out the most ambitious plans for perpetual peace was Immanuel Kant. Kant believed that political prudence must yield to morality if the two are in conflict, and that morality dictates that peace must be pursued in a way that makes it a lasting peace. Since a suspension of hostilities was no guarantee of peace, the state of peace had to be formally instituted through a civil constitution based on cosmopolitan rights of individuals and nations as citizens of a universal state of mankind, one that extended beyond European civilizations. Kant sketched a republican ideal as the foundation for permanent peace and assumed that constitutional democracies were less likely to wage war. This is an Enlightenment ideal that still appeals to us today. Kant's innovation was to propose the achievement of perpetual peace not by revolution but by the gradual reform of states toward a democratic ideal.

The Enlightenment found its Machiavellian realist in the Prussian military thinker Carl von Clausewitz, who served for twelve years as director of the Military Academy in Berlin, writing *On War*, which was published in 1832, a year after his death. Clausewitz understood war as a duel on an extensive scale, a game in which each side sought to compel an opponent to submit to its will using violence as its means. Thus, it was absurd and dangerous to limit war by moral concerns. Famously describing war as "the continuation of policy by other means,"[20] he saw war as a political act that included its political object in its conception. Theoretical speculations about ending war were, therefore, unrealistic. Clausewitz did see prudential political considerations setting some limits to the exercise of war. And he described courage and self-reliance as military virtues that enabled commanders to perform well on the battlefield. Thus, unlike for Machiavelli, war did not serve the sole goal of political survival but also the values of the state. This ethical dimension in Clausewitz's work was to push the just war tradition in the direction of professional military ethics.

We find by the nineteenth century a number of trajectories for the just war tradition: the Christian just war doctrine as developed by Catholics and Protestants, the more universalistic secular law of nations, a philosophical ethics of war, and the alternatives to just war theory in the forms of pacifism, realism, and military ethics. These developments reflected and responded to the impact of historical events and the changing face of warfare. Further changes were to follow in the nineteenth and twentieth centuries as war underwent immense technological changes, and society and world politics were transformed by social and ideological upheavals.

Just war theory and modern warfare

The end of the Napoleonic Wars in the early nineteenth century ushered in a period of relative peace and social reform in Europe, giving impetus to the hope of abolishing war. Peace societies were formed, drawing members from various Christian denominations, and legal and political mechanisms were established to arbitrate disputes between states, in particular the Hague Tribunal in 1899. The tribunal was established after talks on disarmament at a conference called by Czar Nicholas II of Russia. However, all these efforts failed to prevent the First World War that began in 1914. When it ended, the horrors of that war revived the search to eliminate war. The League of Nations was conceived by US President Woodrow Wilson in 1918, although the United States itself opted not to join. In 1929, the Paris Pact, which aimed to outlaw war, was signed by 59 nations. Ten years later, the Second World War began. This was a war that saw an unprecedented level of carnage and loss of civilian life, with the introduction of highly destructive weaponry and tactics, especially obliteration bombing from the air and the detonation of two atomic bombs over Japan.

Just war theorists responded to events in a number of ways. Foremost of all was concern with the requirements of *jus in bello*, in particular the concept of noncombatant immunity. Secondly, as the age of empires drew to a close, warfare often involved non-state fighters seeking to overthrow colonial rule or ferment revolution against tyrannical monarchs. Thus, the requirement of sovereign authority for *jus ad bellum* was subject to reexamination. The nuclear age and the policy of deterrence adopted by the nuclear-armed superpowers also needed to be evaluated as to its moral acceptability.

One school of thought was just war pacifism, with proponents arguing that the requirements of just war could never be satisfied in modern warfare, so that the ethical course had to be to refrain from war. Other just war theorists sought to preserve the relevance of just war theory in two different ways. One was to insist on the applicability of traditional just war doctrine. The other was to adapt just war theory to take into account the changing nature of war. James Turner Johnson[21] defends the use of traditional just war categories to think about both the issue of nuclear deterrence and the problem of discriminating between combatants and noncombatants. He frames the permissible use of force in terms of the protection and preservation of values of a community, and sees *jus ad bellum* as pertaining to the justice of an initial decision to go to war. He believes that it may be worse to fail to safeguard values such as freedom and justice than to engage in war, especially given that most wars are less destructive than a nuclear catastrophe. Once war is legitimately declared, the requirements to avoid harming noncombatants and causing disproportionate destruction set limits to how a justified war is fought. Noncombatants should be spared from direct intentional harm or from use as soft targets, whether or not weapons of mass destruction are used.

Michael Walzer's *Just and Unjust Wars* has appeared in four editions and is frequently cited as an updated version of just war theory. Walzer is admired for rejecting the claims of political realism and taking up the challenge of establishing the relevance of a conception of justice in war. He addresses contemporary challenges to just war theory in areas where the traditional doctrine is silent or unsatisfactory. These include pre-emptive strikes, the right to intervene for humanitarian reasons and the right to secede, as well as the status of neutral states. Walzer pays particular attention to the role of noncombatant immunity in the war convention (international law), and how this is affected by features of modern warfare, such as the use of submarines and aerial bombardment, blockades and sieges, guerilla war, and terrorism.

The moral problem of nuclear weapons has been addressed by Methodist theologian Paul Ramsey, whose writings contributed to reviving the concept of just war from the Christian perspective. Ramsey defended the justice of deterrence, even though the actual use of such weapons can only be morally justified against military forces of an invader and not against civilians. He used the doctrine of double effect to allow for the threat of massive harm to the civilians in enemy cities as side-effects that are not directly intended, but which served to discourage the enemy from launching a nuclear attack. This view was considered too permissive from both the secular just war perspective of Michael Walzer, and the just war doctrine articulated by the

National Conference of Catholic Bishops in 1983. The bishops contra-dicted Ramsey, holding that even the indirect targeting of cities where civilians lived was morally unacceptable. A strategy of nuclear deter-rence can only be accepted provisionally as a step toward progressive disarmament.

The Catholic bishops presented an updated version of just war the-ory that differed significantly from the doctrine held by traditionalists such as James Turner Johnson. The latter objected to the bishops' claim that Catholic teaching implied a presumption against war that did not allow for the use of war as a force for good. Returning to Augustinian principles, Johnson asserted that armed force might be resorted to justly when aimed at peace. Moreover, the bishops had added to the trad-itional doctrine three "consequentialist criteria," namely war as a last resort, with acceptable probability of success, and overall proportion-ality of the harm of war in relation to the good. From Johnson's trad-itionalist outlook, these criteria are concerned with the wise practice of government or the exercise of statecraft, providing guidance as to whether a particular use of force, already deemed just, is wise or unwise. These criteria should not be used to evaluate the justice of going to war.[22] The traditional *jus ad bellum* criteria of sovereign authority, just cause and right intention are deontological and impose duties on those who have ultimate moral responsibility for the common good. When pacifist-minded thinkers use the *jus in bello* requirements of discrim-ination and proportionality to deny the justice of going to war, they misuse the just war doctrine. Johnson criticized the Catholic bishops for effectively rejecting the possibility of war as a means to good in the non-traditional way they set out the *jus ad bellum* requirements.[23]

In international law, the deliberate harming of noncombatants, namely civilians and prisoners of war, is considered a war crime. Such offenses are violations of the Geneva Conventions of 1949, and an International Criminal Court was established in 1997 to enable war criminals to be prosecuted and tried. Military forces around the world are expected to adhere to a standard known as the Law of War or the Law of Armed Conflict that derived largely from the work of Grotius, Pufendorf, and other jurists in developing a secular law of nations out of the Christian just war doctrine. These are positive developments but there are also drawbacks. First, international bodies still have lim-ited power to enforce the law on superpowers and rogue nations. They have to rely on national governments to observe the rules and pun-ish offenders. Second, there is a tendency to substitute legalisms for moral thinking. Just as philosophers in the past have argued for more

restrictions on war than what was permitted by just war theory, philosophers today need to discuss whether the war conventions are too
permissive and provide legal cover for doing things in war that are morally wrong. Even Michael Walzer, who argues against political realism,
seems to have conceded too much to *realpolitik* in accepting "supreme
emergency" exemptions to prohibitions against the deliberate targeting
of noncombatants.

The fact that what began in medieval Europe as a Christian doctrine
to justify and limit the use of force by the state has evolved into a system
of international law that is binding on all nations, although a positive
development, does not represent the end-point of the just war tradition.
War is too serious a moral problem to be left in the hands of lawyers and
politicians. Moreover, war continues to evolve and present challenges
to just war theory. After the Second World War, and throughout the
years of the Cold War, the focus has been on the problem of nuclear
deterrence. Another issue, as Western imperialism receded from Asia
and Africa, was the justification of wars of liberation, including guerilla
warfare and revolutionary war. With the fall of the Berlin Wall and the
collapse of the Soviet Union, new challenges have arisen that demand
a rethinking of just war theory. In the 1990s and the first decade of the
twenty-first century, genocides and ethnic cleansing have taken place
in Rwanda and the Balkan states and are continuing in Sudan. Should
humanitarian intervention to prevent such mass killings be permitted
or required? Who should intervene and under what rules?

By far the biggest challenge has been presented by the rise of non-
state terrorist organizations capable of attacking civilians living in cities
halfway around the world. Almost three thousand innocent lives were
lost in the attacks on the World Trade Center and the Pentagon in the
United States that took place on September 11, 2001. The United States
responded by launching its Global War on Terror that was directed not
just against the Al-Qaeda organization of Osama bin Laden but against
any country deemed to be a supporter or sponsor of groups that engage
in terrorism. The invasion of Iraq in March 2003 was presented as a
justified war of self-defense to prevent future terrorist attacks on the
United States. The legal basis for such preventive wars has been widely
debated. There is a parallel debate in philosophical circles about whether
the requirements of *jus ad bellum* were satisfied, and what adjustments
to just war doctrine are needed to take into account a new generation of
wars that are unlike the conventional wars in history books.[24]

The issue of noncombatant immunity continues to be raised as a
result of recent events in history. Civilians have died in large numbers

in the wars of the twentieth century, and the attacks by Al-Qaeda terrorists and insurgents seeking to drive the United States out of Iraq have echoed the suicide bombings carried out against Israeli civilians in the Palestinian struggle against Israeli occupation. The use of precision weapons and airstrikes has made it possible to wage war by remote control and to carry out "targeted killings" or assassinations. Ostensibly meant to reduce civilian casualties, these weapons have, ironically, resulted in more civilians being killed in proportion to troops who are well protected when on patrol or hidden thousands of miles away in command centers. These weapons have also made it easier for soldiers brought up on a diet of videogames to dehumanize the enemy and kill them. In the war on terror, the treatment of prisoners of war (who are technically and legally noncombatants) has become an issue, with the disclosure of an official policy of torture by the United States as well as attempts by the Bush administration to reject the Geneva Convention. All of these have made the issue of war crimes a subject for lawyers and philosophers.

Most ethicists of war have tried to either adapt the just war theory to account for the recent developments in warfare, or insist that the theory works fine in its traditional form. The remaining ethicists would prefer to abandon the theory and cut the pretense that war can ever be justified. In the next chapter, I will critically assess the just war theory to clear the way for ethicists to proceed beyond just war thinking. I think that in the final analysis, neither the adapted versions nor the traditional just war doctrine could succeed. If I can show this, then the just war theory should be abandoned and a new ethics of war developed that is better equipped to deal with the many difficult moral issues in modern warfare.

2
Just War Reconsidered

The just war paradigm

Theories that belong in the just war tradition propose sets of conditions under which a state engaging in war is morally justified in doing so. Opposed to the theory is pacifism: the view that war is always morally wrong. There are two ways to get from just war theory to pacifism. One is to take as fundamentally correct the view that war is morally wrong and, therefore, unjustifiable. So even if the conditions of just war theory are satisfied, it remains morally wrong for a state to fight a war. Attempting to add or amend the conditions of the theory is a futile exercise because there cannot be a set of conditions to justify what is considered to be morally unjustifiable. The problem with this approach to pacifism is that the view that war is always wrong is certainly not an obvious one that can be accepted without argument. It is based on the idea that any form of violence is morally unacceptable, including violence used to defend one's life or the lives of those that one loves. On the face of it, this is rather implausible. In the context of the ethics of war, the question arises of what, for instance, a pacifist in Britain would do to stop Hitler from invading Britain and spreading the evils of Nazism, such as death camps. The idea that war is impermissible when nothing else works strikes many as unrealistic or plain wrong. In fact, it is said that Hitler was encouraged by the attempts at appeasement by Prime Minister Neville Chamberlain, and by the meekness of the Jews he targeted.

A second path to pacifism concedes the conditions of just war theory but denies that they are ever satisfied. If the conditions could be met, a war could indeed be morally justified. But since no war could satisfy those conditions, there could not be any war that the theory could justify. By default, morality requires us to be pacifists. The problem with this stance is that, even if it is true that none of the wars in history satisfied the conditions, it is impossible to show that the conditions can never be satisfied. It may perhaps be argued that technology such as precision-guided weaponry could make it possible to one day meet conditions of just war theory that are hard to satisfy today. Thus, it is possible to some day fight a just war. It is also a problem that it is a matter of historical dispute whether actual wars have satisfied the conditions for just war. This means that this approach to pacifism is dependent on disputes about facts, not about morality.

In any case, should someone who is dissatisfied with just war theory automatically opt for pacifism? Many critics of particular just war theories in the history of the tradition have responded by offering alternative versions of the theory.[1] They have either reinterpreted the conditions of just war or added new ones. The claim that just war doctrine is too permissive because there are wars that are morally unacceptable even if the conditions of a just war theory are satisfied does not entail that war is never justified. By making the conditions for just war more stringent, we can rule out the counter-examples and arrive at a better version of just war theory. Because the two paths to pacifism that I have mentioned do not preclude this possibility, they have not undermined all just war theories. The first approach assumes that whatever the conditions of just war, war remains morally wrong. How can this be proven? The second approach fails to challenge the conditions of just war, only whether they could be satisfied in reality.

I intend to reject the tradition of just war thinking, but I do not intend to defend pacifism. In my view, just war theory as an ethics of war is in serious trouble because it is too permissive in justifying many wars that are morally wrong. But how can it be shown that the problem cannot be fixed by adding conditions to the theory, as had been done before in the just war tradition? I will show this by rejecting the basic conditions for just war. This would not mean that the pacifist is right that there is no such thing as a moral basis for any war. What it would mean is that the moral basis for resorting to war would look nothing like the theories in the just war tradition. We would need a new approach to the ethics of war. My position is like the response of Copernicus to the Ptolemaic view of the cosmos. The Ptolemaic system that placed the earth at the center of the universe tried to fix mismatches with observations by adding epicycles to the motion of planets. The Copernican revolution came about as a paradigm shift when a cumbersome worldview had to be replaced by another worldview that did not necessitate epicycles because it held that the earth and other planets moved around the sun. In two thousand years of development, the just war theory has become laden with changes that have made it increasingly cumbersome and untidy. It is time for a Copernican revolution in the ethics of war: No more fine-tuning of the conditions of just war theory, but a new way of thinking about the moral acceptability of war as an instrument of the state.

This chapter is about what is wrong with just war theory. But how can I show that the theory is so fatally flawed that it needs to be abandoned? In the first place, there are not only one but many versions of just war theory, and some versions may not exhibit all the flaws that I identify. Secondly, even if all versions can be shown to be vulnerable to at least one criticism, I cannot rule out the possibility that someone in the future could formulate a version that overcomes that one problem. Just war theorists are not ignorant of problems for their theories, including the problems on which I shall focus. In fact, their attempts to resolve problems within the tradition have resulted in a tremendous growth in articles and books on just war theory. It may seem that I have underestimated the task of critiquing just war theory by attempting to do so in just one chapter. I am helped in this task by there being criticisms that have been presented by other philosophers, which I could draw upon. But what enables me to succeed in my task here is that I do not need to discuss every version of just war theory or every detail of any one version of the theory. Instead, I will simply focus my discussion on the central features of the just war tradition that are found in almost every version of just war theory. If the necessary conditions for just war that are recognized throughout the tradition cannot be vindicated, then it looks like anything that is salvageable from just war theory will not resemble the kind of moral view that has a place within the just war tradition. Using my analogy of the Ptolemaic system, what I will take on are not the epicycles but the idea of planets and stars orbiting around the earth. If this idea cannot stand, the point of the epicycles is lost altogether.

I should allow for the fact that what counts as a just war theory may be in dispute. For instance, one thing I am going to do here is to use David Rodin's recent arguments to dismiss the idea of self-defense as a just cause.[2] Rodin sees a need for rethinking the case in international law and ethics for defensive war against aggression and he proposes a paradigm of law enforcement that requires a minimal universal state. Is Rodin proposing an amendment to just war theory or a replacement theory? In my view, an ethics of war that does not appeal to self-defense as the central case of just cause would not be a theory in the just war tradition. Many defenders of just war theory recognize this and have tried to knock down Rodin's arguments. But it is also possible to view Rodin as contributing to the development of just war theory. For one thing, Rodin's ethical framework for evaluating war is a theory of rights, which is a continuation of the legalistic thinking that is characteristic of secular just war theory since the time of Grotius.[3] I shall, after this chapter, propose an alternative approach to moral theorizing about war that does not rest on rules and rights and which would represent a clear break from the just war tradition. But the task in this chapter is to show what is fundamentally wrong with just war theory.

The central tenets of just war theory

Which requirements of *jus ad bellum* and *jus in bello* are central to just war theory in any of its versions? And how many of these requirements must be called into question before we are in a position to declare that the just war paradigm should be abandoned? If all the conditions are individually necessary to justify war, then it would be enough to attack any one condition, as long as it is found in every version of the theory. However, since many just war theorists consider *jus ad bellum* and *jus in bello* to function independently and to attach to different agents – political leaders in the former case and soldiers in the latter case – I should at least critique one requirement in each case. Furthermore, it would be better for me to take on at least two requirements each for *jus ad bellum* and for *jus in bello*, since my objections may be more convincing to some when I take on one requirement and more convincing to others when I take on a second requirement. And it would be all the better if readers are convinced by all my objections.

Having described the requirements of just war in the last chapter, I am now in a position to list the tenets of *jus ad bellum* that are most central to theories in the just war tradition as the following:

1. *Legitimate authority*: Every just war theory must distinguish the violence of war from banditry. The actions may be similar but war is supposedly fought by soldiers who are led by political leaders who have the authority to declare war, unlike bandits who may fight in large well-armed groups but whose leaders do not have the authority of political leaders.
2. *Just cause*: Even sovereigns and legitimate political authorities may declare wars that cannot be morally justified. They may engage in

genocide, power grabs, vendettas, or quests for glory and riches. The reason or cause for going to war is used as a distinguishing factor between just and unjust wars.

3. *Last resort*: This has been a condition of just war from Cicero's time and is also an essential part of modern just war theory as encapsulated in international law. The idea is that a just cause may be pursued by many other means besides war, and when a war is not really necessary, it cannot be just.

4. *Right intention*: This was made a requirement in the earliest versions of just war theory due to the theological roots of the theory. Augustine required that Christians kill out of love and not hatred and that they should aim at peace even when they use violence. In modern versions of just war theory, this requirement is stated in terms of there being no other dominant purpose for fighting besides that given as the just cause in making the decision to go to war. (This principle of *jus ad bellum* is, however, not one that I will critique here.[4])

As for *jus in bello*, it is easy to identify the principles of *proportionality* and of *discrimination* (or noncombatant immunity) as the central tenets. In fact, many versions of just war theory take these principles to be the only requirements for justice in the conduct of war. I shall therefore discuss and critique both these requirements here. And I shall begin first with *jus in bello* and turn to the tenets of *jus ad bellum* after that.

The principle of discrimination

As a principle of *jus in bello*, the principle of discrimination, also known as the principle of noncombatant immunity, requires that soldiers act in such a way that they avoid harm to noncombatants or innocents. These are people on either side of the war who are not engaged in fighting as enemy soldiers and armed combatants are. Many noncombatants are civilians engaged in activities similar to those that they do in peacetime, such as farming, teaching, and treating the sick.[5] Now, although it is logically possible that a war can be fought without harming a single noncombatant, no actual war has been fought in such a way. In fact, it is often the case in war that greater numbers of civilians than soldiers have been casualties because the former are not in a position to defend themselves, because troops appropriate food and other provisions at their expense, and because homes and basic (including dual-use) infrastructure are damaged or destroyed. The principle of discrimination is stated in terms of prohibiting the intentional and direct targeting of noncombatants. The killing of noncombatants can only be permissible if they are not the direct targets of attack and they are not intentionally killed, and if such killing is unavoidable and a proportionate means to achieve legitimate and valuable military objectives. In practice, this means that soldiers are not required to spare enemy targets that they cannot hit without endangering civilian lives. For the killing of civilian bystanders may not be what they intend to do, even if they know that it is something they cannot avoid doing once they launch the attack on the legitimate military targets. The just war theory does not take an absolutist stand in prohibiting any action that could result in the death of noncombatants.

Thus, the principle of discrimination relies on the doctrine of double effect in order to make a moral distinction between intended killing and unintended but foreseen killing. Like the just war theory, the doctrine of double effect (or DDE) has roots in medieval moral theology. It has been attributed to Aquinas, who distinguished between two effects of an act of killing in self-defense: the licit effect of saving one's own life, and the illicit effect of taking the assailant's life.[6] In his view, the moral evaluation of the act depends on the effect that is intended. Hence, the act may or may not be licit, depending on which of the two effects is intended. As with the just war theory, the DDE has been the subject of controversy and has been formulated in many different ways, more so in recent times as philosophers attempted to deal with criticisms and problems.[7]

One way of stating the doctrine as neutrally as possible is as follows: *It is sometimes less morally objectionable knowingly to bring about (or allow) some bad effect in the course of achieving some good end, than it would have been to bring about (or allow) that bad effect with the intention to do so in order that a good end is achieved.* (It should be noted that the doctrine also includes a proportionality requirement that the good achieved is not outweighed by the bad effect, so that one cannot justifiably bring about disproportionate harm just because one does not intend it. But since it appears as a separate principle of *jus in bello*, I set aside discussion of proportionality for the next section of this chapter.) The DDE has been used in the Catholic and natural law tradition of moral theorizing to allow for the taking of innocent life, for instance, in the surgical removal of the cancerous womb of a pregnant woman, which thereby kills the fetus but saves the mother. A favorite example that philosophers discuss relating directly to war concerns the moral distinction between a strategic or tactical bomber and a terror bomber. The former is exemplified by an attack on an ammunitions factory with civilians known to live nearby. The latter refers to deliberate attacks on civilian targets in the hope that severe casualties among them would have a demoralizing effect on the enemy.

The main lines of philosophical criticism of the DDE concern first those examples where the intuitive moral distinction between what is and is not permissible does not match the distinction between what is merely foreseen and what is intended. In other words, contrary to the doctrine, what is foreseen may be impermissible and what is intended may be permissible. Secondly, there is the problem of why the distinction between what is and is not intended should make a moral difference or have moral significance. From a consequentialist point of view, if an equal number of innocent persons are killed as a result of a similar attack, it would not seem to matter whether the killing is intended or not. Would a strategic bomber's action become impermissible if, on the way to his target, he decides that the demoralizing effect of killing the nearby civilians would be a good thing for the bombing to bring about and thereby acquires an additional intention? Thirdly, there is the problem of distinguishing what is intended from what is foreseen. If the killing is certain to happen when one bombs the target and one knows this to be the case, isn't the killing intended? To some critics, those who use the DDE are being disingenuous when they say they did not intend the harm that they did, when they knew full well what they were doing. G. E. M. Anscombe suggests that such a line of reasoning makes it possible for the pilot who dropped the atomic bomb on Hiroshima to deny that the deaths of the city's inhabitants were part of his intention.[8]

Instead of rehearsing the philosophical debate on the DDE between its defenders and critics,[9] I will examine the doctrine from the perspective of its role in the ethics of war. As mentioned earlier, the DDE is crucial for making the principle of discrimination work and, thus, for rendering the conduct of soldiers in the battlefield, where they inevitably kill civilians, morally acceptable. The idea is that if soldiers constrain their actions and tactics on the field to satisfy the DDE, they preserve the justice of their conduct in fighting a war and they act within their rights in so doing. My question is whether the DDE can be used in this way. If it can be used, who uses it?

Jus in bello requirements are supposed to apply to the soldiers doing the fighting, whereas *jus ad bellum* requirements apply to the political leaders who make the decision to go to war. But a modern army is a hierarchy with a command structure and there are different ranks doing different tasks on the battlefield. The lowest ranks of enlisted soldiers are privates who do the "grunt" work. They are on the frontlines carrying out orders and engaging in direct combat with the enemy. The highest ranks are the generals, who make decisions on how the forces that they command are deployed and used. In between are officers and enlisted men of various ranks, taking orders and commanding units of various sizes. What links them together is the chain of command down which orders are passed. Soldiers who are lower down the chain have a lesser ability and a narrower scope to make decisions about missions, tactics, and actions. That would also restrict their ability to make *moral* decisions, including the choice to respect the distinction between those who may and may not be legitimately harmed.

Assume a highly trained army with good discipline and soldiers who have adequate knowledge of the conventions that govern the conduct of war.[10] Let us begin then with soldiers on the ground, the ones who carry out the orders to fight or to bomb. For instance, would a pilot on a bombing mission take care to distinguish between strategic and terror bombing and refuse to carry out the latter? Consider the case of Paul Warfield Tibbets Jr., who in August 1945 commanded the Enola Gay, the B-29 bomber that dropped the atomic bomb on Hiroshima, killing 140,000 civilians in the Japanese city at the end of the Second World War. Until his death in 2007, Tibbets claimed never to have had regrets or second thoughts about his action.[11] If Tibbets had reasoned about his action using the DDE, he should have recognized that the bombing mission was an illegitimate act of terror bombing on a Japanese metropolis with no military target. Yet it is not surprising that he never saw it that way. For, although he had acted intentionally, he could not have chosen to do what he did on the basis of an evaluation of all the effects that had been expected to follow. It was not his place to choose between demoralizing Japan to the point of unconditional surrender and defeating Japan militarily through a land invasion, which were the options that President Truman and his military advisers had the responsibility of deciding between.[12]

Like most other soldiers, Tibbets had been trained to follow orders. This does not mean that he never makes moral choices in battle. Soldiers should have enough moral autonomy to tell when something they are told to do is blatantly wrong and refuse to do it, for example, shooting prisoners or raping women. But when they are given orders where the bad effect is not directly stated, it is commonplace for soldiers to carry out the orders without taking the effect into account, or if they do, to simply take for granted that the commanders had considered it and judged the action as a morally acceptable one. Even when they do not make this assumption, they may view the moral blame for any wrongdoing as falling upon the commanders and not themselves. Thus, any moral thinking that they do is limited and need not extend to choosing to act on the basis of the DDE.

If lower-ranked soldiers follow orders and assume that their commanders have moral responsibility for the orders that they execute, then would the DDE be of use in the latter's decision to, say, order a bombing mission that they know would kill civilians? It depends on what the decision is and how it is made. The DDE is supposedly relevant for making a moral decision, but how would it enter into the decision-making process of a military commander? Consider this example of aerial bombardment in the Korean War:[13] When an American battalion comes under fire from a distant hillside, the commander has two options. He can send a patrol to outflank the enemy and take their position, or he can call for an air strike. The commander orders the air strike. Why? Because the air strike would achieve the goal of allowing his troops to advance without risking their lives. But what about the civilians who are killed in the air strike without any serious attempt at discriminating them from enemy soldiers, as required by the principle of discrimination? Since the commander is acting from a legitimate concern for the safety of his troops and it is not his intention to kill civilians, then assuming proportionality, the DDE can be used to justify the aerial bombardment of the enemy position.

However, I doubt that the DDE features at all in the reasoning behind the decision of the commander. For that assumes the morality of the choice is relevant to his decision. We cannot tell whether it is when the case is one where the commander favors the choice that is deemed permissible by the DDE. What if civilians have to be killed as a *means* and not a side-effect to save the lives of the troops? According to the DDE, this is not morally acceptable. Is there any reason to think that the commander will be guided by the doctrine to make a decision to sacrifice some of his troops rather than to kill civilians? As a matter of fact, the killing of civilians as a means to achieve military objectives has been all too frequent an occurrence in war. An obvious case of this is the very example of the atomic bombing of Japan that was ordered because commanders were concerned about the cost in American lives of a land invasion to defeat Japan.[14]

It may be objected that the failure of commanders to use the DDE only shows that they must be trained to use the doctrine. Suppose the DDE is given the role of a moral constraint that bars decisions that involve killing civilians as the means to achieve a military objective. Imagine the commander who intends to kill civilians (because he judges it to be necessary to achieve his objectives) realizing or being told that it is wrong according to the DDE for him to do so. I would suggest that, if he has already formed the intention, it is too late in the day to introduce the moral doctrine to constrain his choice. Assuming there is no error in his reasoning concerning military necessity, how could it be reasonable for him to give up on the very intention that his deliberation led him to form? Either his intention would have to be frustrated against his will or he has to change his intention. But we should expect morality to do more than blocking or changing intentions. To require the commander to choose a different action given that his reasoning about the best means toward his end led him to prefer the killing of civilians is to demand that he go against the balance of reasons that favors his choice, all things considered.[15] If he does not have desires that lead him to willingly sacrifice his other ends so as to avoid killing them, he cannot be relied upon to choose in a way that satisfies the DDE unless he is prevented from acting on his preferences. To be constrained in this way by a rule is not genuinely choosing to do the right thing on the basis of moral considerations.

A more disturbing aspect to the demand that the DDE constrain choices on the battlefield involves a change of intention in response to the DDE. If the commander seeks to do what by his lights is the most prudent thing, which is to choose the option that involves killing civilians, he may get around the DDE by choosing to do what he would have intended to do *without intending it*. That is, he can "redirect" his intention, assuming that this can be done at will, away from the act of killing civilians. But if this were possible, it would render the DDE useless as a moral standard. It is doing what Anscombe calls "double-think about double effect."[16] If the commander still believes that killing civilians is the best option and does so as the means to achieve his goal, it is disingenuous to deny that he intends to kill them. If he could narrow down his intention to exclude the killing of civilians, what is there to prevent any terror bomber from doing the same?[17]

It seems to me that it is not possible for any military commander to take the DDE seriously in his moral thinking unless he is already strongly disinclined in the first place toward options that involve killing civilians. But if so, he does not need the DDE to constrain him from acting on his intention after he has formed it. He just would not form the intention to kill civilians in all but the most exceptional circumstances, given the kind of person he is; that is, given his moral character. But it is likely that he (and people of similar character) would not join the military, given the kind of person he is, and given that the killing of civilians, whether intended or not, is part and parcel of war. If he does join the military, he will be trained to function in a system where orders from superiors are unquestioningly followed[18] and a deep sense of comradeship among the troops is instilled. This makes it unlikely that individual soldiers would choose to risk the mission or the lives of fellow-soldiers for the sake of protecting enemy civilians. Once again, there does not seem to be a role in decision-making for the DDE that could constrain prudential choices so as to meet the requirements of the principle of discrimination.

It might be thought that the DDE can still be used by ethicists of war to evaluate actions taken by soldiers in war after they happen. Whether this is feasible depends on how the doctrine copes with the theoretical challenges in formulating and justifying the DDE. In particular, there are different views on whether the concept of intention can separate the merely foreseen effects from the intended effects, and on what the rationale is for the moral distinction between what is intended and what is not intended. It would go beyond the scope of this book to examine these issues here. But to limit the use of the DDE to ethicists is to deny that the principle of discrimination can be used in the way that just war theorists and international jurists have proposed. The principles of *jus in bello* are supposed to make it possible to make better moral choices in war. They form the basis for international humanitarian laws that make war crimes punishable offenses. But to hold soldiers accountable for violations of the principle of discrimination requires that it is possible for them to choose to follow the laws of armed conflict. It is not enough that the DDE is used in hindsight to evaluate actions that have already taken place.

The main point here concerns not the DDE specifically, which may well have other uses in moral theory, but the principle of discrimination in just war theory. As I have said before, war has always been disastrous for civilians throughout history. It is important for just war theory to show that the killing of civilians can be kept within morally acceptable limits. To do that, soldiers must be able to judge whether their proposed actions are within or outside these limits. It is too easy in war for soldiers to persuade themselves that they do no wrong when they are tempted to risk the lives of noncombatants. Unfortunately, the principle of discrimination fails to provide clear signposts or out-of-bounds markers to tell soldiers where the moral limits to killing are.

Most people nowadays do not view human life as expendable, even during wartime. Why then do men and women from modern civilized nations still enlist as soldiers, knowing full well that they may be sent to kill, and the people that they kill often includes noncombatants? Is it because they think that civilians will only be killed when such killing is necessary to achieve a goal that is a greater good? Two ideas are involved here: such killings are proportionate and they are not intended. The problems I have raised here for the DDE show that the intentional killing of civilians in war cannot be constrained by the DDE in a way that ensures that soldiers in battle satisfy the principle of discrimination. The just war doctrine is, thus, criticized for implying that there is such a constraint and for providing a rationalization or cover for the killing of civilians that are a very repugnant and persistent feature of war. I turn now to a discussion of the principle of proportionality.

The principle of proportionality

The idea behind the principle of proportionality is that there are limits to what one can do if one is acting justly. Justice is partly determined by a balancing of costs and benefits in specific situations, and proportionality is an idea found in the earliest theories of justice.[19] In war, combatants can do the most horrendous things to the victims of armed attack unless they are restrained by rules of war. Some realists about war think that there cannot be moral limits to acts of war. Clausewitz suggested that there is a propensity to escalate and use the most extreme force once war begins.[20] But there are a number of reasons why military commanders and ethical thinkers would not endorse this way of fighting. From a prudential perspective, success on the battlefield often goes to the side where the soldiers are disciplined and have control of their aggression (as seen from ancient times in Roman military victories over barbarian armies). In addition, how one's side fights has an influence over how one's enemies act in response. It is easier to get besieged cities to surrender if the inhabitants believe that they would not be abused. Conventions that govern the behavior of soldiers in war were developed to ensure that mutual obligations exist to protect soldiers and civilians from inhumane treatment. From a theological point of view, unrestrained violence was bad for the soul. In medieval Church doctrine, soldiers were required to do penance, the severity of which depended on how many they had killed on the battlefield, but unrestrained killing could not be indulged by the Church. Finally, from the customs of war, there existed a code of chivalry and honor that had to be upheld for knights to keep their status in society.

The just war theory incorporates the idea of proportionality in more ways than one. And because proportionality was derived from more than one source, the idea had a variety of interpretations, leading to plenty of confusion about its meaning and application.[21] We are here considering the principle of proportionality as a requirement of *jus in bello*, but a similar principle has been presented as a requirement for *jus ad bellum*. If so, proportionality may be necessary for the justice of war in both its aspects.[22] It was noted earlier that proportionality is a condition for applying the doctrine of double effect when it is used in the principle of discrimination. What is problematic is that the diverse applications of proportionality add to the confusion about how it applies to the evaluation of war. As a result, what seems proportionate to some is considered disproportionate by others. And if the criterion of proportionality is imprecise, subjective, or relative, it does not provide a good basis for restricting what soldiers do in war.

Let me begin a critical examination of the principle by stating some versions of proportionality:

- (*Ad bellum* proportionality) The destructiveness of war must not be out of proportion to the relevant good that the war will do.
- (*In bello* proportionality I) The collateral killing of civilians is forbidden if the resulting civilian deaths are out of proportion to the relevant good one's act will do (i.e., excessive force is wrong).[23]
- (*In bello* proportionality II) The force used against the enemy must be no more than required to attain the justified end.[24]
- (*In bello* proportionality III) Avoid the escalation or broadening of conflicts and refrain from the use of weapons of horrendous destructive potential.[25]
- (*In bello* proportionality IV) The means employed must not destroy the possibility of peace or encourage a contempt for human life that puts the safety of ourselves and of mankind in jeopardy.[26]

It can be seen from these statements that proportionality may concern many different things in war. It may be used to evaluate the decision to go to war or the actions of those who fight the war. It may attempt to maintain a balance (a) in the weapons used, or (b) in the lives taken, or (c) in the necessity of the violence in relation to the goal of war and the possibility of peace. Regarding lives, what are counted may be civilian lives (collateral damage) alone, or combatant as well as noncombatant lives. Even if it can be decided what should count, there are still difficult questions about what weight to give to each human life – civilian, combatant, ally, and enemy.[27] Regarding the use of force, the goal that necessitates violence may be the military objective or the achievement of the cause that justifies going to war or the avoidance of future wars. Again, there is a serious difficulty in judging how many lives is the goal worth. There can be wide differences in opinions when what are being compared are values that are incommensurable.

One thing can be agreed upon: if one believes that the achievement of one's goal in war is highly consequential and of immense value, a lot more violence and killing can be justified in terms of proportional harms that result from the means and methods of fighting a war. If civilization as we know it is at stake, then innocent lives are worth very little and are readily sacrificed. In fact, Michael Walzer goes so far as to lift the *in bello* restrictions when a state is faced with a "supreme emergency."[28] The cases are far from hypothetical. The idea of a supreme emergency came from Winston Churchill when Britain alone faced the might of Nazi Germany and was used to justify deliberate aerial bombing of civilian inhabitants in major German cities in violation of the principle of discrimination. In the present day, the US Global War on Terror has the twin aims of eradicating every terrorist group on the planet and the spreading of freedom to countries in the Middle East and elsewhere in repressive societies that have little or no experience with Western forms of democratic governance. Such a broad definition of the objective of war, against a threat that is said to be capable of acquiring and using nuclear weapons for terrorist attacks, has been used to justify much greater use of force and the abrogation of international standards that protect innocent lives and prohibit atrocities in wartime.[29]

A serious problem for interpretations of proportionality that measure all evils of war against the just cause that is a condition of *jus ad bellum* is that justice is in the eyes of the beholder. Although it cannot be likely or even possible (though this has been debated in the just war tradition) for both sides in a war to be just, and it is quite likely that there is guilt all around, most belligerents will claim to have a just cause in going to war. To get around this problem, some just war theorists have advocated the independence of *jus in bello* conditions from the requirements of *jus ad bellum*. The idea is that whether or not the side that one is fighting for has a just cause, soldiers act justly when they adhere to the principles of *jus in bello*. This is a thesis known as the moral equivalence of combatants.[30] It is obvious that excessive violence and brutality can be limited when the good that justifies the harm is that of achieving a military or tactical advantage and not the lofty aims of the entire war. There is also the recognition that soldiers are not in a position to evaluate the just cause for the war, nor are they able to measure what they do on the battlefield against the overall good of victory in war.

Even then, there is still a possibility of justifications for escalating the violence inflicted on the enemy. Military objectives can be specified in ways that justify more indiscriminate and unrestrained attacks. Force protection and the political need to keep casualties low on one's side have led to the use of weapons and tactics that would otherwise seem disproportionate. In the NATO bombing campaign against the Serbs in Kosovo in 1999, the attacking planes flew above the range of Serbian anti-aircraft guns, with the result that they were less precise in hitting their targets and avoiding harm to civilians.[31] In the US invasion of Iraq in 2003, heavy bombardment of Baghdad and other cities using the most technologically advanced weaponry preceded the boots on the ground. This tactic of "shock and awe" was highly successful in demoralizing the Iraqi defenders and the US-led forces faced a low level of resistance. In a matter of weeks, Baghdad fell, with American troop casualties of about 150. But estimates of civilian casualties ranged from 5,000 to 10,000 in the same period.[32] The US military policy of "overwhelming force" seems to be a negation of proportionality, yet this method of fighting may be necessary if the objectives of the military included minimizing their own casualties.

One criticism of the use of superior forces to overpower the enemy is that the principle of proportionality is opposed to any escalation of war. The introduction of new weapons and the deployment of forces superior in numbers and equipment may in the long run encourage other countries to negate such advantages by acquiring similar or better weapons. This may prolong the conflict or set the stage for greater devastation in future wars. The weaker side also harbors resentment and a sense of injustice, especially when it suffers a much larger number of casualties and more severe destruction. This bodes ill for the preservation of peace after the stronger side has won the war. Peace as the goal of a just war is undermined by the way that victory is secured. There is also a temptation for countries with superior forces to eschew diplomacy and to rely on military means to settle international disputes or to escalate a border incursion into an all out war.

This way of interpreting proportionality as requiring some sort of a balance between opposing forces has struck those who disagree with it as counter-intuitive.[33] Why should the stronger side be required to fight with one hand tied, so to speak? The idea of fighting with roughly equal forces and using the same weapons may make sense in the medieval code of chivalry. But if the stronger side is able to press home its advantage, would not the overall outcome be an earlier end to the fighting and, therefore, result in the saving of lives? This, however, is not the only consequence that matters – and we have just discussed the resentment of the defeated side, especially if they had a just cause for fighting. The unrestrained use of violence in the name of a quick end to fighting would result in a more dangerous world in which might makes right. And the use of greater force may result in more civilian casualties. A trade-off in which the lives of soldiers are saved at the expense of enemy civilians is difficult to justify, whether or not the killings are unintended.[34] The use of the atomic bomb against Japan at the end of the Second World War and the killing of thousands of Iraqi civilians in the campaign of "shock and awe" before the American invasion in 2003 are troublesome instances which strike many moral thinkers as clear violations of proportionality in the use of force.

I think the disagreement about whether overwhelming force can be justified on the basis of military necessity stems from different views of consequences. When one does all that is necessary to win a war as quickly as possible and with the least casualties on one's side, one may not consider overwhelming force to be excessive or disproportionate in relation to the objectives. But if proportionality requires consideration of the consequences for future peace or conflict, then overwhelming force and the introduction of new weapons may bring more harms than good. History has frequently proven this point. In the Six Days War of 1967, Israeli forces went beyond the goal of pre-empting an Arab attack on Israel, taking advantage of their military superiority to occupy large swathes of Arab territories. Those military actions went beyond what was required by the just cause of self-defense or the battlefield objective of neutralizing the Arab threat. The consequence that resulted from the continued occupation of Arab lands has been more than forty years of unceasing conflict without lasting security for any of the countries in the region, with no end in sight.

We have been considering the implications of the *jus in bello* requirements independently of the *jus ad bellum* requirements. We did so in order to disqualify the excessive force that may result when proportionality of one's means is measured against the achievement of victory for a just cause. When the just cause is preserving civilization or defeating terrorism, such a measure of proportionality places hardly any constraints on what can be done. But now we see that comparing the harms that one inflicts in fighting against the *military* objectives also does not necessarily constrain the amount of force or prevent the escalation of war. Not only are there objectives such as minimizing casualties on one's side that can justify overwhelming force, but freed from consideration of the cause for which one is fighting, the military may actually take actions that cannot be justified in terms of what is needed to achieve the just cause. In the Six Days War, military commanders decided to not just defeat the Arab armies but take over control of East Jerusalem, presenting political leaders with a *fait accompli* from which they and their successors have been unable to extricate themselves.

It is hard to escape the conclusion that the principle of proportionality is quite useless as a moral restraint on the conduct of war. The brutality of war cannot be ameliorated by the requirement that combatants fight only in ways that the harms they do are more than balanced by a proportionate good. Proportionality itself is a confusing and muddled concept. Depending on how one interprets it, the principle can be satisfied even when one is fighting in ways that escalate conflicts and that undermine the just cause for which one is fighting. The language of proportionality is used to provide moral cover for actions in war that are extremely harmful to the lives of combatants, civilians, and the cause of peace. Yet it is hard to see what could replace it as a requirement of *jus in bello*.

Legitimate authority

Legitimate authority was supposed to distinguish war from large-scale banditry. Otherwise, how could one distinguish an act of war from the actions of criminals? In Colombia today, the drug cartels have sufficient well-armed and organized fighters to control cities and take on the state army. But the drug lords do not have legitimate authority. They are not fighting to establish a government or to take over the running of a state. Whatever their fighters do, they are not combatants fighting a war. And anyone fighting without legitimate authority to declare war cannot be fighting a just war.

How exactly can legitimate authority be used as a condition for just war? The word "legitimate" seems to beg the question. Just war theory also uses the term "sovereign authority," implying the authority of a head of state. Walzer has interpreted sovereign rights to mean some degree of control over a chunk of territory.[35] But what has being a sovereign ruler got to do with justice in war? Throughout history, it was often the case that kings were leading their armies to fight for their own personal gain or glory rather than for the good of their subjects. Rulers such as Alexander the Great or Hitler or Saddam Hussein clearly fought wars to benefit themselves or to fulfill their personal ambitions. Moreover, it is easy to see the similarities between the drug lords and those rulers who were into exactly the same criminal business – for instance, Manuel Noriega of Panama (until his capture by US forces and his trial for criminal activities) and the Taliban regime in Afghanistan (before its overthrow by an American-led invasion after 9/11).

Obviously, the requirement for legitimate authority cannot stand on its own to justify war in the absence of just cause and the fulfillment of other requirements for *jus ad bellum*. It is clearly not a sufficient condition. But even its status as a necessary condition for just war can be challenged. A problem that has been raised for this requirement is that it seems to favor those in power against those out of power. Why should tyrants have legitimate authority, but freedom fighters not? The latter would seem to have more legitimacy as representatives or defenders of the people in a state under tyrannical rule. Although they are not yet in power and have yet to gain international recognition, could they not be in a position to go to war on behalf of the people and do so justly? Wouldn't denying them the right to fight serve to perpetuate the rule of abusive tyrants or colonial powers? Just war theorists have attempted to refine the meaning of legitimate authority to include non-state actors such as revolutionary groups and anti-colonial liberation movements. But moves in this direction seem ad hoc unless a deeper reason and criterion can be provided for deciding who has legitimate authority. If we decide that tyrants do not have legitimate authority but freedom fighters do, then we are deciding on some other basis than sovereign rule or control of territory. If we are deciding on the basis of the justice of the cause they are fighting for, then the legitimate authority condition for just war is rendered secondary or redundant.

To get at the basis of the legitimate authority condition, it helps to understand where the condition came from and how it was traditionally used. When the just war theory was being developed in the early years of the Catholic Church, the sovereign's authority was believed to be conferred by divine blessing. In Augustine's version of just war, killing that is commanded by God is not wrongful murder. When the ruler of a state goes to war, he or she was thought to be carrying out God's command. If someone was not the sovereign, he or she could not claim to be acting at the behest of God. Thus, if such a person leads a group of armed fighters into combat, it would be unlawful.

Just war theory has now evolved into a secular doctrine that is accepted as the basis for international law. But without the appeal to a divine being, the distinction between a sovereign fighting a war and the use of violence by organized criminals no longer seems intuitive. In fact, it seems that we have to consider *why* violence is being used, not who is doing it, in order to evaluate the justice of a war. That is, we have to examine what the goals are in fighting and how the person or persons in authority chose to use violence as a means to achieve these goals. To ask whether a goal can justify war is to ask if there is a just cause. To ask how it is that the authorities resorted to war in preference to other means to their goal is to ask whether war was chosen as a last resort. It seems that we have reason to say that if a rebel group that controlled no territory had just cause and was fighting as a last resort, its use of violence can be justified. That is why we are tempted to declare such groups to have legitimate authority. On the other hand, a head of state that either did not have a just cause or used war in preference to more peaceful alternatives to achieve the just cause would not satisfy the requirements of *jus ad bellum*. And when that is the case, we tend to find ways to disqualify the authority of the regime, using terms such as "rogue nations" or "failed states."

The traditional idea of sovereigns vested with divine authority provided moral cover for those who fight for them. No matter how wrongly these rulers acted, they were ultimately "right" in that they served a divine purpose. Once this idea of sovereign authority was rejected, the ruler's actions in declaring and fighting wars had to be judged on their own merits in terms of what their purposes were. The secular version of just war theory vests legitimate authority in the Westphalian system of sovereign nation-states. But this is a legal and political arrangement, not a basis for moral authority. There is, then, no reason to think that justice in going to war somehow depends on satisfying the principle of legitimate authority, in either the traditional or modern sense.

Just cause

What constitutes a morally acceptable reason for fighting a war? In the just war tradition, war is appropriate as a response to injustice, wrongdoing, or a violation of rights. In the earliest versions of just war theory, the just causes for war included both self-defense and the punishment of an offending party. With the latter goal, war could be justifiably continued even after the threat of the opposing side has been neutralized, in order to punish the people deemed responsible for an offense that led to war, to obtain reparations to compensate for the harm caused by the offense, and to prevent a repetition of the offense in the future. Punishment as a just cause for war meant that wars often lasted longer than what was needed for the purpose of self-defense. It also meant that wars could be fought when there was no unjust attack on a nation's territory, as the offense that had to be punished may be a dispute over commerce or honor. The traditional view partly reflects the Christian roots of the just war theory that was developed by Augustine who viewed the punishment of sinners as a Christian duty (and act of love) that can be achieved by the use of war.

As just war theory became secularized and integrated into international law, and as the idea of state sovereignty under the Westphalian system took hold, punishment in itself was no longer regarded as a good enough justification for states to resort to violence against other states. For a state to punish another state (beyond warding off an attack and removing a serious threat to a state's security) presumes that it has judicial authority over other states and that the sovereignty of another state did not seriously limit what it could do within the other state's borders (as opposed to its own territory when invaded). In the words of David Rodin, "self-defense is central to modern international law: it is currently the *sole* legal justification for the use of force by states without the authorization of the United Nations."[36] This means that if it cannot be maintained that war could be morally justified on the basis of self-defense, there may not be anything that counts as a just cause for war initiated by individual states.[37] And given the central role of just cause in the many formulations across the long tradition of just war thinking, the just war doctrine would then be seriously undermined.

I will first discuss the problems for national self-defense that Rodin has presented. Then I will argue that there are implications that are more dire for just war theory than what Rodin himself describes as "a serious challenge to the traditional Just War doctrine of international morality."[38] Rodin examines how the right of self-defense by a state under attack could be understood. Such a right seems to draw on the more intuitive idea of a personal right of self-defense when violently attacked. So how does the moral legitimacy of personal self-defense (simply called self-defense by Rodin) provide a basis for the state's right to respond with force to military aggression by another state (called national-defense by Rodin)? One way, the reductive strategy, is to view national-defense as the collective form of self-defense, "an application, *en masse*, of the familiar right of individuals to protect themselves from unjust lethal attack."[39] An alternative way, the analogical strategy, is to consider states as right-bearers in the way that individuals are, so that, by analogy, the state has the right to defend itself against aggression in the way that an individual person has the right to act in self-defense.

Rodin argues that both strategies fail. I will show that the way they fail can be instructive. The reductive strategy is confronted with two counter-examples. The first example is humanitarian intervention, that is, military intervention in another state without authorization by that state's authorities, with the purpose of preventing widespread suffering or death among its inhabitants. Either the basic human rights of many of the people (often a minority ethnic group) are being violated by their repressive rulers, or there is a failure by their government to protect these rights. The intervention of outside forces coming to protect them can be resisted as an unjust attack on a state's sovereignty and provides the basis for the state intervened with to oppose the intervention by exercising its right of national-defense. But if national-defense were reducible to the right of individual citizens to act to protect their own lives, then "not only would national-defense and humanitarian intervention share an underlying moral structure but the latter right could be derived from the former."[40] Thus, the reductive strategy does not succeed in making personal self-defense a sufficient basis for national-defense. A second example is that of a bloodless invasion where only territory is violated and no citizen of the state that is invaded is personally threatened. Rodin imagines that this could happen if a remote and uninhabited piece of territory was seized, or there was an armed incursion into a state's air space or territorial waters that did not threaten any citizen of that state. Although in international law, there is justification to use force in response to attacks against a state's territorial integrity and political independence, this seems logically independent of whether any individual citizen has been threatened by the attacks. The conclusion here for Rodin is that when the state makes it case for national-defense as a just cause for war, there may not necessarily be a case for personal self-defense.

With the failure of the reductive strategy, Rodin turns to the analogical strategy. The idea is that national-defense is a state-held right that has a similar moral content to the personal right of self-defense. Just as the individual has the right to defend his or her own life, the state by analogy has the right to defend the "common life of the community." What does this common life have to be to justify defending it with the use of force? There are two requirements: particularity and objectivity. As Rodin puts it, "The value which grounds national-defense must be particular in the sense that it provides a reason for defending one form of common life against another, but its value cannot be so particular as to be simply subjective."[41] The problem is that a Hobbesian understanding of the value of the common life in terms of the state's legitimacy based on its role in securing order for its citizens' lives does not justify defending this particular order against the order that may be provided by an aggressor state taking over. A second interpretation views the common life as the embodiment of a particular cultural and historical heritage, recognizing our identity as partially defined by the cultural and linguistic traditions in which we locate our lives. The problem here is that the value of any particular form of common life is evident only to those within that common life. As a value, it is not for outsiders to judge. The value of a particular common life is a relativized value and the right to national-defense is construed to correspond with a duty on others of non-interference based on the illegitimacy of judging the value of another's common life. But if a relativism of value is maintained, the notion that non-intervention is objectively valuable and applies to all is objectionably ad hoc.

Rodin considers one other interpretation of a common life on which the right of national-defense rests, one that could be both objective and particular. Since "freedom, autonomy, and self-determination are objective transcultural goods...there is an important realm of self-determination which is necessarily collective" and which is disrupted by foreign intervention.[42] It does not matter that the intervention may be aimed at bringing democracy or at ending oppression, for "it violates the rights of peoples to determine collectively the form and nature of their common life."[43] But Rodin thinks that this notion of self-determination is stretched beyond recognition as it allows, for instance, civil war to count as collective self-determination – even though it reduces self-determination to coercion. So even if collective self-determination in the abstract could be objectively valued, the concept in some of its particular forms could not provide an adequate moral basis for a right of national-defense, a right that supposedly justifies the use of violence when the common life is threatened from outside the community.

Rodin concludes that national-defense or the self-defense of the state as it is used in contemporary just war theory and in international law as the sole just cause for individual states to resort to war is without a moral foundation. The right to personal self-defense does not provide a basis or an analogy for the state's right to use violence when faced with external aggression. Instead, Rodin believes that if military action against aggression could still be justified, it should be considered not as a form of self-defense but as a form of law enforcement. For this to work, a minimal universal state would need to be established. This is a radical proposal that would be very difficult to pull off. But it is a proposal that maintains the right of a proper authority to use military force in the right circumstances, while conceptualizing this right differently from the self-defense justification found in almost all versions of just war theory. In this book, I am proposing an even more radical proposal than Rodin's, namely the complete abandonment of just war theory as a paradigm for the ethics of war. Perhaps Rodin is already doing this, but he does not seem to go far enough since he seeks to preserve the *right* in international law to fight a war and be justified in doing so. What I need to explain here is why I think Rodin's arguments have provided a basis for the more radical move of rejecting the just war paradigm altogether.[44]

As mentioned before, just cause has been a requirement of *jus ad bellum* from the beginning of the just war tradition and self-defense is now taken in modern just war theory and international law to be the sole just cause for states to go to war. Rodin's arguments show that the just war tradition has been mistaken all along about what counts as a just cause. His proposal is a new way of justifying the use of military force to repel aggressor states. Such use of force may well in practice be co-extensive with the use of force in self-defense as justified by the just war theory. But because Rodin's justification requires the existence of some kind of universal state, the "justification" for states that act in self-defense actually takes the form of a counterfactual: *if there had been a universal state at the time that military force was used against an aggressor*, it would have been justified to fight against the aggressor. But given that there is no universal state at the time, the actions of the state that goes to war in self-defense are, in fact, unjustified. In other words, no wars with just cause have taken place in the past and present, though there could be such wars in the future, and there could have been one in the past had the past been different. I think that such a conclusion would provide little comfort to the just war theorists, be they traditional or modern, religious or secular.

Notice, however, that pacifism does not follow, even in the absence of a universal state. For Rodin's arguments not only leave the right to personal self-defense untouched, but his arguments to reject national-defense rests on there being a right of self-defense by individuals facing attack from aggressors. Throughout history, the lives and safety of individuals have been placed under serious threat of violence from aggressors. These individuals are justified in using force to defend themselves against violent attacks and threats to their survival. In my view, the significance of Rodin's argument is that it shows that there is no plausible way to translate the justification for individuals to use force in this way to the justification for states to act in national-defense. There is, I think, a simple reason why this is so, namely that war as experienced throughout most of history is not really about defending individuals who are under attack. Wars take place when armed warriors go to fight because they have been compelled to or rewarded for doing so by the people in their society with power or wealth. In my view, the only morally relevant change in the use of collective violence in history was from individuals in a community banding together to take up arms in self-defense when actually attacked, to armies of full-time soldiers organized and trained to fight on the orders of a military leader in the form of a state or tribal authority. It is actions of the latter kind that are properly described as war and that require special moral justification because such actions go beyond those of individuals acting together in self-defense.[45] Although soldiers act in personal self-defense in war when they face attack on the battlefield, the fact is that soldiers in war place themselves in such situations by going to war, often in faraway places, and they are attacked because they pose a threat to other people. What Rodin's arguments succeed in showing is that going to war is not about personal self-defense at all, so it is no surprise that war cannot derive justification from the individual right of self-defense.

Once we recognize that war is about fulfilling the political will of leaders, whatever their claim to power, and consists of actions such as taking control of territory and influencing the policies of adversaries or overthrowing them, it seems ludicrous to appeal to self-defense as a just cause for war. One of Rodin's examples discussed earlier illustrates how fighting to defend a piece of remote territory need have no bearing on the lives and safety of citizens. And in making the point that the common life does not have an objective and particular value that it is justified to fight a war to defend, Rodin shows that a fight over who should be in charge of the state is not analogous to a fight for the survival of an individual, where the objective and irreplaceably particular value of human life is at stake. In showing the illegitimacy of appeals to self-defense as just cause, Rodin has actually exposed as a fiction the claim that a just war is about people fighting for their own lives. Because of the true nature of war and the way that armies are designed to fight, the actions and aims of war are hardly ever solely defensive in nature. When a state is attacked, it may "defend" itself by launching a military attack on the territory and citizens of the aggressor state and by finding ways to influence the actions of other states that have ties with the adversary and ways to change the leadership or the policies of the political leaders of the adversary. These are actions designed to harm or threaten to harm individual citizens of the adversary and are hardly defensive at all. These are not actions that should be included under just cause, except when falsely disguised as self-defense.

Last resort

According to the principle of last resort as a condition of *jus ad bellum*, the use of force by a state is justified only when all non-military means of conflict resolution to deal with the matter in dispute have been tried without success. The state's leaders are required to make a choice of war based on an evaluation of the evil of war compared with the burden of an injustice that is left unaddressed by non-violent options. As with proportionality, which also requires such comparisons to be made, the requirement that war be used as a last resort is difficult to put into practice or to evaluate correctly. How do the leaders determine that non-military options no longer have a reasonable chance of success or are no longer available? What is the time frame during which alternatives to the use of force should continue to be pursued?[46] In one sense, war is never truly the last resort. Suppose that State *A* faces aggression from State *B* and the aggressors reject all diplomatic overtures. War could still be avoided if State *A* chooses not to fight against the aggressors. Of course, this would reward aggression and the citizens of State *A* would suffer the loss of their autonomy. The requirement that war be a last resort may have more practical utility if we take "last resort" to mean having tried everything else to settle international disputes short of surrender or appeasement. But what does "everything else" include? Does a state have to literally go down a list of options? This may seem as imprudent as appeasement, since any delay in going to war may let State *B*'s aggression succeed as a *fait accompli*. If it is justified to fight, then it may be better to do so quickly, with a minimum of delay.

So maybe we should have a shorter list of options, or we should reach the point of last resort at an earlier point on the list. Not "everything else" must be tried. But is there a principled reason why trying some things is required but trying other things is not? It cannot just be a matter of opinion that the failure to try something to avoid war makes going to war unjust and the failure to try another thing to avoid war does not make it so. On what basis do political leaders who decide on going to war deem the requirement of last resort to be satisfied? If there is any non-arbitrary basis for their decision, is the basis grounded in morality? Since the choice of which options to try before going to war seems subjective apart from some obvious options, it could be argued that the judgment that a state has no choice but to fight is a matter of prudence rather than justice.[47] That is, the requirement of last resort does not have to be satisfied for there to be justice in going to war, but where there is justice in going to war (after satisfying the other requirements of *jus ad bellum*), the leaders must decide whether it is prudent to fight by considering whether there are less costly alternatives that may achieve the same goals as fighting. But no matter whether it is prudent to fight, the war would be a just war based on fully satisfying the other requirements and an unjust war otherwise.

Because last resort is such an imprecise concept, it seems to contribute little to the ethical evaluation of a decision to go to war. But a further problem with this condition of just war is that even those who take it seriously end up resorting to war too easily. Apart from the question of how many things must be tried before going to war, there is the question of how we know that the alternatives to war that have been tried cannot succeed in achieving the goal, for example, of getting the aggressor to back down. It is often the case that items on the list of options are checked off too quickly and the option of war surfaces as a "last resort" too readily. The theologian John Howard Yoder describes the dishonesty of deciding that all alternatives to war have been tried without success when "the decision that nonviolent means will not work for comparable ends is made without any comparable investment of time or creativity, without comparable readiness to sacrifice, and without serious projection of comparable costs."[48] When countries have invested so much into building up their military assets to ensure success in wars, and so little into training and equipping diplomats and peacemakers, then any peaceful means seems unlikely to succeed, in comparison with military means. Yoder's point is that this is not a fair test of the last resort requirement.

In summary, the last resort requirement seems to contribute little to the justification for going to war. Even when it is taken seriously, it is difficult to apply with any precision, and any results are of questionable value, given that peaceful alternatives are too easily dismissed. It is also unclear what the ethical basis of the requirement is. In particular, does failure to satisfy the requirement undermine the justice of going to war, or does it only show the imprudence of choosing war over a less costly alternative? It may be that because war was thought to be justified as a form of self-defense, the last resort requirement is included by analogy with personal self-defense where the defender is required not to use force in the face of aggression if it is possible to flee from the attack. But given that the analogy of national-defense with personal self-defense was rejected in the previous section of this chapter, there is no basis for using the analogy to argue for including last resort as a condition for *jus ad bellum*.

* * *

In examining three central requirements for justice in going to war, and the two main requirements for justice in the conduct of war, I have shown in this chapter that there are deep and serious problems with each of them. Since these requirements are central to the just war tradition and are found in almost every version of just war theory, it presents the just war theorist with a difficult choice. To remain in the tradition, the just war theorist may tinker with some of the other requirements, adding some and amending others. But he cannot give up on the central tenets that I have critiqued here. He will then have to stick to a seriously flawed ethics of war. If, on the other hand, he acknowledges that he is unable to deal with the problems that have been raised in this chapter, he needs then to offer an ethics of war that does not include the problematic requirements. But such a theory would no longer be a theory in the just war tradition. In my view, this is the path that the ethicist of war should follow and one that I will proceed along in the remainder of this book.

3
From Rights to Virtues

How one responds to the flaws in just war thinking set out in the last chapter depends on which moral theory one holds. Theories within the just war tradition are concerned with justifying what is done in war in terms of rights and duties. Thus, one may think, for instance, that one should reexamine what the right of self-defense and the duty not to kill innocent people involves. Other moral theories, for example utilitarianism, treat rights and duties in a different way or they do not use these concepts at all. Either there are other ways of deciding on right and wrong action, or there are other concepts to be considered, such as those of good or bad character, that are more important. In the following chapters of this book, I shall be presenting a new ethics of war that makes use of the concept of a virtuous person instead of those of rights and duties. In this chapter, I will provide a contrast between deontological ethics and virtue ethics in order to make clear what the shift from rights to virtues means in terms of moral theory.[1]

Deontology and rights

The standard account and source of deontological ethics is that of German philosopher Immanuel Kant.[2] Kant is famous for his Categorical Imperative, which is the supreme principle of morality used to evaluate maxims of action to determine what a person's duties are. There is a connection between a person's will and the rightness of what he does. In his view, an action is right and has moral worth if it is done for the sake of duty and not out of desire or inclination. That is, if the action is done because the agent wants to do it or has some goal he wants to achieve by doing it, then the action does not have moral worth. The actions that do have moral worth are those actions that are chosen on the basis of reason alone, which is objective and not dependent on what the agent desires to do. However, as humans are not purely rational beings, their desires may conflict with reason. So the actions that they have objective reason to do may not be what they want to do. Nevertheless, as a rational being, a person will feel compelled to do what he has a duty to do, whether or not he wants to do it. Since he has these conflicting motivations within him, he has to determine what it is that he has a duty to do or a duty to avoid. Specific categorical imperatives are principles that state what a person's duties are. These are objective principles in contrast to the subjective maxims of action that may be hypothetical imperatives applying when he acts out of inclination.[3] According to the supreme principle of morality that Kant calls the Categorical Imperative (capitalized), what makes a maxim categorical is that it has the form of a law: it is universalizable and holds without exception. The agent's maxim of action can be tested as to whether it has the form of a law by asking whether everyone can act on the same maxim without contradiction. The contradiction may arise because it is impossible to conceptualize everyone willing (that is, intending) to act on that maxim, or because if everyone wills to act on that maxim, the agent is prevented from acting on another maxim that he also wills. Contradictions of either kind are contrary to reason and, given that a moral being is one that acts from reason and not from desires, he should avoid doing those actions that do not pass the test of universalizability.

Kant provides more than one formulation of the Categorical Imperative. Another formulation commands that persons be treated never simply as a means but also as an end. What this means is that a rational being should be respected as an autonomous being with its own ends, not just used as an object or tool that serves the purposes of others. Again, maxims of action can be tested using this formulation of the Categorical Imperative. If the maxim describes the action as one that makes use of other persons for the purposes of the agent in a way to which they cannot in principle consent, then the maxim does not pass the test and the action is forbidden. That is, if people are treated in such a way that they either are not asked for their consent or are tricked into consenting through manipulation and deceit, they are being used as objects and are not respected as persons. Kant thinks that the same maxims that do not pass the first formulation of his Categorical Imperative also do not pass the second formulation, and vice versa.

One issue in philosophical discussions of Kant's ethics concerns how the testing of maxims works and what the test shows regarding our moral duties. Assuming that it is supposed to work in the way Kant uses it, the Categorical Imperative test of maxims will determine in a negative way the actions that are forbidden, that is, those actions that a rational agent has a duty not to perform. Where a maxim passes the test, the action is permissible, not obligatory. For instance, the maxim of killing innocent people in war by bombing cities would not pass the Categorical Imperative test, as the people killed have their lives taken for the purpose of furthering the bomber's purpose of winning the war for his nation. Therefore, the bombing violates a duty not to kill people in that way. The same idea can also be stated in terms of the innocent person's right to life, which is violated in being killed in that way.

Another characteristic of Kant's account of duties is that they have to be carried out no matter what the consequences are. His ethics lays down absolutist requirements for rational agents, since he views moral principles as laws of reason. The duties also hold for every person with no exceptions, since each person is a rational being and cannot escape from the requirements of reason, which moral principles are supposed to be. Thus, the rights of persons that are supposed to be respected are universal rights that every person possesses, regardless of the person's race, gender, status in society, occupation, and age (except for children before maturity).

It should be clear from my brief account of Kant's ethics how the just war theory, especially in the form of international law, has a strong deontological flavor.[4] The principles of just war theory tell us who can be attacked in war on the basis of actions of the enemy that have made them liable to be attacked. That is, people on the enemy's side are also rational beings, with the same universal rights to life, protection from harm, self-determination, and so on, and they could only be attacked if they had done something that placed them outside the protection of these rights or stripped them of these rights altogether. The model used here is self-defense and punishment on the individual level. An unjust aggressor renders himself liable to be at the receiving-end of his victim's violent defensive actions. A murderer forfeits his right to life and it is just to execute him. Similarly, a nation that has been attacked has just cause to fight a war of self-defense. And individual soldiers are liable to be attacked because of the threat they pose by the actions that they take.[5] But noncombatants who are engaged in nothing threatening but are merely caught up in war cannot be justly killed, since attacking them would be a violation of their right to life.[6]

I have already presented a critique of the just war theory that showed how the conditions required for just war cannot succeed in making war ethical. If the rules of war have a moral basis in a theory of rights, then it is important to get a correct account of basic human rights and explain which rights are more important. This is because rights conflict with each other in many circumstances and very often do so in war. When fighting begins, the right to life of persons comes into conflict, as defending the lives of some including oneself means taking the lives of others. Other rights – such as the rights to freedom, to have essential needs met, to be protected from bodily harm, and to have a say in the affairs of the community one lives in – may conflict with each other and also with the right to life. When rights conflict with each other, a way must be found to resolve the conflict in a justified manner. If there is a hierarchy of rights, the more basic rights trump the less basic ones. If the same right of different people conflict, then there must be some way to prefer one person over the other. For instance, when two people are in a fight to the death, their respective rights to life conflict with each other. However, if one person is an unjust aggressor or is in some way the cause of the fight between them, the innocent person's right to life may be more deserving of respect and protection. Another factor to consider is the intention of each agent involved. The doctrine of double effect makes it more permissible to violate someone's rights, including the right to life, if it is not done intentionally.

Given these complexities, an ethics of war formulated on the basis of a rights-based moral theory can take different forms. Since killing is the most salient moral violation in war, just war theory is concerned with when the right to life may be justly disrespected and with whether innocent life can be justly taken. Since it is recognized that individuals may have to kill when attacked, self-defense seems to be the most obvious exception to the moral prohibition on killing people. If the right to life means anything, it should include the right to do what is necessary (within limits that exclude, for instance, the killing of innocent bystanders) to protect that life.[7] Unsurprisingly, self-defense has been considered a just cause for war since the beginnings of just war theory and it is now the only legal basis for a state to go to war without United Nations authorization, under the UN Charter. But the concept of self-defense is itself a complicated one and gives rise to different views about when killing in self-defense is justified.[8] In addition, it is not clear how the individual right of self-defense when attacked translates into a right of self-defense by the state.[9] As we saw in Chapter 2, an outside aggressor need not attack individuals when it attacks the state and the state can attack its citizens without outside interference. This led us to be skeptical about the state's right of self-defense as the basis for just war. One possible response to this is to work out an account of just war on the basis of rights in a different way. Instead of articulating a right of self-defense by the state, war and the killings entailed by war can be justified only when the basic human rights of individuals are at risk and must be protected. Many basic human rights depend on others in society to be satisfied. Those that are socially basic human rights include security rights and subsistence rights. Thus, war that is fighting to effect social change may be justified to protect and to advance socially basic human rights.[10]

Despite such attempts to work out alternative versions of rights as the basis for just war, there remains a feature of war that a rights-based morality does not handle well. I may be within my rights to harm or kill an aggressor when I act in self-defense to protect my right to life, but in doing so, I will cause great suffering. On a deontological ethics, the suffering that I cause does not count against the rightness of my action if I am doing something that I have the right to do. When I exercise my right of self-defense, the harm I bring to the aggressor is deserved. If I were to torture him or make him suffer a slow and painful death, then I would have inflicted more suffering than he deserved and I would be wrong to do so. But as long as I do what is within my rights, I do no wrong. Now in individual self-defense, I need not do great harm, even if I have to kill the aggressor. He loses his life and he may have loved ones who suffer from the loss. But wars are on a much larger scale and are much more harmful. If there is a right to go to war and to do certain violent actions in war, then in exercising the right, very great harm and suffering could and usually does result.[11] The rights-based account is concerned with whether the state and those fighting on its behalf are acting within their rights to do what is done in war. So long as the conditions for just war (both *jus ad bellum* and *jus in bello*) are satisfied, the state can do no wrong in bringing about the harms and suffering of war. But, as is more than obvious in history, such harms and suffering are on a different scale from those that are caused when an individual kills in self-defense. The killing of millions and the massive destruction of property and disruption of life combine to make war much harder to justify than killing in defense of the life of an individual. The harmful effects of war must be taken into account in an ethics of war in a way that the rights-based account of just war cannot possibly do.

In arguing for the moral relevance of the harmful effects of war, I may appear to be moving in the direction of a consequentialist moral theory. This is not the case. Consequentialists are also blind to certain morally relevant aspects of the world and the application of a consequentialist theory such as utilitarianism to war would be a moral disaster. For one thing, the difficulty of measuring and comparing benefits and harms makes it likely that states would go to war giving more weight to the benefits for themselves and less weight to the harms to the other side. But the most serious shortcoming of consequentialism is that it permits people to be harmed for the greater good. So, even though the theory counts the harms caused by war, these harms are aggregated and could be offset by benefits. If the good to be achieved is important enough, or if a large enough number of people benefit, great harms could be imposed on some people and it does not matter whether they deserve to suffer these harms. Under consequentialism, war would actually be more common, as all that is required to justify war is that the net benefits of war are greater (by a little bit) in comparison with any other alternative. The nature of the benefits and the harms are not considered if the cost-benefit analysis only takes into account the quantities involved as measured on a scale of utility.

   I shall now turn to virtue ethics which I think is a moral theory that does take into account the harm of war in a way that rights-based moral theories are incapable of doing. But the way that virtue ethics does that is different from consequentialist moral theories. Virtue ethics is an account where moral decision-making is not a matter of calculations of benefits and harms. But neither does it leave moral choice to the following of rules or to the satisfaction of conditions that provides a person with the right to do harm.

Virtues and agent-based ethics

Until the past few decades, the standard philosophical approach to ethical problems has been either utilitarian or deontological. Since then, virtue ethics has experienced a resurgence of interest and a number of important books and articles have furthered the development of virtue ethics as a third main moral theory that rivals utilitarianism and deontological ethics. Yet there remains misapprehension and skepticism toward virtue ethics, especially among applied ethicists. The problem for virtue ethics is the challenge of showing how it can provide practical guidance. Before I turn to that, I shall present an account of virtue ethics to show how it is different from its rival theories.

   The main versions of virtue ethics today draw from the writings of the ancient Greek philosopher Aristotle, and his *Nicomachean Ethics* is usually cited for many of the central ideas of the theory. What Aristotle provided was an account of what a good human being is and what such a person aims toward in his or her actions. The human good is an objective good that is determined by the essential nature of a human being. Aristotle observed that humans differ from other species of animals in their ability to use reason to choose their actions. Thus, human excellence consists in the ability to use reason well in both theoretical (scientific and philosophical) and practical matters. A virtuous human being is one who has all the characteristics that enable him or her to function well in doing the activities that constitute the good life of a human being. These qualities or virtues are acquired by a process of habituation in which the human agent goes through the repeated experience of doing what is the virtuous thing in the circumstances, usually by following an exemplar of that virtue. After gaining enough experience, the agent would himself want and choose to act virtuously not for the sake of something else but for its own sake.

A human agent cannot learn to choose correctly by making a calculation of benefits and harms or by following a set of moral laws. In making a calculation, he would be choosing to maximize whatever is used to measure the value of the benefits and harms and not choosing the right action for its own sake. The use of moral laws to make choices presumes that the right action is the same one, regardless of who the agent is and what his circumstances are. Aristotle defines virtue as a mean between vices of excess and deficiency. The agent chooses correctly only when what is done is appropriate in several ways: he is the right agent to do it and it is done to the right person, at the right time and place, to the right degree, in the right way and for the right reasons. For instance, courage in battle is not simply following a rule of standing one's ground to fight no matter what the circumstances are. Sometimes, doing so would be rash and the right thing to do is to flee and fight another day. At other times, running is cowardly. Yet soldiers can become brave with enough experience in battle. By doing courageous actions, they acquire an ability to judge correctly whether they should stand or they should run. Aristotle says that this ability is a form of perception that the experienced agent uses to determine the particular thing to do in the circumstances, without needing to deduce it from a universal principle. Thus, his criterion of right action is that which a person with practical wisdom, that is, the ability to reason well, would choose in the circumstances.

On this view of practical choice, unlike in utilitarianism and deontological ethics, an account of right action cannot be provided in advance of an account of a good agent. A virtuous action is one that a virtuous agent would choose because it is choice-worthy in itself. We do not say of an act of killing that it is always wrong because it violates a universal rule against killing (deontological ethics), or that it is right when the benefits outweigh the harms by more than any alternative course of action and wrong otherwise (utilitarianism). We need to first provide an account of the virtuous agent and examine how such an agent would choose. We need to know what such an agent aims at in making choices and understand the moral character of such a person. That is, we need to know what human excellence or human good is. But there are big challenges to the completion of the virtue ethics project. Some of those who object to virtue ethics say that there are different moral exemplars, each of whom does different things in the same circumstances so moral choice is indeterminate under virtue ethics. It is not helpful or practically useful for agents to decide what to do in the way that is suggested by virtue ethics. Moreover, the idea that there is such a thing as the good for human beings or, if there is, that it is objectively the same for every human, fixed and unchangeable, strikes many critics as absurd. Some critics view human good as a social construct or a matter of subjective choice. They point out that Aristotle's concept of human good follows from his teleological view of nature that explains changes and events in the world in terms of the essential nature of things. It is assumed that what a thing naturally aims at is its good.[12] Teleological explanations no longer make sense in the science of the natural world since the advent of Newton's physics. So the use of Aristotle's metaphysics of nature to ground his virtue ethics seems to ground the latter in an obsolete worldview.

Modern virtue ethicists have tried to provide an account of human good that does not require Aristotle's metaphysical assumptions about human nature. Instead, some have proposed a naturalized account of goodness that is modeled on the biological good of every living thing.[13] Another proposal is that the virtues are human characteristics defined for every sphere of those human activities that are necessary for human well-being.[14] But regardless of whether these ideas to improve on Aristotle's account succeed, the problem remains that it is much easier, more determinate, and more straightforward to decide what the right thing to do is by making use of a utilitarian calculus or by following deontological rules. It takes a lot of philosophical work to figure out what a virtuous agent is like and how he would choose, and too many of these questions remain unsettled. (However, readers of this book will find in the later chapters when I apply virtue ethics to the ethics of war that I have a way of avoiding some of these problems.)

I should point out here that what was presented by critics as an objection to virtue ethics could be turned into its strength. The simplicity of the decision-making process proposed by utilitarians and deontologists may fail to take into account morally salient facts and to recognize the moral complexities of hard choices. Thus, determinacy may be purchased at too high a price. The ethics of war is concerned with many complex dilemmas and it may be to the advantage of virtue ethics that it does not oversimplify the choices that are faced in wartime. In fact, my criticisms of just war theory as a rights-based deontological ethics include the problem that the conditions providing a leader or a soldier with the right to do certain things in war do not give sufficient consideration to the intolerable harms that result when these things are done. Utilitarians do weigh the harms in their calculations, but they make it too easy to offset the harms. The complexities of moral choices such as those that are made in war should be reflected in the decision-making process proposed by a moral theory. Virtue ethics does well on this score.

How would an ethics of war based on virtue ethics proceed? The focus has to be on what kind of person makes the moral decisions and what virtues are needed in such a person in order to do it well, not on rules that can be followed mechanically by anyone, good or bad in character. The correct moral decisions on war are ones that a virtuous political leader would make in the particular circumstances of the choice. However, the problems for virtue ethics that have been mentioned pose obvious obstacles for the virtue ethics approach to war. One way to figure out what is the right thing to do is to consider the wartime decisions of morally admired leaders. But how do we know which political leaders are virtuous? Do we not need to know which decisions are right in order to tell whether the leaders who make them are virtuous? If so, we end up abandoning the agent-based approach of virtue ethics for an act-based ethics with criteria for right action that are independent of or prior to the concept of a virtuous agent. In order not to do this, we must provide criteria for a leader's virtuous character directly. We can do this if we have a reasonably complete account of what human goodness is which can be used to pick out good human beings. Without such an account, we can only rely on intuitions about who are and who are not virtuous. This opens the door to the critics who claim that virtue is a relative concept that lacks objectivity or universality, so there is complete indeterminacy about what the right moral choices are. These critics think that an act-based ethics is the only way to avoid either moral skepticism (that is, the view that we cannot tell what is right or wrong) or moral relativism.

If I can do what I seek to do in this book, namely to provide a new ethics of war based on virtue ethics to replace the just war theory, then

I would go some ways toward proving the critics of virtue ethics wrong. In the remainder of this book, I will proceed as follows: I will first explain in what way a decision to go to war is a choice to do something that is very evil. It would certainly be very rare for a virtuous leader to choose to do anything as evil as war, given that there are other less-evil options to protect citizens against attack from the state's enemies. But I will show, in examining the nature of moral agency and how choices are made, that it could be rational and morally correct of a virtuous leader to choose to go to war under extreme circumstances when faced with a dilemma of choosing between great evils. Because such decisions are not made by calculation or rule-following, there will be a degree of indeterminacy in some cases when the right choice is too difficult to discern. Nevertheless, I will go on to address many of the recent controversies in just war theory using the virtue ethics approach in order to demonstrate how it is possible to provide practical guidance on these issues and make recommendations that are preferable to the answers we get from just war theory. The critics of virtue ethics are correct about indeterminacy up to a point. But given the shortcomings of just war theory and the better answers I shall be giving on the basis of the virtue ethics approach, it may be preferable to take an approach that lacks some precision than to stick with a just war approach that fails to take proper account of the evil nature of war.

4
War as an Evil

The ethics of war in the just war tradition is one that takes war to be morally neutral in itself.[1] War could be justified if certain conditions were met, and war could be chosen as a morally acceptable means to achieve justified ends. If war is recognized as intrinsically evil, then the deliberate choice of war could not be justified in the way that just war theory attempts to do. Take for comparison how torture of human beings is intrinsically evil. There is consequently no "just torture theory" to distinguish between torturing justly and torturing unjustly. Given this, the only moral question to ask is whether it could be a lesser evil to torture than to allow some other great evil. Some would answer "no," but even those who answer "yes" have to regret the evil they do and be required to make amends or accept punishment for doing evil, even if what they do is the lesser evil.

I think that the ethics of war should be concerned with a similar moral question as the one about torture. Before I raise this question in the next chapter, I must present reasons for taking war to be intrinsically evil and to explain what I mean when I make this claim. In a way, it should strike readers that this chapter is unnecessary. Surely, war is an evil, if anything is. Not only that, it is an evil that has been inflicted a lot more than torture and affected lots more people in history. But as I said, that war is an evil is not obvious to many ethicists, theologians, and jurists who have been thinkers about war in the past and the present, especially the many who do their work in the just war tradition. In fact, some who deny that war is an evil belong among those who are skeptical that anything is intrinsically evil and who may even think it is nonsensical to describe war or torture or Hitler as evil. Hence, there is a need for this chapter of the book.

First, we must understand what is meant by "evil." It is useful to examine how philosophers think about evil and distinguish it from bad things that are not evil. How are evil deeds related to evildoers? What do the moral theories of utilitarians and Kantian deontologists say about evil? Can evils be compared, and how do we judge what is the greater evil? Thus, the first part of this chapter will discuss how evil is conceptualized. Without a clear concept of evil, it would be difficult to settle arguments about whether war is an evil and how it compares with other evils. If war is an evil, does that mean war should never be fought? The concept of evil can guide us on how to deal with evil and identify for us the circumstances under which evil deeds can be allowed.

In the second part of this chapter, I present evidence about war that shows it to be especially evil. Although the terrible things that take place in war are well known, my purpose is to identify the ways in which war is not just a bad thing in being harmful to human life and well-being, but satisfies the conditions to count as a very serious evil. This will set the stage for the discussion in the following chapters of whether war can be allowed or justified as necessary to avoid greater evils, if there are any.

What is evil?

Evil is opposed to good. So too is bad. Evil connotes the extreme in badness. In many religions, evil is associated with the devil or demons, who are supernatural beings that are in conflict with God and angels. In the course of history, human beings have experienced all kinds of hardships and misfortunes, such as earthquakes, droughts, floods, famine, and epidemics. Those who believe in supernatural forces attribute such events to the agency of evil beings. They try to avoid being the victims of evil by offering sacrifices and building temples of worship. By doing so, they hope to gain favor from the evil beings or to enlist the help of good deities to ward off evil and to protect them.

For a religion such as Christianity that postulates a single omnipotent, omniscient and benevolent creator God, the existence of evil in the world presents a philosophical and theological problem. It seems to be in God's power to create a world without evil, so it seems that God is responsible for evil and the suffering that evil brings to human life. But this seems to contradict God's absolute goodness. One way out of the problem is to hold humans responsible for evils that result from their misuse of free will. However, this solution does not explain why God allows or inflicts natural disasters on humans. Even if they are punishments for human sin, is it compatible with God's justice that infants and young children are afflicted by these evils?

Some religious views that were held before the development of science can strike the modern mind as primitive. Advances in understanding how things work in the world have led to a recognition that no supernatural being is needed to explain natural disasters. This does not mean that there is no problem of evil. Instead, a distinction has to be made between natural and moral evil. The latter are evils that result from human agency. If war is an evil, it is a moral evil. The problem is why humans choose to do evil things. Are humans irrational to so choose, or are they simply wicked? It was suggested during the Enlightenment by the philosopher Rousseau that humans were basically good and that it was corrupt political arrangements that were responsible for human wickedness.

In more recent times, moral philosophers have focused on the concepts of good and *bad*, rather than good and evil. For secular philosophy, evil seems an obsolete concept derived from or closely connected with religion and belief in supernatural beings and explanations. The use of the term is to be avoided as it tends to demonize those who do bad things, which is not seen as helpful when one is seeking to identify social and psychological causes of behavior. When "evil" was mentioned, it would simply be used interchangeably with "morally bad". However, philosophers who have recently written about evil have argued that we need a concept of evil to distinguish trivial wrongdoings such as not paying the fare for a subway ride, from very serious wrongdoings such as slavery in eighteenth- and nineteenth-century America and the Holocaust perpetuated by the Nazis during the Second World War.[2] Without a clear concept or a good definition, it is difficult to provide answers on philosophical issues to do with evil, such as the relation between evil deeds and evildoers, and the morally appropriate response to evil. The failure to provide satisfactory answers is a shortcoming in the dominant moral theories of utilitarianism and Kant's ethics. If evil is simply a matter of harmful consequences, it should be evaluated in the way that all consequences are evaluated in utilitarianism: is it more or less harmful than its alternatives? No action with harmful effects is absolutely prohibited for the utilitarian. On the other hand, in Kant's ethics, evil is a matter of the will, not of consequences. All that is required of a moral agent is to have a good will. Now, it is often the case that an action can be motivated by a good will but have very harmful consequences. Such action is not only permitted but may actually be required in Kant's ethics. I will argue later that the inability of moral theories such as those inspired by Kant's ethics to recognize war as intrinsically evil accounts for some of the deficiencies in ethical thinking on war.[3]

Following Claudia Card's "atrocity paradigm," I will define evils as *foreseeable intolerable harms produced by culpable wrongdoing*.[4] This definition emphasizes both harms and wrongdoing, thus improving on both the utilitarian and Kantian views that focus on one or the other. An evil involves harm that deprives persons of the basic necessities for a tolerable life, a life at least minimally worth living for its own sake from the standpoint of the being whose life it is. The paradigm of evil is an atrocity, which, unlike a natural catastrophe, is the result of agency. Harms that count as evil are inflicted or tolerated by moral agents who are culpable in that it is reasonable to expect them to foresee the harms, and it is inexcusably wrong for them to be the agents of such harms.[5]

Who is evil?

Given that there is agency involved in evil, are the agents thereby evil? A distinction must be made between evildoers and evil persons. Not all evildoers are evil persons. This can be seen by distinguishing between motives and intentions. To be an evildoer is to be culpable for doing evil, which means that he succeeds in acting from an intention to do intolerable harm or to do something with that foreseeable result. To be an evil person is to have a character such that one has persistent evil motives, where the object of the motive is the evil that results from his actions.[6] Why would someone who is not an evil person do evil deeds? One possibility is that they have misjudged the choice of means to their ends. Such a mistake may be culpable if it is due to a failure to recognize the risk of intolerable harm to others where such a risk is reasonably foreseeable. Another possibility is that seemingly reasonable actions to achieve one's legitimate goals need not be morally acceptable. John Kekes has suggested that those who do evil are motivated by psychological propensities that are common to human beings, such as faith, ambition, envy, and honor, but circumstances and opportunity may conspire for these propensities to cause evil.[7] A view similar to this was summed up by Hannah Arendt in the phrase "the banality of evil."[8] Arendt reported on the trial of Adolf Eichmann, who had the job of arranging the transportation of millions of Jews from across Europe to labor and death camps during the Holocaust. At his trial, Eichmann turned out to be a thoughtless bureaucrat who simply focused on doing his job well, rather than a Jew-hating monster. (Yet in Eichmann's case, it can be convincingly argued that he was really an evil person, given his persistent evil-doing that continued even after he found out what happened to the Jews he transported. He must have had an evil character to choose this way of advancing his career and gaining favor from his superiors.)

The point of the distinction between evildoers and evil persons is that the absence of agents with evil character does not prove that no evil was done. Culpable wrongdoing involves intentions that could be faulted for the intolerable harm that can be foreseen to result when they are carried out. When the intention succeeds, evil follows. This is so even if the intention is not an intention to bring about the evil. In other words, evil can flow from the best of intentions. The relevance of the point I am making here to the ethics of war is that some people may claim that wars are evil only when they are waged by persons with evil motives, such as Hitler. There are "good" wars, in particular the wars fought to defeat tyrants and despots. The people who wage "good" wars have good motives, and if there are foreseeable harms in these wars, these are not intended. The conditions required for just war are just the sort of thing needed to ensure that the war one is fighting is "good." But contrary to this, if there are evildoers who are not evil persons, then a war could be evil without finding the agents responsible for the war to be evil persons.

Comparing evils

Card rightly points out that comparing evils is a morally sensitive issue and "an atrocity is already so evil that in some contexts it seems disrespectful of victims to point out that another was even worse."[9] I agree that sensitivity is needed to avoid trivializing or justifying the evil. There should be no implication in making the comparison that those who suffer a lesser evil are fortunate or that action should not be taken against those responsible for the evil. However, there are degrees of evil, given the definition of evil as intolerable harms due to culpable wrongdoing. Harms may vary in their severity and there are more or less bad motives for evil deeds. The danger in saying that an evil is not as bad as another is that it overlooks the impact on the victims. An evil may be a lesser one because it affected fewer people or lasted for a shorter period of time. But, for the person who is a victim, the suffering is experienced at the time as intense and intolerable, regardless of how many others are affected or how long the evil lasts.

The world confronts us with hard choices. Not all evils are avoidable. If we do not compare evils, we cannot choose and not choosing might itself be an evil. In the story of *Sophie's Choice*, a woman in a Second World War concentration camp must choose which of her two children to save, condemning the other child to die. Not choosing would result in the death of both children.[10] The US decision to drop two atomic bombs on Japan in August 1945 was a choice to kill hundreds of thousands of civilians in order to avoid fighting the war in the Pacific to the bitter end. For decades after that, the dreadful attack was officially explained (and thought justified) as the choice of the lesser evil. Abraham Lincoln faced the choice of continuing the war on the American South with its human toll or allowing the Confederate states to secede and continue their evil institution of slavery.

Where war is concerned, I think that the degree of harm is more important for evaluating an evil than is the degree of culpability. As mentioned in the last section, we may overlook the evil of war if we focus on the evil of those who wage war. We may also miss the severity of the evil of war if we focus on the culpability of the people responsible for the war. This problem is aggravated in moral theories that use intention as a yardstick for culpability. Does the fact that an agent did not intend the evil he brings about lessen the evil of what he does? The traditional doctrine of double effect used in just war theory to justify the killing of large numbers of civilians in war relies on the premise that great evil can be inflicted without the intention to do evil. But the severe harms suffered by civilian victims of bombing raids are not lessened in any way by the absence of an intention to kill them. Given that the atrocity paradigm view of evil places moral weight on the harms suffered and stresses the victims' perspective, it makes good sense to prioritize the degree of harm in comparing the evil of war with the evils that can be eliminated through war.

Choosing between evils

As I have already said, we want to be able to make moral choices, even if there are no good options. The possibility of comparing evils provides a way to choose between evils. The utilitarian would compare the harms involved in each option and choose that which produces the least amount of harm. This option is not only permissible but is the right thing for the utilitarian to do. The problem is that a distinction between the bad and the evil is not recognized in making the choice. Always choose what is less bad, even if what is less bad has crossed into the realm of intolerable harms. I am in agreement with Claudia Card when she writes, "The 'greater good' justification for harm sets no upper limit to the extremity of harm that any individual might be made to suffer in order to produce benefits for others."[11] The idea that doing evil might be morally obligatory seems not just counter-intuitive but reflective of a failure to appreciate what evil is.

Utilitarian calculations give weight to the suffering of victims of evil but not to the victims as individual human beings who are made to suffer. What is the lesser evil overall because fewer people suffer may be the greater evil for the individuals who have to bear the suffering. The idea that intolerable harms can be traded for a larger number of smaller harms ignores the damage that the former does to individual human lives. In effect, there is no evil that utilitarians would absolutely prohibit, as the harms involved could always be outweighed by the greater (number of) harms involved in another option. With respect to the ethics of war, wars and many of the things done in war may be unjustified when the result is more harm than if those things were not done. But a war could involve a great deal of harm and still be justified as the lesser evil. In the D-Day landings at Normandy on June 6, 1944, the Allies obliterated the French city of Caen, killing thousands of innocent French citizens.[12] Even though for France, liberation from Nazi occupation ended more suffering than those inflicted on the people of Caen, the Allied bombing is an evil for those who lost their homes and families on D-Day. The fact that it was not carried out by evil persons does not lessen the severity of the harms.

Kantian practical reasoning is supposedly the antithesis of utilitarian calculation. In Kant's deontological ethics, a moral agent is absolutely forbidden to will acts that violate the moral law. If he has a duty not to kill, then he should not kill, no matter what the consequences are and even if more people are killed in the state of affairs that result. In other words, morally culpable wrongdoing must be avoided at all costs and cannot be justified as the lesser evil in terms of its consequences. The only times the agent may be required to violate a moral duty is when moral duties conflict with each other. One would hope in such cases that if a duty is prioritized, it will turn out that a less-serious moral wrongdoing will occur in violating the other duty. This, however, does not seem to be the case. Not telling a lie turns out to be a perfect duty that has priority over saving lives, an imperfect duty of beneficence. Does that mean that a moral person must truthfully reveal the hiding place of Jews when asked by a Gestapo officer? It has been suggested that the duties against murder and mayhem also count as imperfect duties and can be overridden by perfect duties, which seems to indicate that the order of priority of Kantian duties does not correspond with what we intuitively take to be the seriousness of the wrongdoing.[13]

So it seems that many of the evils of war could be justified from a Kantian point of view. Even though they are prohibited as wrongful acts, the duty to avoid them may have less stringency than other duties that involve less harm. Consider as an example how in 1914, the major European powers of Britain, Russia, and Germany were drawn into conflict by leaders who felt duty-bound to keep promises made to their allies. As a result, Austrian sanctions against Serbia for the murder of Archduke Ferdinand of Austria in Sarajevo quickly led in just five weeks to the start of the First World War.[14]

The Kantian emphasis on right intention instead of good effects has influenced much of modern just war thinking. For instance, the principle of discrimination relies on the doctrine of double effect that distinguishes between intended and foreseen harms, allowing for many wartime atrocities to be justified on the grounds that these harms are not intended.[15] The principles of *jus ad bellum* include that of right intention. And the just war theory as a whole is a legalistic doctrine that stresses formal requirements and discounts the harmful consequences of war once these are met.

That war is an evil does not mean that war cannot be legitimately chosen. Pacifism only follows if war is the worst evil in every circumstance. My complaint against the just war theory is that it has become more a matter of law than ethics, and that it permits a lot of avoidable evil. The doctrine draws the line between the morally permissible and the morally impermissible use of war in the wrong place and ends up justifying wars that have turned out to be worse evils than the alternative of not fighting one's enemies. It does not follow that there is no line to be drawn except the one that places all war beyond moral acceptability. The line must permit war against an implacably and irredeemably evil regime such as Hitler's, which was capable of repeatedly carrying out shocking atrocities on a large scale that victimized millions, but recognize that war is so evil in itself that it should not be used against other less exceptionable but more common threats to a state's security. Even in a war against a Hitler-like adversary, there must be limits on what can be permitted, so as to reduce the evils of war. There is good reason for war to be a last resort, but even when it is exercised as a last resort, victory cannot be pursued regardless of the human costs of war that are measurable in terms of intolerable harms that are deliberately inflicted. It cannot be justified to destroy a village to save it.

So how great an evil is war? The remainder of this chapter sets out my answer to this question.

The evils of war

It would be redundant for me to rehearse the details of wars in history to illustrate the evils of war. The reader can simply open a history book and read about any of the numerous wars to find ample evidence of evil. It should be obvious that the deliberate killing and maiming of large numbers of human beings constitute intolerable harms, and the actions that cause these are wrongful and culpable when the victims do not deserve or need to be harmed to the extent that they are. In other words, war should not be pursued for its own sake. There has to be a purpose in going to war, but the purposes of most wars in history fail to excuse the evils of war. I have argued in Chapter 2 that self-defense cannot justify most of the violent actions carried out in war. In order to figure out what, if anything, could legitimize war, we must say something about how great the evils of war are. How does war rank among evils? As we saw, Card's definition allows for evils to be compared in terms of both the severity of the harms and the degree of culpability for wrongdoing.

Is there a distinction between war as an evil in itself and the evils of war? The evils of war are the evil of things that happen in war. If these evils can be avoided, would war still be an evil? Suppose that war could be fought without any killing or at least not the killing of any innocent person. That is what a just war would look like if the conditions for just war were all satisfied. Technology might very well make this possible. But the weapons of war would destroy buildings and infrastructure, even if somehow they do not kill innocent people. So people would still be harmed if they were deprived of shelter, electricity, or clean water. Also, a military intervention would restrict the movement and activities of civilians, affecting their freedom to travel unhindered and subjecting them to searches of their homes and body searches and all sorts of other humiliations. On the other hand, it could be argued that such non-lethal harms to noncombatants are not intolerable harms and do not, therefore, constitute evils.

But what about soldiers who are killed? If they are killed in large numbers, then many spouses would be widowed and children orphaned. Losing your loved one is a serious and irreversible harm. So for war not to contain evils would require that the war not be fought with soldiers. We can imagine futuristic scenarios of battles fought using automated machines, following rules that prohibit attacks on humans. It is not clear whether these would still count as wars. If in the distant future, political differences between states could be settled by a battle of machines, why not settle disputes today bloodlessly through a chess match or computer simulation? And if we were to do that today, would that still count as going to war? Occupation and control of territory and attacks on the humans living there, or defending the territory and repelling the occupying force, are necessarily part and parcel of war.[16] Therefore, when hostilities reach the point where war is resorted to, the point has also been reached where it would not satisfy either side to decide the outcome by a coin toss or a game of chess. War necessarily involves the use of force in the form of threats and actual violence on humans on the other side. Even when violence is not used in an unrestrained manner, it is in the nature of war to use a degree of violence that is sufficient to cause intolerable harms to combatants and noncombatants, and there is culpability for resorting to war and for the actions that cause the harms. The evils of war are inseparable from war itself.

There are many human activities besides war that are considered evil because of the harms caused through culpable wrongdoing. We have already mentioned American slavery as an evil. In *The Roots of Evil*, John Kekes discusses six examples of evil, only one of which is an act of war. Other than the crusade against the Cathars, he describes examples of political violence (the Terror following the French Revolution, Hitler's death camps, and Argentina's "dirty war" on political dissidents) and of crime (multiple murders committed by the Manson Gang and by the sociopath John Allen). There are numerous other evils we can add if we try to expand the list. Corporations poisoning drinking water and the air we breathe, organized crime rings trafficking in sex-slaves and drugs, religious fanatics denying women basic rights, homophobes terrorizing gays, children abused by priests.... The list goes on. People with common moral sensibilities and priorities would surely like to see such evil ended, and we do indeed condemn these evil activities. But it is not always in our power to stop them. With so much evil in the world, why should war be singled out for special attention?

The special evil of war

I shall now list a number of reasons for thinking that as an evil, war should rank above almost all others. To claim this is not to diminish the need to confront other evils, nor to deny the seriousness of the harms and the culpability of the evildoers outside of war. As I will explain at the end of the chapter, it is necessary to fully understand how evil war is in response to those who would sanitize war and treat it as a morally neutral and justifiable means for humans and states to conduct their business.

1. *War is worse than other evils because it includes and combines with other evils. In this, it multiplies both the severity of intolerable harms inflicted, and the amount of moral culpability for the multiple incidences of wrong-doing by large numbers of agents.*

Mass killing is an evil. The worst mass murderers who commit their crimes in peacetime have managed to kill dozens of innocent victims. Some of these commit their murders at one place and time, for example in the Columbine school shootings. Others commit their murders in serial fashion over a number of years. Killers who work for organized crime also commit multiple murders. But comparable mass killings take place repeatedly in war. The killers and their victims number in the millions. The killings take place both as single events and as repeated events over a number of years. In ancient and medieval wars, cities were besieged, bombarded, starved, and then sacked after the walls were breached. Inhabitants of cities that fell were usually massacred or enslaved. In the twentieth century, major cities that have suffered heavy damage from artillery and aerial bombardment include London, Coventry, Stalingrad, Dresden, Berlin, Hamburg, Tokyo, Hanoi, and Baghdad, to name but a few. Ground troops have carried out large-scale acts of genocide in war, ranging from the My Lai massacre by US troops in Vietnam, to the Serbian ethnic cleansing of Sarajevo, to the Japanese army's Rape of Nanjing during the Sino-Japanese War.

Rape and sexual assault are some of the worst forms of physical harm short of murder. Many women and children around the world suffer from the evil of rape in peacetime. In the present day, organized criminal groups arrange the abduction of women and girls in Eastern Europe, China, and Southeast Asia, and sell them to brothels in the United States, Western Europe, and the Middle East, where they are imprisoned, abused, and forced to provide sexual services. Individual sex predators pursue victims through the Internet and attack vulnerable women on the streets. Pre-teen girls have been abducted and found dead after they have been raped, or confined for years to serve as sex slaves. Rape is certainly a common occurrence in war, sometimes as deliberate policy and sometimes from undisciplined soldiers who expect to rape as a reward. During the Second World War, the Japanese set up "comfort stations" for their soldiers by forcing Korean and Chinese women to serve in army-run brothels. During the Balkan wars at the end of the twentieth century, the

Serbian authorities used rape as a method of ethnic cleansing to instill fear in their enemies from Bosnia and Kosovo, and to destroy the lives of a generation of women from the ethnic groups that were targeted. In ancient wars, when a city was taken, the men were killed and the women were raped. The women were then either killed or sold as slaves.

It is also an evil for people to suffer horrendous injuries that they have to bear for the rest of their lives. It is an evil for people to lose their homes and their ability to fend for themselves. It is an evil for people to die from diseases because they have been deprived of proper medical care and sanitary living conditions. All these are also evils that result from deliberate actions that take place because of war. Soldiers come back from war with scars and lost limbs. Children get blown up when they pick up unexploded bombs or step on landmines years after combat ends. Refugees are driven from their homes and live for years in horrible conditions in camps. They can no longer work or grow their crops. Those who fall sick in war do not get the medical attention they need. The unsanitary conditions created by war help to spread disease and cause epidemics.

2. *War inflicts not only physical damage on populations affected by war, but also moral harm on both victims and perpetrators of war crimes. War has a corrupting influence that brings out the worst in people.*

Moral dilemmas and conflicts of duty are facts of human life. In wartime, the moral certainties that guide choices are threatened by traumatic life-and-death struggles experienced by those who serve in the military. Soldiers risk their lives in battle and their survival depends on their training, loyalty and trust between comrades, and willingness to follow orders. They have only a narrow view of what they are doing and are under tremendous stress. When they think they might be doing something wrong, they find it hard to disobey orders or to expose the wrongdoings of others because they may feel that doing so would be an act of disloyalty or betrayal. When fellow-soldiers are killed by the enemy, they feel enraged and have the urge to take revenge. Prisoners and civilians have been killed as a result of such feelings.

Civilians, too, end up doing things that they would not choose to do in peacetime. There are shortages of basic necessities and individuals have to think of themselves and their families first. Some people hoard and others steal. When they live under enemy occupation, they may be under pressure to collaborate in order to survive. They may betray friends. Wartime refugees have been known to prostitute wives and daughters to get money for food. In the Nazi concentration camps, some inmates helped to operate and clean the gas chambers and to police fellow-Jews in order to postpone being put to death themselves.[17]

There are many more examples from every war in history that demonstrate the power of war to corrupt and to dehumanize. Such evil was best described in the plays that the ancient Greek dramatist Euripides wrote about the Trojan War. Although works of fiction, the plays *Hecuba* and *The Trojan Women* described what the Greeks had experienced in real wars. Remarkably, Euripides wrote about the losers as well as winners, and showed how both sides were morally damaged by the ten-year siege of Troy by the Greek army.[18] In *The Trojan Women*, as the Trojan captives are marched into slavery, the Greeks execute the infant grandchild of the dead King Priam out of irrational fear. In *Hecuba*, the victorious Greeks in their desperation to go home decide to make a human sacrifice of Polyxena, the daughter of Priam and Hecuba, to gain a favorable wind for their ships. The Greek commander Agamemnon justifies the sacrifice as a matter of military necessity and honor. The Trojan queen had already lost her husband and all her other children, save a boy sent to the safety of Thrace to be cared for by its king, Polymestor, a friend of the family. When it is revealed that the boy had been murdered by Polymestor, the previously virtuous queen carries out a vile act of vengeance on him by blinding him and murdering his two sons.

3. *Just war theory makes the claim that war is fought for peace. War usually has the opposite effect. Ironically, what happens in war often lays the conditions for future wars.*

Perhaps the most famous example is the relation between the First and Second World Wars. In the Treaty of Versailles at the end of the first war, the victorious Allies set down humiliating and punitive conditions on the defeated Germans. To enforce the "war guilt" clauses of the treaty, the economic blockade of Germany continued for some months after the Armistice that ended the war. Tens of thousands of German noncombatants died from starvation and epidemics in that short period. As a consequence, Germans saw themselves as victims, and their resentment contributed to rising German nationalism and support for Hitler's policies when he came to power.

In the Middle East, the conflict today between the state of Israel and the displaced Palestinians seeking their own state has deep historical roots in earlier wars and periods of violence. Since the Six Day War in 1967, Israel has occupied the West Bank and Gaza, where millions of Palestinians live. Instead of withdrawing to internationally recognized borders after victory in the war, the occupation of Arab land and the building of Jewish settlements have become obstacles to lasting peace in the region. Whole generations of Palestinians grew up knowing nothing but the humiliation of occupation and the lack of economic opportunity. Without a state army to face the might of the Israeli army, young Palestinians have turned to other means of violence, including terrorism, which in turn is used by the Israeli government to justify continued suppression.

The 1967 war itself reflected unfinished business from the birth of the Israeli state in 1948 in a war with Arab states, which resulted in Palestinian residents being uprooted and becoming refugees. The Jewish settlers were granted statehood by Britain, who had a mandate to govern Palestine, only after a campaign of violence and terrorism by militant Zionists. The impetus for granting these Jews a homeland was the genocide that European Jews suffered at the hands of the Nazis during the Second World War. The British had become the authorities in Palestine as a result of the First World War defeat of the Ottoman Turkish Empire. And the Turks had ruled Palestine for centuries after seizing control from the Mamluks who had taken over when European Crusaders were driven out after more than a century of war.

Considering how the cycle of violence is repeated in war after war, and how the roots of many wars can be traced to an earlier war, it is obvious how short-sighted it is to imagine that war could be the means to achieve peace. When weighing the pros and cons of going to war, leaders do not think of consequences beyond victory in the war that they declare. It is true that there are other evils besides war that also spawn further evils. Some victims of child abuse or rape grow up to become mentally and emotionally disturbed individuals who harm others as a result. It is unfortunate that they end up repeating the evils that they had earlier suffered. But the evil of war is worse in that the repetitions that follow are often of greater magnitude and continue for generation after generation. The Second World War was much more destructive than the First. Some historical grievances that can lead to war may go back thousands of years. Greeks and Turks have a mutual distrust for each other going back to the battles between the Byzantine and Turkish empires, and Greece and Turkey were nearly at war as recently as the 1970s over the island of Cyprus.

4. *War helps to perpetuate other evils when it is used as a diversion and a pretext not to correct them. If not for war, these other evils may well be reduced or eliminated.*

In peacetime, the evils that must be confronted include crime, corruption, racism, sexism, economic and social injustice, and lack of access to basic necessities or primary goods. Governments grapple with these problems with varying degrees of success. In democracies, leaders who fail to deal with such problems are voted out of office. In non-democracies, leaders face revolution or revolt if these problems build up. One way that incompetent and corrupt leaders rally support is to engage in hostilities with another state. When Argentina's military junta ordered the invasion of the British Falkland Islands in the South Atlantic in 1982, these leaders were diverting attention from their failed policies in managing the economy in the face of growing dissent among the people of Argentina. They were also attempting to strengthen the hand of the military, which was losing its honor in fighting a "dirty war" in which thousands of dissidents were abducted, tortured, and murdered.

Even when war is not a deliberate attempt to divert attention from failed government, the cost of fighting a war leads to insufficient resources for dealing with other problems. The US invasion of Iraq in 2003, and the many years of occupation, has cost more than a trillion dollars. Meanwhile, little was done to make health care available to more than 45 million uninsured Americans, or to protect the people of Louisiana from Hurricane Katrina and help them rebuild after that, or to address the problems of gas emissions that poison the air that people breathe and contribute to global warming, or to safeguard American schoolchildren from gun violence and to fund programs to improve their proficiency in language, math, and science.

5. *War costs lives, and destroys the possibility for the good things that people whose lives are lost could have enjoyed and provided for others.*

Loss of human life is a tragedy. A life cut short is a waste when such a life has the potential to flourish. The totality of war dead in human history is astronomical. When a country goes to war, it is sending its soldiers out to kill or be killed. When cities are attacked, the lives cut short include children who have their whole lives before them and young women who could have brought many more children into the world. Many human lives are lost in peacetime due to accidents, risky activities, and misfortune. When death is caused by culpable wrongdoing, the loss of life could be considered evil. Examples of evil include murderous rampages, such as US school shootings at Columbine High School and Virginia Tech, or reprehensible corporate behavior, such as that of tobacco companies concealing the addictive and carcinogenic properties of their products. The deaths that are caused in war are the result of deliberate decisions by leaders to wage war, and by commanders to attack enemy targets, fully anticipating that soldiers and civilians on both sides will die in large numbers.[19] The development of new armaments and fighting techniques has been taking place throughout human history as armies pursued greater effectiveness in their methods of killing and maiming people in large numbers so as to achieve a military advantage over their enemies.

Sometimes, those who choose war or choose to target population centers or choose to use more destructive weapons declare that they are actually doing so to save lives. The excuse for dropping atomic bombs on Japan was to bring the war to an end sooner and thereby save the lives that would have been lost in a lengthier war. But if the United States had been serious about ending the war quickly, it could have dropped its demand for "unconditional surrender" and accepted Japan's offer (apparently made through Russian diplomats) of a negotiated surrender that would safeguard the position of the Emperor. More lives would have been saved in this way. Instead, the use of the atomic bombs simply substituted the killing of soldiers in a protracted war with the killing of a quarter-million innocent civilians, including women, children, and the elderly.

As a justification for its invasion of Iraq, the United States argued that it needed to fight terrorists there so that Americans did not have to fight them at home.[20] Once American forces had been deployed in the Persian Gulf, any delay in launching an attack in the hope of a diplomatic solution would cost more lives because it gave the enemy time to prepare its defenses while American soldiers grew weary waiting in the desert heat. Rationalizations such as these should be rejected. The idea of saving lives by taking lives is a morally perverted logic.

To appreciate the perversity of fighting wars to save lives, consider the practice of human sacrifice in primitive societies where it was believed that regular rituals of sacrificing human lives would make the world safer for the rest of society. Such practices were clearly evil. But sending Americans to fight and die in the Middle East to keep Americans safe at home is in effect making use of the soldiers in a similar way, comparable to making human sacrifices. Americans know that many of the soldiers sent to war will not come back alive. They are chosen to be among those who will die so that those at home will be safe. The justification of ancient human sacrifices is undermined by the need to do it over and over again. If the number of victims sacrificed were added up, it should be obvious that too high a price was being paid and that other ways of safeguarding society should be preferred. It was only ignorance and superstition that prevented ancient societies from finding these other ways. Similarly, wars overseas have to be fought over and over again, since the logic is that if we stop fighting, our enemies will attack us at home. This is a recipe for endless wars and long-term occupations. Unfortunately, the ability of the Bush administration to exaggerate the threat from foreign enemies such as Iraq prevented people from realizing the futility of such wars. Only after several years in Iraq did the majority of Americans finally recognize that the cost of keeping America safe by fighting overseas wars was too high in terms of human lives, and that reliance on force is often not the best way to protect America. By the time that they voted for a new president who promised to end the war in Iraq, millions of Iraqis had already suffered the evils of a war that the United States had chosen to wage.

The just war myth

Andrew Fiala points out that the just war theory has in fact been used to shelter war from moral criticism and to make war a moral possibility. The concept of just war is a dangerous myth because it allows those who wage war to provide rationalizations of what they do.[21] Fiala, who is a pacifist, thinks that in reality there may be no such thing as a just war. Yet many people assume that simply because there is an account of just war, there must be (some) just wars. This allows those who use war as a means to political ends to fend off any proper moral accounting of what they are in fact doing.[22]

This is an important point about the just war doctrine. I have already criticized the central requirements of just war theory in Chapter 2. The fact that requirements that have been embodied in the tradition of just war thinking for almost two thousand years have been called into question does not necessarily rule out the possibility of just war. It is possible to argue that there is a morally acceptable form of war with conditions quite different from those in the tradition. I may actually have shown how to devise such a "just war theory" in the following way. Given all the things listed above that make war so evil, there is still the possibility for war to take place without any of these evils. For evil is extreme badness, and war could be a morally acceptable choice if it is merely bad, not evil, and if it is used for preventing something far worse or for achieving a greater good. So there could be a version of just war theory that simply requires that all evils of war be avoided or reduced to the level of mere badness. Such a war would still involve some fighting and killing, but if the new rules of just war (whatever they are) are observed, the harms caused by war need not reach the level of foreseeable intolerable harms that are due to culpable wrongdoing.

I am however skeptical that war could be fought according to rules that prevent it from escalating to the degree that makes war evil.[23] First, there are so many evils of war that it seems unlikely that they could all be avoided. Second, there does not seem to be any war in history that has actually avoided these evils. Third, once war begins, the pressure to win the war and the importance of staving off defeat make it difficult to stick to the rules that keep war from being evil. There is a very real danger of escalation in every war. Clausewitz had made the point that the violence of war must logically lead to an extreme, and that it is absurd to introduce moderation into war. Walzer's more recent version of just war theory allows for what he calls a supreme emergency in which rules of war that forbid the intentional killing of enemy civilians can be suspended.[24] The US war in Iraq provides a good example of how easily the evils of war become acceptable. As the occupation dragged on with no victory in sight and the number of American dead rose (from the 150 who died in the six weeks it took for Baghdad to fall, to several thousand in the years that followed) and as the lives of ordinary Iraqis became so intolerable that many said they had been better off under Saddam Hussein, one of the main justifications that was proposed, by those who want the United States to keep its troops there and to send in more soldiers, was that they had to keep fighting so that those who were already dead had not died in vain.

The problem with those who believe that a just war is possible is that they do not take the evils of war seriously enough. The myth of just war is premised on two false assumptions. First, there is the pretense that evil things do not have to happen in war. It is argued that a "sanitized" war is possible. We are told that it is only when the rules of war break down that war becomes really nasty. And if the rules do break down, it is not the fault of those who fight with justice on their side. It is the injustice of the adversary that forces one's side to fight dirty. So if we can ensure through international bodies and war conventions that all sides follow the rules, war could be fought without the evils that have plagued war throughout history. This is nothing but a set of shallow excuses. If a country is really committed to following the rules, it does not have to break the rules, even if others break them.[25] It does not have to wait for there to be an international authority before it observes the rules that it claims to uphold. Another suggestion to "sanitize" war is that technology could eventually solve the problem. Precision weaponry would enable military targets to be hit while avoiding direct harm to civilians. The irony of this claim seems to have been lost on those who make the claim. Precision in war is also a myth that leads to greater willingness to use weapons in places inhabited by noncombatants, resulting in more incidences of collateral damage. As a consequence, the proportion of civilian casualties in war compared to combatants has sharply increased in many of the wars that have taken place in the twentieth century and since.

The second assumption is that even if evil happens in war, these things do not matter in the moral justification of war. All that matters are that the requirements for just war are satisfied. This assumption is based on moral theories that take rule-following to be the only yardstick of moral evaluation. The fact that when the rules are followed, evil consequences take place is not considered to have independent relevance. This approach to morality is incompatible with the approach to the ethics of war that I am taking here and I have explained why in Chapter 3. In my view, any moral evaluation of war must take account of the intolerable harms and sufferings imposed on people who have not done anything to deserve these harms and for which there is culpable wrongdoing. The most morally salient facts about war are that it is evil in the many ways described in this chapter.

5
The Philosophy of Co-existence

If, as I have argued in the last chapter, war is a great evil, then war should be avoided. Certainly, wars of choice should be avoided and too many wars are wars of choice.[1] But is there a point at which it is morally worse not to fight a war? Or is war always a worse evil than the evils we seek to eliminate through war? And how does anyone provide rational and morally justified answers to these questions? In this chapter, I will propose answers that are different from those that have been used in the ethics of war.

Let us begin by reflecting on what the ethics of war is essentially about. States have enemies that threaten them with violence. They have to choose how to respond to such threats. If violence has to be met with violence, then states must wage wars against their enemies. Are there limits to the use of violence by states? An ethics of war provides criteria for determining what morality permits or forbids states to do. Realism denies the application of ethics to war. For realists, ethical limits make no sense, and war must be fought according to what is politically or militarily necessary.[2] Absolute pacifism holds morality to forbid war altogether. The use of violence by the state is never permitted, even in self-defense.[3] The just war tradition consists of theories regarding the justification for going to war and for taking certain actions in war. Some wars but not all wars are morally justified. When certain conditions are satisfied, states have the right to go to war. But what they do in fighting the war is also limited by the requirements of morality. The attraction of just war theories is that, unlike realism, they show how ethics applies to war but, unlike pacifism, they do not apply ethics in a way that denies the moral legitimacy of every war, even in cases where an enemy would carry out evil designs such as genocide and enslavement of entire peoples.

Since I have argued in Chapter 2 that just war theories in general face serious theoretical and practical difficulties, it would seem that I should endorse the pacifist position. Theoretically, theories in the just war tradition cannot provide a set of conditions under which nations have a right to wage war because the central tenets of the theory are unsatisfactory and they fail to fully acknowledgement the intrinsic evil of war. Practically, the just war theory is overly permissive. I consider many of the wars allegedly justified according to just war theory to be morally indefensible because of the evil nature of war. Where I disagree with the pacifist is on whether war could ever be the morally correct choice. I have to accept the pacifist conclusion only if there is no moral alternative to just war theory apart from pacifism. It may seem that this is the case, since no ethics of war has been proposed that is not either a form of pacifism or a version of just war theory. Thus, the important task for me in this chapter is to propose and defend an alternative ethics of war as a middle path between pacifism and just war theory.

The steps I shall take in arguing for a new ethics of war are the following. First, I want to make it intuitive that we do not have to use violence to eliminate threats to our existence. I do this by using analogies about how we deal with predatory animals and criminals. Second, I will explain how the choice to fight with one's enemies should be made. This is needed as a response to the view that one ought never to do anything that is evil, a view that leads one to pacifism, given that war is intrinsically a great evil. In taking the virtue ethics approach, I will present the choice to go to war as morally right if it is one that is made by a person of exemplary character, that is, a virtuous person with practical wisdom. The key to making the right choice is found in an account of how such a person would choose between evil alternatives that involve either the death of innocent human beings that occur when killing others or the failure to prevent others from killing innocent human beings.

Co-existing with animals

Is it possible to live peaceably in a world where there are people seeking to destroy us or our societies? One of the most frequent causes of violent conflict between states is that people respond to any threats to their way of life or existence by resorting to force as a way to eliminate the threats. Although examples are found in all periods and across cultures, the Romans best exemplified this in their practice of war: to keep fighting until the threat was completely eliminated or the enemy had been forced to become Roman vassals, with armies that fought on Rome's side. There would be no peace with anyone who possibly harbored any hostility toward Rome.[4] Hostility from outsiders is also used as a *moral justification* when an enemy threat is cited as a just cause for war. This justification was recently invoked by President George W. Bush soon after the terrorist attacks of 9/11, and there was huge support at the time for his stand that Americans must respond with force against all enemies, real or potential, wherever they are known to exist.

My purpose in this chapter is to evaluate the assumption that there is always some moral justification for nations to respond to hostile threats with force. To do that, I will discuss the way in which states deal with their enemies, and assess whether military responses are appropriate. I begin by proposing a few analogies that provide some perspective on the use of violence as a response to threats to one's existence. The first analogy has to do with human responses to threats from predatory animals.

We live in a world where unfortunate humans can and do fall victim to predators such as tigers, snakes, and sharks. It seems obviously acceptable for a human to defend himself by killing the predator. But killing when attacked does not eliminate the threat posed by such animals. As their population grows, humans tend to encroach into areas where such predators live, with the inevitable confrontation as the animals wander or hunt in areas of human occupation. To live in safety without the threat posed by such animals would require humans not just to kill when attacked, but also to capture or eliminate all the predators in the area. Humans have sometimes done exactly that in history, for instance in nearly exterminating tigers and wolves, sometimes not just to eliminate the threats but to profit from the sale of animal parts. Why is this no longer a common practice and why do many people in developed countries frown on the notion of eliminating the animals that could possibly threaten human life?[5]

One reason is that there are ways of keeping humans safe without hunting down the wild predators that live on the fringes of human society. There might even be an element of self-interest in efforts to preserve animal diversity, since we are now aware of the inter-connectedness of the ecological world. Another reason is that humans have begun to appreciate the aesthetic and scientific value of animal species, even those that will kill us if we meet them in the wild. In this regard, consider the example of the Monterey Bay Aquarium sharks.[6] The project involved exhibiting white sharks, one of the most fearsome ocean predators. The aquarium was able to keep the sharks for several months, in one case, a record of 198 days in captivity. The sharks were eventually tagged for study and released back into the ocean. The humans who helped in transferring the sharks to ocean waters took enormous risks. The point is that sharks cannot be domesticated and white sharks are natural killing (and feeding) machines. Why not kill the sharks at the end of their captivity? Why risk your life for a predator?

Consider now the paradox that we treat human beings worse than animals. We resort too readily to force when another human or group of humans poses a threat to our existence.[7] Many states are not satisfied just with containing the threat posed by a hostile state by securing their borders but they seek to attack the enemy until they are eliminated or captured or until they surrender unconditionally. Do not any of the reasons we have for respecting the lives of animal predators apply to humans? Surely human life has as great or greater value than animal life. Surely there is cultural and scientific value in ways of life that are found in states different from ours, even if these are states hostile to us. Surely we can do enough to defend our borders so that breaches of our security are no more likely than an encounter with a shark on the ocean or a tiger in the wild.

Perhaps there are some differences between humans and animals that may justify a different response to human threats. Most obviously, humans act intentionally and can be blamed for their actions. A tiger or a shark is doing what it does when prey is available. It is not out to pick on a human victim or to act out of cruelty. Some of the threats that a state faces from outside parties arise from bad motives, such as land or resource grabbing, or out of hatred due to a history of animosity. Hitler was not just a predatory shark; he was evil, acted from evil motives, and could only be stopped by being eliminated. And because he was morally responsible for his evil deeds, he needed not just to be restrained, but also to be punished. We could not just leave him alone as long as we could keep him at bay, as we might do with predators in the wild.

On the other hand, the fact that humans act intentionally makes possible ways of avoiding conflict that are not available with wild animals. Humans can choose what they do so it is possible to give them reasons not to attack us. It is possible to negotiate with a hostile human enemy but not with a shark or snake. This possibility is only closed when the leaders of an enemy state are acting emotionally or are unreasonable in their demands. So the difference between human and non-human animals cuts both ways: there are ways to avoid conflict with humans by reasoning with them, but there is reason to fight with them so as to punish them, even when the threat from them can be contained. From the perspective of just war theory, there are those in the Augustinian tradition who argue that punishment is a legitimate cause for war.[8] But those who hold self-defense as the only just cause would find war unjustified when enemies can be prevented from attacking one's state, either through border defenses or through negotiations and treaties. Wiping out those who pose a threat to us, as the Romans often did, is even less justified with human enemies than with predators in the wild.

The ability of human beings to make intentional choices and to be given reasons to change their behavior provides a way to answer a possible objection to the analogy between predators and human enemies. It could be argued that the containment of threats from predators is only co-existence from the *human* point of view. Animals in the wild do not choose to co-exist with us, and we contain them when we can and exterminate them when we cannot contain them. Now the idea of co-existing with enemies that I will set out later as an alternative to war does not require that the enemies want to co-exist with our side. So it is analogical with how predators behave. But it might also be true that containment only makes sense from a position of strength. The reason we do not have to exterminate predators is that we are able to do so if they cannot be contained. If co-existence with enemies is the basis for an ethics that makes the resort to war less common than under just war theory, it would apply not just to superpowers that have the ability to destroy their enemies, but to all states, including weaker ones that are asked to practice co-existence without being able to destroy the enemy if containment fails. But I would reply to the objection by arguing that the ability to negotiate with human enemies and to provide them with reasons not to attack opens up an option not available with predators. It is not a prerequisite for co-existence that we have an ability to destroy the enemy that is held in reserve since we can affect the behavior of human enemies by influencing how they choose.

A second difference between non-human predators and human enemies is that humans are capable of much greater destruction through the use of tools and technology. Unless we are stranded in the wild, we can usually keep out of reach of sharks and tigers. There are states nowadays that have the ability to use highly destructive weapons to launch massive attacks on their enemies and do lots of damage in a very short time. To defend the state and to protect citizens, it is not enough these days to post border guards and have armies ready to meet an invader. It is necessary to disarm the enemy or to replace the regime with a friendlier one. And if that is not possible, we have to credibly threaten them with similar retaliation for any attack on us.[9]

But the claim here is an instance of the "technological imperative," which is the idea that whatever can be done will be done, or that nothing is invented that will not be used sooner or later. These are questionable assumptions. Non-human predators are found in nature with the fangs and claws that they use to survive. It is not an option for them not to use what nature gave them. But the weapons that humans have invented to use on their enemies are what they need to survive only because they are engaged in an arms race for military superiority. There is nothing inevitable about the doctrine of mutually assured destruction that prevailed during the Cold War in the form of nuclear deterrence. If there is a will to find ways to co-exist with unfriendly states without fighting or eliminating them, it makes good sense to do away with any weapons that make war so devastating that we have to strike first in order to stave off annihilation. If states could agree to do away with weapons that could not be defended against (and they can do this even if they remain enemies), they can return to warding off aggression in the old-fashioned way of border patrols and armies capable of driving off invaders. This is not merely the pipedream of idealists as global agreements have been negotiated in the past to eliminate chemical weapons and landmines and to reverse the nuclear arms race. In the last case, some disarmament and reduction of nuclear stockpiles have been achieved. This shows that human capacities to develop weapons do not force us to respond more aggressively to human threats than to non-human predators.

A third explanation of why human and non-human threats are responded to in different ways is that of competition between humans. Because humans have over-populated the earth and stretched the limited resources of the earth to breaking point, states are inevitably in conflict with each other. There is not enough clean water, land for agriculture, and fossil fuels to meet every state's needs. Humans do compete with other animals and have, in fact, wiped some species off the face of the earth by destroying their habitat or hunting them to extinction. It did not matter whether these animals were threats to us; rather, their very existence prevented us from getting what we need to survive. The greater intensity of the competition between humans is due to the fact that we do not just compete for one or two things, but we have so many essential needs in common. Since the competition between human societies is more critical for our survival than the competition with animals, wars over resources are the unavoidable result.

On the other hand, humans are the most versatile of species and can satisfy their needs in many more ways. When animals are faced with over-population or shortage of food, they must fight each other or die. They have to drive other animals away, and if they are themselves displaced, they cannot survive. Humans, on the other hand, obtain their food, water, energy, and shelter from a variety of sources. If there are not enough caves to dwell in, they can live up in trees. If there is not enough wood to burn, they can burn coal. That is why humans are able to survive in the desert and in the tundra. They can live on open land or in cramped cities. When animals are faced with a loss of their natural habitat due to the encroachment of other animals or humans, they often dwindle in numbers. The only way to save them is to provide them with a similar environment in another location. But human refugees who have moved to very different places in terms of culture and climate have adjusted and been able to meet their needs in new ways. The need for resources does not necessarily force us to fight wars with each other.

So far, it does not seem that there is a difference between non-human predators and human enemies that prevent us from possibly co-existing with the latter. But there is another point of difference to be considered. It seems that competition for resources and fear of conquest by one's enemies are not the only reasons for humans to engage in violent conflict with each other. Even before the world became a very crowded place, human societies were at war with each other. As Hobbes noted, humans are also motivated by a desire for glory.[10] Military superiority, confirmed by victories in battle, seems to be a high priority for the earliest human clans and tribes, all the way to the empire-building nation-states of recent times. Many of these societies were internally organized in such a way that success at war was rewarded with political power. Although many people still take pride in hunting animals, the skills needed to overcome a human enemy are held in greater esteem as demonstrated by the prestige of service in the military in most societies. Not only are human societies driven by the need to prove their superiority in warfare against other peoples, but it is easy to recognize that this is true of their neighbors as well. This creates a mentality of "getting them before they get us." As mentioned, the ancient Romans thought in this way but so, it seems, do some Americans in the twenty-first century.

If we apply the Hobbesian contractarian model of domestic society to the relations between nation-states, the point of the development of a law of nations would be to govern the relationship between states so as to bring order to the state of nature in international affairs. Under these rules, might does not make right. This would establish a way for weak states to avoid being the prey of big powers on the world stage. In other words, it is no longer the case that the only way for any nation to avoid attack by other nations is to defeat all actual and potential enemies on the battlefield. The international conventions of war established on the basis of the just war doctrine require that war be justified as self-defense, as a last resort, and carried out with no ulterior motives (with right intention) by a sovereign authority. Acceptance by all member nations of the UN of the rules of *jus ad bellum* should mean that nations would now be able to co-exist with each other, even with the inevitable competition and rivalries between them.

The discussion in this section has shown that although humans differ from animals in the threat that they pose when they are in competition for resources or when they have political or religious disagreements, there is no reason to think that humans must eliminate their human enemies or competitors who are viewed as potential threats to their existence. So why do states often resort to force when dealing with threats from other states? On the Hobbesian model, it has obviously to do with the absence of a global sovereign with the power to enforce international law in contrast with the way that domestic peace is preserved by the authority of the state ruler. Institutions that substitute for a global sovereign such as the United Nations and the International Criminal Court of Justice are too imperfect and cannot be relied upon to prevent nations from falling victim to aggression from their neighbors. Ultimately, nations must be prepared to defend themselves and fight for their own survival.[11] I will now assess the validity of the claim that, in the absence of a global sovereign, a state cannot co-exist with hostile threats in the way that citizens within the state do with threats posed by other citizens.

Co-existing with criminals

In this section, the discussion will make use of another analogy: the domestic analogy.[12] The Hobbesian model assumes that domestic peace can be preserved by the rule of law. But the rule of law is, in fact, an imperfect system for protecting citizens from domestic threats. Individuals can still be victims of violence by criminals and some criminals do get away without punishment. We cannot assume that everyone we meet on the streets will follow the rules of the social contract. Should not citizens reserve the right to act as vigilantes when threatened by violent crime? Should we (individually and collectively) not wage war on criminals to eliminate them, instead of doing what liberal democracies do in respecting their rights and trying to collect evidence to have them prosecuted by an imperfect criminal justice system which may let some of them off the hook?

There are times when civilian law enforcement becomes ineffective due to a state of anarchy in which order and civil authority break down completely. In such times, civil rights may be suspended and a state of emergency imposed. But in normal times, people in liberal democracies are usually willing to put up with some risk in giving up their right to use vigilante violence against criminals in exchange for the protection of the state. In the Hobbesian social contract, such an exchange is thought to be in the interest of every citizen because, despite the risk, they have more to gain from peaceful co-existence and cooperation with others, in comparison with the state of war where everyone maintains the right to act for their own interests at the expense of others. But there is a flaw in the contractarian view that concerns the possibility (and rationality) of being a free-rider: someone who breaks the rules when it is in her interest to do so and she can get away with it. Although it is better to play by the rules most of the time, the temptation to violate the rules is always there. And if we recognize that others are similarly tempted, we may have difficulty fully trusting that they will refrain from violence.

Nevertheless, there is something we can learn from the domestic scenario about what we ought to do in responding to human threats. In dealing with lawbreakers, it is not morally legitimate in a liberal democracy to use unnecessary violence or to endanger innocent people. It might be more effective and make sense prudentially to eliminate the threat from criminals by granting the police greater leeway in going after the bad guys. But in a liberal democracy such as America, most people have traditionally preferred to live with a bit more risk of being victims of crime than to grant the police more power for the purpose of getting rid of crime. For one thing, citizens could well be innocent victims of overzealous police actions. In other words, in the domestic situation, we prefer to err on the side of protecting the innocent, even at the risk of letting some criminals get away. Now admittedly, there is not a hundred percent consensus about how much power the police should have in a liberal democratic state to deal with lawbreakers. There are quite a few Americans who think that their government and the courts are too soft on crime and are overly concerned with the rights of criminals, at the expense of victims.[13] They do not see law-abiding citizens as in any danger from an increased use of force by the police. On the contrary, they feel safer knowing that the police have greater ability to deal with crime. The question is how far we can go in the direction of empowering the police to act and to use force before we become a police state. There is a line to be drawn, even if we disagree about where to draw it, that if crossed, would be a betrayal of ideas about the value of human beings that are central to the liberal democratic ideal.[14]

The community of nations is arguably different from the community of citizens so that the domestic analogy cannot fully apply. As I said, there does not seem to be a powerful enough authority to maintain peace on behalf of individual states. There is no international police force. Moreover, individual nations do not see themselves as obligated to uphold the rule of international law in their relations with one another when it does not serve their interests to do so. Political leaders do not see the obligation to abstain from the use of military force as having as much weight as the obligation to protect their own people. The risks of not acting quickly or of waiting for help from allied nations seem too great when faced with a threat of military attack by another state. What we describe as a state of anarchy in the domestic situation when civil authority completely breaks down is considered the norm in international relations, where potential adversaries lurk all the time. It would seem that the only safeguard that individual states can have against threats from outside enemies is by deploying an effective military force to defend themselves and to engage their enemies before they get across the border or get their hands on weapons of mass destruction.

There is admittedly lots of evidence concerning the ineffectiveness of international institutions in maintaining peace and protecting weaker nations. There have been many territorial incursions that have not been reversed, such as in Palestine and Cyprus. There have been people who have lost their statehood, such as the Kurds. And big powers have carried out invasions when it suited them, as did the former Soviet Union in Hungary, Czechoslovakia, and Afghanistan, and the United States in Afghanistan and Iraq.

So the realist view of international politics maintains that morality is impractical and inapplicable to the relations between states, and that nations should be free to pursue their own interests by any means, including war. War is simply politics by other means.[15] On the moralist side, a Hobbesian view can justify citizens restraining themselves from using violence in a state that upholds rules and agreements and punishes those who break them. But the community of nations is closer to that of a state of anarchy, where civil authority breaks down, given the absence of a world government and police force, and the seriousness of the threat of aggression from other nations. As for the law of nations, the secular version of just war theory that has taken root in international law does, in fact, allow for the use of force to deal with threats from other nations. Much of the debate about just war has been about when and to what extent the use of force is acceptable: Is it only when attacked or is it legitimate to strike preemptively? What kind of force can be used and against whom?

In Chapter 2 of this book, I have rejected the just war theory. In this chapter, I am arguing for the possibility of co-existing with enemies who pose a threat to us. I suggested that we do co-exist with non-human threats such as tigers, snakes, and sharks. To some extent, we also co-exist with human threats that take the form of criminals in domestic society. We are willing to live with some crime rather than have the police act in more brutal ways that may harm innocent lives. But to have nations co-exist with enemy states without exercising the right to use military means to ward off and eliminate hostile threats seems too risky and imprudent. If so, the domestic analogy fails, except in reference to the breakdown of civil authority in a state of anarchy.

Co-existing with enemies

I think, however, that there is another lesson to be learned from the domestic analogy. The reason that liberal democratic societies do not use more force against criminal elements is not just based on some sort of bargain, as the contractarians would have it. Of course, tyrannical states that usually resort to force to get what they want may be restrained only by a calculation of the costs of violence. But I think that there is another reason for liberal democracies to reject the use of unrestrained violence to eliminate crime and to protect citizens. The reason is that such violence by officials of the state would change the nature of liberal democracy and undermine its moral values.

Consider why the arguments in favor of the use of torture to extract information from terrorism suspects have not gone down well with a lot of people in the United States. Some have argued against torture because there is evidence that it is not effective in obtaining accurate and timely information, since experienced interrogators believe that other means work better at getting the suspects to talk. There is, however, no agreement on this and it is conceivable that torture has worked in some cases.[16] Others object to torture of prisoners because it is illegal in domestic law and is a violation of international law for the United States to engage in torture. Defenders of torture, on the other hand, argue that the Geneva Conventions and other humanitarian laws are outdated in the era of "new wars" against enemies who do not observe legal niceties and are not uniformed combatants fighting on the side of a sovereign state. This has led to debate about which enemy combatants are covered by the Geneva Conventions in the "War on Terror."[17]

The objection to torture that I find most compelling is one that holds that compromising our values in order to protect our security undermines what is worth protecting about our liberal democracy in the first place.[18] It is not just the value of the rule of law, since the law could be changed so that torture and police violence against possibly innocent suspects and bystanders could be legalized.[19] It is the *moral* values of a society that are at risk when the state carries out torture. Such values determine the kind of people we are, the kind of community we live in, and the kind of relations we have with fellow citizens. I think it is clear that life in a police state would be intolerable for most people who live in America today, even if there is no street crime in such a state. It is intolerable for ordinary citizens, who could be subjected to actions against them by the police or the state without doing anything to justify such actions. Thus, we cannot accept that one can be detained and questioned on the basis of one's ethnicity where there is no evidence of criminal activity.[20] For when one lives in a liberal democracy, one should be able to make choices on the basis of one's values and legitimate goals without having to fear the interference of the state unless one is violating the law. Clearly, one's moral autonomy and integrity would be undermined by the excessive use of coercion by the agents of the state, even if those agents are acting to protect our lives and property.[21] Moreover, the agents of the state are themselves corrupted and prevented from achieving decent human lives. The use of violence, even if carried out in the name of law enforcement, can be psychologically and morally damaging, and particularly so if it is excessive and results in loss of innocent lives.

The actions of a state against the citizens of other states also have an effect on the moral life of those who carry out these actions. Whatever the disanalogies between the preservation of domestic civil order and the maintenance of international order among nations as recited earlier, there is an analogy between the policeman and the soldier. Both are being asked to engage in coercive acts to defend the state and its people. It is important for the citizens of a liberal democracy that there are limits to what the policeman and the soldier are asked and allowed to do in carrying out their duties. These limits are not set just by considerations regarding what is effective and what is on balance more beneficial than harmful. They are set by the moral values of the society that they purport to defend.

I have explained how excessive police violence in domestic law enforcement is intolerable and detrimental to the moral integrity of citizens and the agents of the liberal democratic state. It may be argued that the analogy does not apply to war since the soldier acts against those outside of the state. If they kill civilians or torture prisoners, is there an effect on the moral values of the state that they fight to protect? One response is that as soldiers represent the state they belong to and serve, they should act in ways that are consonant with the state's values. But then, the debate turns into one of whether the values of the state are more threatened by defeat on the battlefield or by the hypocrisy of those who fight to defend the state. I will argue instead that it is a mistake to try to isolate what happens on the battlefield from what happens at home. There are a number of ways in which the failure to practice moral values that the state claims to uphold when the state is at war affects the moral integrity of the state and the survival of those values.

First, soldiers return home. Much has become known in recent years about the adverse effects of post-traumatic stress disorder (and survivor guilt) suffered by American veterans returning from Iraq. Suicide rates have soared, as have incidences of domestic violence and divorce rates. Returned reservists have had trouble functioning in civilian jobs and living with their families. We cannot expect human beings to transition from months or years of wartime duty to life in their communities at home. This is true even for soldiers who have not committed atrocities and who have maintained their moral integrity. But it is difficult for soldiers to keep their moral bearings when they fight and kill. History books on war describe civilized Greeks executing all the men and enslaving women and children after taking a city; Christian crusaders looting, raping, and murdering their way through the Holy Land; and American soldiers on rampage in My Lai and Haditha.[22] It is not just when the laws of armed conflict are violated that soldiers suffer moral harm. The moral values of a liberal democracy are more restrictive than what international conventions of war permit. A soldier can be damaged in a way that prevents him from functioning as a citizen in his own community, even if he has not violated the rules of war. This is because the rules of war permit those in the military to take actions that involve killing of civilians as a form of collateral damage.[23]

Second, those who give orders to the military that disregard or discount the harm done in the killing of civilians or the destruction of homes are the people who run our country. Ethicists of war have pointed out that, by definition, a noncombatant is innocent, in the sense that she is someone who poses no threat to us and has done nothing that entitles us to override her right not to be harmed by our actions.[24] If the leaders of a state can "justify" violating enemy non-combatant rights for the sake of military advantage, it does not take much for them to similarly discount the rights of citizens for the sake of national security. This is the path to tyranny, and is a real and grave threat to the values of a liberal democracy. It is not a hypothetical threat as in the American experience during the Vietnam War years as well as in the current "war on terror," domestic spying and extra-judicial arrests and detentions have been carried out against those citizens who disagree with the policies of the state. What is sown abroad is eventually reaped at home.

Third, citizens at home are not unaware of what the troops are doing. If they are ignorant, they are in a position to find out. To the extent that they know and do not object, they are implicitly endorsing the killing of innocent people in other countries. The endorsement becomes explicit when they declare that they support the troops without distinguishing between actions that they support and actions that they object to. There are some who would attempt to rationalize the killing of innocent people in other countries by appealing to the fact that our enemies do not respect innocent life either. But that would be to grant that we share the values of our enemies, not those values such as respect for human life and autonomy that we claim to uphold.

The line of argument that I have been presenting is that the same reasons we have for limiting the ability of the police to use coercive powers against criminals in ways that harm innocent people also apply to the use of violence against the people of other countries when we send soldiers over there to defend our country against hostile states. The fact that the innocents who may be harmed in other countries are not our citizens does not change the fact that the moral values of our liberal democracy are at stake. So the position of domestic law enforcement and military action by the state against its enemies are analogous in this respect. The use of force must be limited to prevent harm to innocent lives. We would not allow our police force to blow up a building or fire into a crowd in pursuit of criminals because doing so would cause many innocent people to be injured or killed. We should not allow our military to bomb civilian areas or take other actions that are foreseen to cause "collateral damage" because doing so would cause the deaths of innocent people. The fact that these people belong to another country does not lessen our moral obligations, and damage is still done to our moral values and standing when we fail to avoid killing them. If we treat innocent life with less respect just because they are not our people, we undermine the moral values that we claim to uphold.

The possibility of co-existence

It is not up to us whether or not another country wants to threaten us. It is up to us how we respond. The threats posed by humans are harder to deal with than the threats posed by wild animals. But when we face threats from human criminals, those of us who live in a liberal democracy are able to find a compromise between the need to protect ourselves and the need to respect innocent human life and even the life and rights of the criminals, who should not be summarily killed but should be apprehended and punished only after due process. The question is whether we can transfer our practice in dealing with domestic threats to our practice in dealing with hostile states that threaten us.

To protect ourselves from criminals, we try to protect our homes and property. We also keep away from places where criminals lurk and avoid situations that provide them with opportunities to harm us. We also expect the police to locate the criminals and to arrest them, as well as to keep them away from places where people live, work, and play. It is not realistic to expect the police to eliminate crime altogether. The police cannot capture every criminal and anticipate every crime. Nor can they violate the rights of citizens in order to facilitate police action. We are not willing to let the police do more to reduce the threat of crime, for to do that would undermine the values we uphold.

We have to recognize that there is an analogous situation with the use of force against people from other countries that threaten our state. We cannot defeat all our enemies on the battlefield or eliminate all threats from hostile states or non-state groups. What we can do to protect ourselves is to secure our borders and limit the opportunities for our enemies to harm us. Fighting and killing can be avoided as far as possible, and the possibility of negotiation with enemies and of finding compromises that would defuse an immediate threat should always be explored.[25] But if war is really unavoidable, respect for innocent lives should be paramount. To do otherwise would be to damage the liberal democratic values we claim to live by and to uphold.[26]

Is such a scenario too idealistic? If we believe in our values, then by standing up for them, we can triumph in the long run. The United States did not defeat the Soviet Union militarily, but its liberal democratic values withstood the test of time better than did the values of a totalitarian state. In the short term, the American people have been and will be tested. They will suffer losses and they will endure greater risks. But I would argue that a liberal democracy that upholds values that include the sanctity of innocent human life is a society that cannot do otherwise than to try to outlive its enemies while trusting that its moral values will ultimately be proven superior. To compromise a state's values in exchange for greater short-term security or in the hope of killing all its enemies would mean giving up on what citizenship in that nation stands for. We may save the state but sacrifice the values that define it as one worthy of saving.[27]

The limit of co-existence

The analogies that I have used to make the case for co-existing with enemies that threaten us do not show that we are always morally required to avoid killing them. There are times when co-existence becomes impossible and we will (regrettably) kill predatory animals. There are times when the police must be given special powers in order to stop particularly heinous criminals. In both analogies, there are limits to co-existence. So we should expect there to be times when a nation that is practicing co-existence fails to keep a hostile enemy at bay without going to war. A foreign threat can be so serious that it is no longer possible to stop the enemy without weakening them militarily or to tolerate the evil carried out by the enemy. The problem is how we are to determine whether war is the morally right choice. We cannot base the right choice on what political leaders actually do, as many are too ready to use force.

War is an evil, but I do not think it should *never* be right for a political leader to choose to fight a war. On the basis of virtue ethics, the question to ask is: Would a political leader with all the moral virtues such as compassion, courage, and justice ever choose something as evil as war? Suppose such a leader was faced with Hitler's advance across Europe. How could it be right for him not to engage Hitler in battle to stop his advance? The triumph of Nazism was rightly seen as so evil that it had to be stopped. This may not be so obvious when we consider today how terrible the Second World War turned out to be. That is because many morally unacceptable things were done, such as the terror bombing of cities. If we assume that the choice of war was made by a morally virtuous leader, the war would be prosecuted in a way that was more respectful of innocent lives. She would recognize the taking of innocent lives in war would damage the values of her society and the psyche of the soldiers, preventing her citizens from flourishing as human beings.[28]

Moreover, she would also end the war at the point where Nazism was no longer a threat with which she could not co-exist. Thus, the war that a virtuous political leader would have fought against Hitler would have been far less evil than the actual war that was fought.[29]

The judgments that I am assuming the virtuous political leader would make depends on her using practical wisdom to make the right choices.[30] She will not be a pacifist committed never to use force, but she will be less likely to choose war than those who decide on the basis of who has the right to go to war according to the just war theory. In order to support this claim about the virtuous political leader, I must explain how her moral choice is made. It is not enough to say that some evils such as Nazism make war a preferable choice. We need to know what it is about Nazism such that fighting against it is an acceptable choice and what else would also make fighting acceptable. And we need to answer this in a way that shows war to be ruled out in many more cases than those that are ruled out by just war theory. One way to argue for pacifism is to appeal to the claim that by allowing the justified use of war in some cases, we end up allowing many morally unacceptable wars. For the pacifist, the only way to avoid justifying too much is not to permit any use of violence altogether. I do not agree with this, but I do agree with the pacifist that just war theory allows too many wars. So I must now show that there is a way to make war an acceptable moral choice without opening the door to many of the wars that are justified by just war theory. I have already argued that just war theories are not sufficiently restrictive, and that one reason for this is the failure of the just war tradition to properly recognize the evil of war. What I must provide here is a different basis for the moral acceptability of choosing something as evil as war. By doing this, I will at the same time be able to locate the difference between the philosophy of co-existence and the pacifist position, thereby making room for a new ethics of war that is neither in the just war tradition nor a form of pacifism.

To explain how war is chosen, I will first consider the morality of killing and saving lives. Is it ever right for someone to choose to kill in order to save lives, and if not, why not? This is a question that has been much discussed by moral philosophers but usually in terms of the rights involved in killing and letting die. Would virtue ethics recognize a moral difference similar to the one between killing and letting die? By understanding whether killing may be chosen by a virtuous person, we will be in a better position to understand how war may be chosen. For as discussed in the previous chapter, the evil of war can largely be attributed to the killings that take place on a massive scale in war.

Such killings destroy the possibility of a flourishing human life for the victims as well as for the killers. And they damage the relationships between human beings that are necessary for establishing and maintaining a decent human community.

Virtue and killing

As explained in Chapter 3, in virtue ethics, right choices are not determined by maximizing utility or following rules. The standard is the choice that a fully virtuous person would make in the situation. To be fully virtuous requires that the agent possess practical wisdom – an ability derived from experience to make correct practical choices in a reliable manner based on a discernment of the human good that is the goal of action. An agent is motivated to seek the good when she has the moral character of someone who desires that good and makes it the object of her choice of action.

For critics of virtue ethics, the problem with this account of choice is that it seems vague and indeterminate. It may even seem circular: Do we need to know what is the correct choice before we can tell who the person of good character is? To avoid such criticism, a common move to make is to provide an account of human good or goods. If this could be done, then both the person of good character and the correct moral choices could be determined in relation to the good. Unfortunately, an account of human good has been a source of serious difficulty for virtue ethics. There are doubts as to whether the same things are good for every human being. Why should we assume otherwise? Aristotle provided a metaphysical account of human nature that is no longer appealing today. Contemporary virtue ethicists have tried instead to provide a naturalized account of human good. Even then, it is a challenge to find agreement on what natural facts about human beings (if any) should be used to figure out what is good for human beings. And it is a puzzle why such facts could have normative import.

Thus, it remains controversial what exactly constitutes human good. If I need to know this before it can be decided whether a virtuous person would be correct in choosing to kill, then the project would be too big to deal with in this book. I do not, however, think answering the questions about killing in war requires me to carry out the task of specifying the human good in advance. We may not agree about every virtue of character that the virtuous human being would have to have. But there is little disagreement that a strong reluctance to kill other humans is a virtue. There are both empirical and conceptual reasons for thinking this. As a matter of fact, almost every human society has some form of prohibition against homicide, and the ones that do not (or the ones that have too flexible rules against homicide) are societies that have not thrived.[31] The conceptual reason is that humans must live with other humans in order to flourish as human beings, as Aristotle noted. But for humans to form relationships that are strong and deep enough to support human flourishing, the people that they live with cannot have so little regard for human life that they do not hold back from killing others.

If I am right, then whatever else we think count as virtues, we would expect the virtuous person to have a strong aversion to killing humans. This claim about human good is all that I need to give an account of what a virtuous agent would do when making choices that involve killing humans. Before I go into the account of practical choice, I should explain what I mean by a strong aversion to killing humans. First, an aversion to killing is a desire not to kill. But we need to distinguish between intrinsic desires and extrinsic desires, which is the distinction between a desire for something for its own sake and the desire for something for the sake of something else that it is needed for.[32] The aversion that is part of a person's character is an *intrinsic* desire. When something is chosen not for its own sake but for the sake of something else, the choice of that thing need not impugn a person's character, for it may be the most rational thing to choose it, given the alternatives and the other things that the person desires. The distinction between the two kinds of desires is best seen in how a person may say, "I wanted to do it because of the good that it will bring, but I did not really want to." We would evaluate such a person very differently from one who did it because they wanted to (period).

The second clarification is that a strong aversion to killing does not necessarily override every other (intrinsic) desire. We would expect a virtuous person to have a character with a whole slate of virtues. This means that the person would choose and act on the basis of a number of desires that are relevant to her choice. The achievement of some other desires may necessitate killing. The virtuous agent may end up choosing to kill, despite her strong aversion to killing. Her choice could be the right one to make in the circumstances, so long as the intrinsic desires motivating her are virtuous ones, and she did not reason badly nor did she choose killing as a result of her aversion to killing not being what it should be for a virtuous person.

So what kind of goods could a virtuous person intrinsically desire that could override her strong aversion to killing and thereby motivate her to choose to kill human beings? The most obvious and strongest candidate is the good of saving lives, including one's own. This is an intuition shared by other moral theories that recognize the right of self-defense as a form of justified killing. There are also accounts in moral theory of justified killing in order to save a greater number of other lives. Where does the virtue ethicist stand on the choice between killing and saving lives? Unlike the utilitarian, it is not a matter of counting the value of each life and choosing the alternative with the greatest value. Unlike the deontologist, it is not a matter of deciding if the duty not to kill is more stringent than the duty to save lives. I have said that the virtuous person will have a strong aversion to killing other human beings. I would suggest as well that it is a virtue in a person to intrinsically desire to help other people whose lives are in danger. All things being equal, someone who ignores the cries of help from a person about to lose his life has a deficiency in moral character compared to the one who is motivated to help. In an ideal world, the virtuous person can act in character by not killing others and by saving others. Unfortunately, there are moral dilemmas in the real world where the agent can only save lives by killing. Can such killing be morally right?

It does not seem to me that the virtuous agent is one who would never choose to kill, no matter how many lives could be saved. Suppose the two relevant desires for her moral choice are her desire not to kill and her desire to save lives.[33] The person would be lacking in virtue if her desire to save lives has so little weight that she would not kill the mass murderer about to detonate a nuclear weapon in the middle of a metropolis. But would she kill one innocent person to save a few innocent people? We find philosophers thinking about such scenarios by devising examples such as the Trolley Problem.[34] A rights-based theorist would criticize the utilitarian view that one should kill whenever greater utility results from killing. But the rights-based theorist who holds that the negative right not to be killed always outweighs the positive right to receive aid when one's life is endangered would also hold that one should never kill to save any number of lives, however large the number. I said that the virtuous agent would choose to kill a mass murderer to save the lives of millions who would be killed by the nuclear weapon that he is about to detonate.[35] Such a choice is not made by simply counting lives and maximizing utility. Instead, how she chooses is a reflection of the relative strength of the desires that are relevant to her choice. If her desire not to kill is very strong and her desire to save lives is very weak, then the agent is unlikely to choose to kill to save lives unless the number of people saved is very much larger than the number of people killed. If on the other hand, the desire not to kill is very weak and the desire to save lives is very strong, then the agent is much more likely to kill whenever there are a few more lives to be saved. It is also possible that the desires are roughly equal in strength, in which case the agent's readiness to kill falls between the earlier two cases.

I do think that the desire not to kill is more important for virtue than is the desire to save lives. Ideally, a virtuous person should desire both. But it is a greater fault if the desire not to kill is too weak than if the desire to save lives is too weak.[36] So I think a virtuous person will be reluctant to kill just because a greater number of lives will be saved. Her moral reasoning differs from that of the utilitarian. Yet, there will be situations where killing is the morally right choice because there are so many lives at risk that her desire to save lives will motivate her to kill, despite her strong aversion to killing. I cannot specify in advance how many lives must be at risk for the virtuous agent to choose to kill in order to save lives. Virtue ethics is a theory that leaves moral choice partly indeterminate, a matter of intuitive decision-making based on experience and an appreciation of the particularities of the situation. For my purposes, I do not need to say more than what I have said here: that sometimes, for the virtuous agent, the morally right choice is to kill, despite her strong aversion to killing.

Moral choice and war

The choice of war is a choice to kill. But war is different from the killing that a virtuous agent may choose in particular situations. An individual agent may face a situation when he has to kill one or a few persons to save her own life or the lives of others. This may be over in a matter of minutes. It is unlikely that he would have to get other people to join in the killings. And he should not be killing innocent bystanders. A political leader making a decision for his country to go to war is choosing to send tens of thousands, perhaps millions, of soldiers out to do battle where they will kill or be killed. Wars can last years, decades, or even centuries. And many of the people who end up being killed are civilians who are not taking part in hostilities. These differences between individual killings and organized warfare are some of the reasons provided in the arguments in the last chapter that war is intrinsically evil.

Thus, it cannot be assumed that just because a virtuous person may correctly choose to kill to save lives, a virtuous leader may correctly choose for his country to go to war. It seems right that a virtuous person is one who would kill the person about to detonate a nuclear weapon in the middle of a big city. It is not so clear that she would also kill the person's entire family, if needed to stop the detonation. It is even more doubtful that she would kill an innocent bystander's family for the same purpose. And it seems quite unacceptable for her to get other people to kill other families. It may be true that the outcome of doing all of this is a better set of consequences than the results of a nuclear explosion. But the virtue ethicist is not a utilitarian. These other acts would constitute vices or defects in the character of the agent because they reflect an insufficiently strong aversion toward the killing of human beings.

Since war involves a number of acts that seem wrong for the individual person to choose, we need a further argument for the choice of war beyond those in the last section that were used to show that the virtuous person may choose to kill. My argument will not provide a set of necessary and sufficient conditions to justify a political leader in going to war. That would be what would be expected of a theory in the just war tradition. I have shown that a virtuous agent can make a correct moral choice in choosing to kill by providing an example when this is the case, namely the killing of a mass murderer to save the lives of millions who would be killed by the nuclear weapon that he is about to detonate. However, because practical wisdom is partly a matter of intuitive judgment and sensibility to particularities, I did not try to draw a sharp distinction between cases where killing is the right choice and cases where it is not. I shall now use a similar strategy in presenting the example of the choice of war against Hitler and the Nazis as a clear case where a virtuous political leader would be correct in going to war. I will explain why co-existence is not possible in this case and how it is that a political leader can exemplify virtue in choosing something as evil as war. But I will also try to use my explanation to show why many other wars would not be chosen by a virtuous leader, even if they satisfy the requirements of just war theory.

What were the alternatives to fighting a war against Hitler's Nazi Germany? The answer depends on which nation we are discussing. Unlike Japan, Germany had not attacked American territory, although many of its actions had caused damage to American interests.[37] The United States could have chosen to stay out of the war. Britain was at war with Germany from the time it invaded Poland, and Hitler, in fact, sought to invade Britain. For Britain, the alternative to fighting was surrender. The Soviet Union had a peace treaty with Germany and stayed out of the war until Hitler broke the treaty. From then on, the Soviets were in the same situation as Britain and had to fight to defend its territory and citizens. As for France and the rest of occupied Europe, they would have to accept Nazi occupation permanently if they had not resisted the occupiers.

So, for the Western Allies in the Second World War other than the United States, the alternative to a war of resistance was to live under a harsh foreign regime. Life under Nazi rule bore similarities to life under a tyrannical police state. The occupied people lost their political freedoms and rights, and were subjected to the rule of a foreign leader. The Nazis had a secret police, the Gestapo, and encouraged collaborators and secret informants. They imprisoned, tortured, and executed those who worked against them, and subjected families and communities suspected of supporting the resistance to collective punishment. The Nazis were also criminals who plundered and looted works of art and jewelry from rich homes and museums. But the worst crimes for which they were notorious were the state-organized murder of millions of people that they judge to be inferior races, particularly the Jewish people and gypsies. These people were hunted down, deprived of all possessions, and transported to concentration camps, where they were systematically annihilated.

It would be grotesque even to ask whether conceding to the Nazis the freedom to do what they were already doing in Europe prior to their defeat is a worse evil than fighting a war against them. The Second World War in Europe exemplified all the evils of war that I have listed in the previous chapter. The uncertainty for a political leader at the start of a war is how much of those evils the war would contain. But, given the weapons and the size of Hitler's army and the extent of the theater of war in Europe, it would not have eluded the leader that the war was going to be extremely costly in human and moral terms. If the Nazis had simply wanted political domination of Europe and not the murder of whole races of people, it might be arguable that war was too evil to use as a means of defeating Hitler. But the genocide taking place on an unprecedented and inhuman scale, added to the criminal activities and sadistic cruelty of the Nazi leaders and officers, made the choice of war against Hitler a clearly acceptable choice for a virtuous political leader.

In evaluating the choice of the virtuous leader, we should not use the actual scale and violence of the Second World War as the basis for judging how evil a war against Hitler had to be. As I noted earlier, a virtuous leader would not have prosecuted the war in the way it was fought by the Allies. Innocent civilians would not have been killed in such numbers, and the war would not have continued once the occupied countries were liberated and the Nazis had been deprived of the ability to continue their atrocities against the Jewish people. With the Germans on the retreat, Hitler would have faced greater dissent at home and his authority would have been challenged. During the Second World War, the Allies were motivated to continue the war partly out of a desire for revenge and partly to fight for control of post-war Germany. The German people were also less willing to surrender because of atrocities by the Allies in bombing raids on civilian population centers. This would not have been the case if a less-evil war had been fought by the Allies. Any war is intrinsically evil, and a war against Hitler would be no exception. But many of the evils of the Second World War as it was actually fought could have been avoided if virtuous leaders had made the decisions.

Given Hitler's policies, co-existence was not an option and surrender would have left Hitler unencumbered to continue and to expand the evils of Nazism, especially the genocidal Jewish Holocaust. Just as a virtuous individual with a strong aversion against killing can be correct in choosing to kill in exceptional circumstances, a virtuous leader who desires not to go to war could still correctly choose to go to war against Hitler. War for her is not desirable for its own sake or even morally neutral. Although the choice of war in the circumstances need not impugn her character, she will not think of it as a just war. As I said before, evil cannot be justified. She would recognize that in going to war, she has chosen to begin something that is a great intrinsic evil. She will regret having to choose war, but she would regret even more if she did not choose war and left Hitler to do his evil deeds without a military challenge. In seeking to turn back Hitler's advance across Europe and to free the people in the countries that he had occupied, she is acting out of virtues such as justice, courage, and compassion for Hitler's victims. She is motivated by her desire to save a larger number of innocent lives.

There are few wars in history that compare to the fight against Hitler and the Nazis. Leaders of Western democracies going to war have often attempted to liken their enemies to Hitler.[38] Take the American invasion of Iraq in 2003, in which Saddam Hussein was portrayed as the equivalent of Hitler, and those who stood against the war were compared with British Prime Minister Chamberlain, who negotiated peace with Hitler in 1938, a year before the Second World War started. At the time of the invasion, the Iraqi regime was not even occupying anyone's territory. Saddam ran a police state and did kill many political opponents. Many of his deeds were evil. But it is hard to argue that leaving him in power (while subject to UN sanctions and weapons inspections) is a great enough evil to make it correct to choose to invade Iraq and depose him. A virtuous political leader who appreciates the great evil of war is not likely to prefer war, in those circumstances.[39]

What I am saying is that once we consider how evil war is, in the ways described in the previous chapter, it is very difficult to find cases in which a virtuous political leader would choose war. The choice of war can be a correct choice only when the alternative to war involves such great evils that the virtuous desires of the leader may lead him to choose the evil of war in order to act against these other evils. I have tried to show that this requirement is clearly met in the case of fighting a war against Hitler. But it is hard to find anything comparable in evil with what Hitler and the Nazis were doing in the 1930s and 1940s. Perhaps the Romans were evil enough with their murderous spectacles in the Coliseum. Perhaps the Aztecs were evil enough with their rituals of human sacrifice carried out on captives from neighboring tribes. These are already less-convincing cases for waging war than in the paradigmatic Hitler test case. Even less convincing are those enemies, such as Saddam Hussein, used to justify wars in recent history.

Just as for individual killings, I will not try to draw a clear line that can be used to decide every case. That is not how moral choices are made in virtue ethics. What I have done here with the example of Hitler (even if this is the only clear case) is enough to show that a virtuous political leader need not be a pacifist. War may be a great evil, but it is not the only great evil. However rare the cases are, evils such as Nazism do exist in the real world. The problem of too many wars is the result of many leaders choosing to fight wars against enemies that do evils that are comparable neither to what the Nazis did nor to the evils that happen if war is used against them. In that case, the choice of war is due either to a mistake in moral decision-making or to a failure to appreciate the evil of war or to a leader who is lacking in virtue. The leader who is not virtuous in making decisions to go to war is comparable to an individual whose defective character leads him to kill too readily, given that he does not have a strong enough aversion to killing.

It may seem paradoxical to say that a virtuous person may choose to do evil. A virtuous person would not desire to do evil for its own sake. Neither would she do evil for the sake of goods that can be achieved without doing the evil. But the right choice is not always a choice of things that are desired for their own sake. The world presents agents with moral dilemmas and tragic choices where the agent ends up choosing to do things that go against her intrinsic desires.[40] If she could only avoid one evil by doing another evil, she should use her practical wisdom to choose the "lesser" evil.[41] What I have argued is that there could be situations where the choice of the virtuous leader, who reasons correctly from her intrinsic desires that include a strong aversion to killing, is to go to war. When she does this, she is not choosing evil for its own sake. And she would not justify the evil of war by the good that can be achieved by fighting a war. One of the evils of war is the moral corruption of people on all sides, combatants and noncombatants. Those who kill and those who order killings damage their ability to flourish as good human beings.[42] Those who suffer severe harms in war and those who witness the harms are also hindered from achieving the human good. A virtuous leader would recognize that her choice of war involves a sacrifice of her own goodness.[43] Thus, she would only choose this when it is a matter of great moral importance to prevent the evil that would take place if she did not choose war. A virtuous leader would not take the choice of war lightly. It is her role to make this difficult decision with full sensitivity to the nature of war and the burdens and sacrifices for everyone affected by the war. To get the decision right, she must locate the mean between the evil of fighting and the evil of not fighting. Her ability to decide correctly would depend on her experience and character, not on a set of rules and conditions of the sort found in just war theory.

6
Theoretical Implications and Challenges

The philosophy of co-existence that I proposed in the last chapter as an alternative to both just war theories and pacifism will draw many objections. In this chapter, I will address some likely objections that are theoretical in nature.

First of all, there is an issue concerning the nature of war. If war has taken a completely new form in recent times, there are two possible responses that do not require the kind of ethics of war that I have proposed. One is that just war theories are always in a process of evolving to take into account the changing nature of war. Granted, the traditional forms of just war theory have difficulties with issues such as asymmetric warfare and humanitarian intervention, but the failures should not indict the tradition of just war thinking. Instead, ethicists of war should continue working in the just war tradition to address these difficulties. I have already partly responded to this when I showed that the central tenets of just war theory are seriously problematic, so that any version of just war theory will share these problems. But there is a second response to the claim that war has taken a completely new form. In this view, just war theory should be replaced because we need moral theories for human conflicts that have not been seen before recent times. So a view such as mine that is not tied to the features of recent conflicts but is meant to apply to the wars that just war theory deals with would be as obsolete as just war theory itself.

The thesis of new wars originated from the ideas of a political scientist that have influenced some of those writing on the ethics of war.[1] I reject the view that wars in recent times are so different that no ethics of war could apply to both "old" and "new" wars. My discussion of this issue will involve both an attempt to conceptualize war and an examination of the reasoning and examples used to support the "new war" thesis.

A second theoretical issue that I will deal with here is something carried over from the previous chapter. I argued against the state using violence in a way that fails to adequately respect the lives of innocent people in dealing with either domestic or international threats. My argument assumed a state with liberal democratic values. This might seem a major limitation for the philosophy of co-existence. There is disagreement about the superiority and universality of the values espoused in liberal democracies, especially since liberal democratic societies seem to have evolved into existence in the Western world. These values may instead be a cultural and historical phenomenon that need not be appropriate for societies that are very different.

The third theoretical issue that I will respond to concerns what a virtuous leader would do in the face of threats to her society. There are obviously views on this that differ from mine. Historically, there have been virtuous people who have chosen in a variety of ways. For instance, Gandhi, a man of undeniable moral virtue, thought that war could not be chosen as the means to end the evil of British colonial rule in India. On the other hand, the ancient Greek philosopher Aristotle, one of the originators of virtue ethics, thought that courage was a virtue that is acquired and exercised in war when one's city, an essential human good, is threatened or attacked. And many people of excellent character differed on whether the enemies of Nazism should fight or make peace with Hitler – the theologian Dietrich Bonhoeffer participated in a plot to murder Hitler, while believing killing to be a sin. There is also a problem arguing from what an individual person may rightly choose to what a political leader ought to choose. The problem of "dirty hands" arises when political leaders are thought to be justified in doing what it would be immoral for an individual person to do. To put it in the context of virtue ethics, the question can be asked whether a person who assumes the role of a political leader should choose differently on the basis of the same virtues. Would courage or justice require different actions from an individual than those required from a political leader?

The new war thesis

Mary Kaldor uses two related lines of argument for what I will label as her New War Thesis. She presents a set of differences between wars of the eighteenth, nineteenth, and twentieth centuries, up to the Second World War, and the wars that have taken place in the post-colonial era, in particular after the end of the Cold War. She also examines in depth a paradigm example of a "new war," namely the conflict in Bosnia–Herzegovina in the last decade of the twentieth century as the federal state of Yugoslavia dissolved into a number of independent nation-states.

Kaldor identifies a number of differences in the characteristics of new wars as compared with those found in the wars between states that were fought by regimental armies, wars of the kind that Clausewitz had written about. According to Kaldor,

> the processes known as globalization are breaking up the cultural and socio-economic divisions that defined the patterns of politics which characterized the modern period. The new type of warfare has to be understood in terms of this global dislocation.[2]

As she explains it, globalization has the effect of erasing a number of distinctions found in the old wars between public and private, internal and external, the economic and the political, the civil and the military, and combatant and noncombatant.[3] The first distinction is that between state activity and non-state activity. Old wars were an activity of the state. Private acts of violence were criminal acts. New wars involved the actions of militias and mafia-types. The second distinction is between threats to the state from within and outside the territory of the state. Internal enemies may ferment civil wars against the regime, while external enemies may threaten the interests of the country. In the new wars, internal enemies are financed, equipped and supported by state and non-state agencies and individuals through global networks. The third distinction is between private economic activities and public state activities. Rather than being fought solely for political objectives, war has become an economic activity for many of the groups fighting the new wars. The fourth distinction is between non-violent legal intercourse between citizens and the violence used in external struggles. In new wars, the politics of identity divides citizens and leads to armed conflict. Finally, the bearers of arms in new wars are not just soldiers in uniform under the control of the state but mercenaries, private militia, and criminal organizations.

Kaldor sees the features of new wars illustrated by the war in the former Yugoslav province of Bosnia–Herzegovina that took place between April 1992 and October 1995.[4] She describes the conflict as the result of economic collapse and the disintegration of the Yugoslav federation following the end of the Cold War. The warring factions were a mixture of army units, militias and criminal groups that essentially preyed on the civilian population and benefited from looting, extortion, black market trading, and "taxation" of humanitarian aid. Instead of a strategy of winning the people's hearts and minds, the various parties to the conflict subjected people in the areas they controlled to fear and hatred, culminating in the process of ethnic cleansing in which many thousands were murdered, raped, or forced to flee. The intervention by foreign governments in the form of peacekeepers and political mediation only provided legitimacy to those who had committed war crimes and ultimately solidified the ethnic partition of the country. Kaldor attributes the mistakes of the international community to a misperception of the conflict in terms of the old wars between warring states, rather than recognizing them as the new wars that she has identified.

I do not dispute the facts on the ground that Kaldor had carefully documented. But does she succeed in depicting the Bosnia–Herzegovina conflict as a new war that is fundamentally different from the wars of earlier times? That depends on what we think those earlier wars were like. The problem is that she focused on wars of the eighteenth, nineteenth, and (most of the) twentieth centuries (call them ENT wars for short) as exemplars of old wars. Her argument can be formulated as follows:

1. Wars of the ENT were old wars.
2. Wars of the late twentieth century and since are different from the wars of the ENT.
3. Therefore, wars of the late twentieth century and since are new wars.

The problem with this argument is that the conclusion only follows if in premise (2), the differences between the wars of the two periods make old and new wars conceptually different in an essential way. And that in turn depends on whether a focus on ENT wars is enough to identify the essential features of old wars.

There is obviously a feature of ENT wars that made them look different from the wars of earlier centuries. This was the role of the standing regimental armies of citizen conscripts that fought on behalf of nation-states in this period. The existence of nation-states as a sovereign political entity that became the basic political unit in international relations followed the development of the Westphalian system of European nations in 1648. The treaty that set out the system was a significant historical event that put an end to conflicts that Europe had experienced at the hands of the titled elite who used hired armies to fight for their right to rule, for the expansion of their territories, and for spreading their religious beliefs.

It seems to me, however, that the wars that prevailed in the many centuries prior to the Westphalian system were not dissimilar to the conflict in Bosnia–Herzegovina and other "new wars." The war historian John Keegan pointed out that "war antedates the state, diplomacy and strategy by millennia," and that Clausewitz's account of war as the continuation of policy by other means is an "incomplete" thought that happened to reflect the relations between states in Europe at the time.[5] So what were wars like throughout human history? As old wars, what did earlier wars have in common with the ENT wars? And are not the essential features of old wars also found in the so-called new wars?

As a philosopher, I can best answer these questions by first defining what war is and differentiating it from violence that is not war. Individuals and groups have fought with each other from the beginning of humankind and still do. When they fight, they may use weapons that are similar to those that soldiers use in war. The concept of war requires more than just fighting in groups and the use of weapons. Warfare is organized fighting, with warriors "put into the field in formation, when they work as a team under a commander or leader rather than as a band of leaderless heroes."[6] Moreover, it is characteristic of these warriors that they fight for reasons that usually diverge from the reason for the wars that they fight. For instance, soldiers fighting in the Roman army in places like Britain or Palestine were not doing so because Britons or Israelites had shown up at Roman homes and threatened them. Similarly, the United States may have declared war on Japan after the attack on Pearl Harbor, but most of the Americans who were sent out to fight against Japan had no personal experience of the attack or other threats from Japan, and their livelihood did not depend on the United States keeping its bases in Hawaii or the Philippines. Instead of individuals or groups fighting for their own lives, families, homes and means of livelihood, soldiers that fight in wars do not necessarily share in the reasons of the leader or ruler who orders them to fight.[7] They may be fighting because they would be punished for disobeying, or because they would be rewarded in the form of pay or loot, or because they were seeking adventure. The enemy soldiers that they fight and kill have not usually done them any personal injury prior to facing them on the battlefield. It is the choice of the leader to send them out to fight to further his goals.

Before the advent of the nation-state, the idea that the leader chose what was good for the state rather than for what was good for himself made little sense. For the leader was the state. The people under his control were his possessions or his hirelings, who had little choice but to do as he commanded. They were the tools that he used to get what he wanted. So the goals of a leader in war could be whatever he chose to fight for. The reason for a war might be to satisfy his honor or his desire for glory or his greed. Many of the five distinctions that Kaldor lists as features of old wars are not found in the wars that I am describing here. In particular, there was nothing private in the lives of those who lived at the mercy of their ruler. Nor was there purely economic activity to be pursued in private. Anyone could be sent out to fight so no one was purely a civilian. And internal enemies were hard to distinguish from external ones. They usually had to be dealt with in the same way, by force of arms. Rivals for the throne usually fled to other countries when defeated and could count on support from other rulers based on kinship, religion, or political interests.

Hence, the features on Kaldor's list do not seem to be essential features of old wars. From ancient times, the idea of fighting and dying for one's country was a fiction. In reality, a soldier fights and dies for his leader. I would contend that this is true even of the wars of the modern era, despite appearances. The birth of the nation-state simply provided those in power with another ideological tool (and a rather effective one) to persuade an increasingly wealthy and educated population to sacrifice their lives in war. As I said, it is characteristic of war that those who fight were not doing so because they had to, in the sense that their lives, homes, and livelihood (food and resources) were in the process of being taken from them. I am drawing a contrast here between what hunter-gatherers do when others encroach on the places where they hunt or shelter, and what soldiers do when they march off to battle at their leader's behest in the name of religion or the state. War is a dangerous business – so what could convince people to take on such risks when they do not have personal reasons to hate or fear those that they face in war? Some people have gone to war as a result of poverty or under compulsion. Others were seeking adventure, glory, or loot. But another means that made possible the enlistment of large numbers of healthy young men is the narrative that leaders could provide to make war respectable and attractive. One ideological tool that had been used in many wars in history is the elevation of the ruler into a deity or the chosen defender of religion. For instance, the strange thing about the Crusades is how tens of thousands of people in Europe could be persuaded to abandon their families, farms, and possessions to fight and die in a faraway place that they knew little about and with which they had nothing to do.[8] It was the ideological power of the Catholic Church that made the Crusades possible.

In the ENT wars, rulers of nation-states used the concepts of state sovereignty and national identity to persuade subjects that they belonged to something that was worth fighting to defend. In reality, they would be fighting in wars that their rulers chose to fight for their own reasons, just as the case had been in earlier wars. What they were doing was not essentially different from what soldiers in earlier periods of history were doing.

So what happened at the end of the twentieth century was not a change in the nature of war, as Kaldor claimed, but was instead a change in the ideology of war. The rulers that came to power in newly independent nations after the Second World War as a result of decolonization and the division of Europe could not rely on an ideology of national sovereignty that worked so well in Europe in the previous three centuries. In a number of countries, the competing ideologies of capitalism and communism had been used to prop up governments and send men to war. After the collapse of the Soviet bloc at the end of the Cold War, these ideologies lost much of their appeal. Instead, forms of identity politics based on tribe, race, and religion were used by those politicians who wanted to replace those in power or to set up their own states by breaking away from established nation-states or to profit from the local or global arms trade and other criminal activities. Although the post-ENT wars were of smaller-scale and involved irregular forces fighting in populated areas, we could still distinguish between the causes the leaders fought for and the reasons individual fighters got involved. True, the fighting often caused people to be displaced from their homes, so they ended up having no choice but to defend their homes and livelihoods. But the wars began when leaders mobilized people who did not have to fight but were persuaded to fight through a narrative of identity politics that disguised the leaders' own motives of seeking power, land and wealth. In Rwanda, villagers who had been living in peaceful communities where neighbors posed no threat to each other ended up murdering other villagers on the basis of race. In Bosnia, as noted by Kaldor, there were Bosnian Serbs who shelled their Muslim neighbors by day and called them on their phones at night to check if they were all right.[9] Clearly, they had little personal animosity against the people they were fighting.

My main point is that the new war thesis is in reality a new ideology thesis. At the most basic level, all wars in human history essentially consist of warriors who fight for reasons that usually diverge from the reason for the wars that they fight.[10] And it is because war is of such a nature that ethics is relevant to war. When primitive groups of hunter-gatherers had to fight with other groups or early Greek farmers had to ward off intruders, there was no need to justify the fighting in moral terms. Moreover, such fighting usually ended once the enemies had gone away. These were people who fought when they had no choice and stopped fighting when there was no need to fight. The ethics of war is about whether the *choice* of fighting can be ethically correct. This question applies when there is a choice about fighting and when fighting takes place where there is no need to fight. Thus, the same ethical questions apply to all wars – pre-ENT, ENT, and post-ENT. Kaldor's new war thesis cannot sustain an argument for a different ethics for ENT wars and for post-ENT wars, respectively. If just war theory fails for post-ENT wars, as some ethicists of war think, it is because it is a deficient ethics for all wars in any period and not because the nature of war has changed.

Democracy and justice

In the previous chapter, I argued that just as police violence undermines the values of a liberal democracy that respects individual lives and choices, violence by soldiers at war puts those same values at risk, even if the battlefield is far away from home. This prompts the following challenge: To what extent should an ethics of war appeal to a particular political theory or theory of justice? Is it a limitation on the universal application of the moral theory if it is based on a view of the value of the individual in relation to the state that had originated from the European Enlightenment?

I could, of course, point out that just war theory is also an invention of Western Christendom, but this did not prevent it from evolving into a secularized version that became the foundation of international conventions and laws governing the relations between states. But such a development was not pre-ordained and the influence of the theory did not necessarily reflect the strength of the arguments and reasoning behind it. I should not, in lieu of an argument for liberal democracy, be suggesting that the philosophy of co-existence be allowed to evolve for several centuries to see if it could gain broad international acceptance! There is in addition a crucial difference between just war theory and the philosophy of co-existence. Nations, whatever their view of individual rights and the value of life, must deal with other nations under the framework of international law, and the just war theory in its secular form provides the basis for such a framework. The philosophy of co-existence is however a *moral* theory that governs the choices of a political leader and suggests how she should choose on the basis of certain values. Thus, the leader's (and her society's) views of individual rights and the value of life is crucially relevant to the moral theory.

It is clear that different societies just do not share the same views of individual rights and the value of life. For instance, there are disagreements about how much the state may intrude into the lives of individuals, and to what extent individual choice should be allowed. There are, for example, disagreements about the right of the state to execute convicted criminals. The moral choices of a political leader who does not accept liberal democratic values would be very different from those of a leader who does. So to justify the philosophy of co-existence, I must explain what it is about the ethics of war that necessitates a political leader to make choices about war on the basis of liberal democratic values. This is an immense task, since there have been philosophical disputes about this question for hundreds of years and nothing seems to have been settled by thinkers up to the present day. I do not intend to enter into those debates. Instead, I will take a position on the moral legitimacy of liberal democratic values. My position is that an ethics of war only makes sense if such values are accepted. Let me explain.

Suppose a society does not respect the autonomy of individuals and it does not value human life for its own sake. What ethical principles could justify limiting the power of the state to send its citizens to war? Obviously, there will be questions of prudence as to whether the state or the ruler would be better off as a result of the war, and whether the war aims could be achieved. But would there be moral limits? In this society, going to war would not be seen as wrong just because the citizens were against the war and the soldiers did not want to fight. For the leader's choice in this society automatically trumps the choices of individual citizens. It also could not be argued that the achievement of war aims would come at too high a cost in terms of the loss of lives. For the lives of people in this society are valued only for the contributions they make to society and not for their own sake.

As I defined it in the previous section, war by nature is fought by individuals who do not find themselves needing to fight because they have been personally attacked by those that they fight in war. The reason for the war is distinct from the reason for which a soldier goes out to fight in a war. The ethics of war is about distinguishing what are morally acceptable reasons for leaders to choose war as a means of achieving their goals and about evaluating war on that basis. If we discount individual autonomy and the value of life, what *moral* limits can be placed on the choice of war? If we do not appeal to liberal democratic values, war would be acceptable whenever the leader or the state has goals that can be prudently achieved by war. This is essentially the view of a realist – a view that effectively excludes morality from the evaluation of war.

All this, of course, does not constitute a full defense of liberal democratic values for their own sake and for other purposes. Such a defense would require me to discuss the role of these values in other aspects of human society, not just in the choice of war. It may seem that my position that an ethics of war only makes sense if such values are accepted does not provide me with the tools to argue that the philosophy of co-existence should have universal application. Many past and present societies do not accept liberal democratic values. Some of these societies view such values as a Western imposition and a violation of their traditional cultures.

However, the philosophy of co-existence that I am presenting in this book does provide a genuine basis for universal acceptance. What is universal across cultures is the experience of war as a great evil. It matters not what a society's political or value system is. People in non-liberal democracies suffer the harms of war just the same as do people in liberal democracies. War was an evil for people living in ancient China, medieval Europe, and communist Russia. People cannot have too little war. For people in any society, it is not enough that war is limited by reasons of prudence. But on what basis would someone evaluate the moral legitimacy of war and critique the reasons for war? If, as I stated above, an ethics of war only makes sense when the values of individual autonomy and respect for human life are accepted, then there is a reason internal to the society to introduce such values into any society. This is not the same as imposing Western values or making a tendentious claim that such values are morally superior. It is, rather, a choice of values that comes with the need for the moral evaluation of war – a need that begins with a common experience of war as a great evil that it would be better for any human being not to have to endure.

Historically, periods of prolonged peace in any society had been viewed as "golden ages," in which there was wealth and prosperity, and the arts, culture, and sciences flourished. True, there have been militaristic societies such as the Romans, who built their success on conquest. But as history shows us, such societies could not in the long run maintain their fortunes by military means. Eventually, they ran out of enemies to plunder or stretched the borders of their empires too far. Their people also grew weary of a continued state of war.[11] I do not, therefore, think that it is a culturally biased perspective that leads me to claim that people and societies everywhere prefer to limit war and to choose peace whenever they can.[12] And in seeking to limit war, they will have to appeal to liberal democratic values.

Virtue and politics

How would a political leader who is a virtuous individual choose to deal with enemies who threaten to destroy his state? I have presented one answer to this question in the philosophy of co-existence – such a leader would seek to avoid the killings that make war such a great evil and, therefore, choose to co-exist with enemies where it is possible to contain the threats without resorting to the violence of war. However, the leader would choose to go to war when the alternative to fighting was submission to the kind of evil exemplified by Nazi Germany's death camps and oppressive criminal regime. My answer is based not on an account of human good that determines what all the virtues of character are and how important they each are. Rather, I simply discussed the desires of a virtuous person to avoid killing innocent people and to save the lives of others. Whatever one's view of human good, there is enough of a consensus that a virtuous person would have a strong aversion toward the killing of other people. I suggested that this aversion is so central to virtue that in moral reasoning, it often overrides a desire to save others. Thus, unless the enemy is so greatly evil, a virtuous leader will correctly choose not to fight a war against the enemy, even if fighting was necessary for saving some lives.

The challenge I want to discuss here is posed by the likelihood of disagreement about where the line between fighting and not fighting should be drawn, especially given the lack of precision in decision-making on the virtue ethics approach. I had deliberately left it vague by focusing on an extreme evil like the Nazis. How much less of an evil can still be judged evil enough to fight against? Would it be virtuous to be reluctant to fight to prevent evil? Because I did not set out an account of human good and of all the virtues of a good human being, I cannot provide a set of necessary and sufficient conditions to demarcate cases where a virtuous political leader should fight and cases where he should not fight. In fact, providing such conditions is more in the spirit of just war theory than of virtue ethics. Instead, I will begin my response to the challenge by discussing some examples where it seems a

virtuous person chose differently to show that these examples of different choices do not really show what many may take them to show.

Consider first a virtuous leader choosing not to fight to stop a great
evil. Gandhi lived during the period of colonial British rule in India
when indigenous Indian people were victimized by policies that were
terribly harmful and exploitative. Besides the fact that Indians had
no political freedom to run their own affairs, they were subjected to
economic policies that served the interests of the British East India
Company, such as those that forced them to pay taxes on basic necessities such as salt, revenues on their land, and duties on foreign imports.
The British also tried to instigate religious conflict between Hindus and
Muslims, to prevent their colonial subjects from uniting against them.
Those who opposed the British or advocated the end of colonial rule
were imprisoned or massacred. After the Second World War, the British
increased their oppression when faced with growing opposition to their
rule. Many Indians who had already had experience fighting against
the Japanese were prepared to fight a war of independence against
the British. However, Gandhi, who had deep spiritual influence over
ordinary Indians, advocated a policy of non-violent opposition to the
British.[13]

Gandhi was a moral exemplar for Indians. He lived a simple and fru-
gal life and was considered to be a man of wisdom. His philosophy of
non-violence has influenced many other great men of the twentieth
century, such as Martin Luther King, Jr. and Nelson Mandela. There are
many anti-war pacifists today who draw on Gandhi's ideas. His moral
choices should be taken seriously as we attempt to figure out how a
virtuous person would choose between war and co-existence. Does he
represent a different view of moral choice from the one in the philosophy of co-existence?

Gandhi did not support the use of violence to achieve political goals.
But it does not follow that he thought people's lives should not be protected from criminals. He did not seek to do away with civilian police,
though obviously he would object to excessive police violence. This
means that it can sometimes be necessary within limits for the state to
use force to deal with lawbreakers. Since the philosophy of co-existence
draws on such a domestic analogy to determine what the state can do
when threatened by external enemies, it would seem that it is not necessarily objectionable to use military force when it is really necessary and
on balance right to do so. This, however, does not mean that Gandhi
would have supported any actual wars. In particular, he did not support
a war of independence against the British. In this, I think, he has been

proven right. India was able to eventually secure its independence from the British without fighting a war that would have been a very great evil for the Indian people. It is on such a point as this that the advantages of a virtue ethics approach can be seen. The Indian people may have just cause and maybe the right to fight, but it could still be wrong to fight if the evil of war was so great that it was preferable to pursue a possible non-violent course that required living with the evil of colonialism for a bit longer.[14]

The fact remains, however, that before the Second World War, Gandhi advised the Czechs to surrender to the Nazis and the Jews to offer themselves to be massacred.[15] It would appear that he would carry non-violence much further than I would stretch the possibility of co-existence. If Gandhi saw absolutely no limit to his policy of non-violence, then he was a pacifist and not an example of a virtuous person drawing a line as to where the choice of fighting is morally correct. But if he did see a line to be drawn, then he was sadly mistaken to place the Nazis on the side of enemies that one could co-exist with. From the evidence of his writings (including an open letter to Hitler on December 24, 1941, in which he praised Hitler as a brave and devoted man and not "the monster described by your opponents"), he was clearly ignorant of actual events in Europe and failed to appreciate the extent of the evil posed by Hitler.[16] So one may speculate about what Gandhi would say had he understood more about what the doctrine and practice of Nazism meant. When we take into consideration Gandhi's philosophy, it is more likely that he was simply a pacifist on spiritual grounds. He seemed to believe that no one, not even Hitler, was beyond redemption and that everyone's heart could be changed by the "soul-force." Moreover, he believed that violence on the body does not touch the soul, the seat of honor and dignity. To me, these are indulgent metaphysical assumptions that contribute to the dreamy idealism of pacifist thinking such as that espoused by Gandhi.

Next, consider a virtuous leader choosing to fight against an enemy that the state could have co-existed with without fighting. What I need to discuss is an example where the leader used moral reasoning, which led him to a different conclusion in making the choice for the state to go to war. I cannot use an example that does not even satisfy the requirements of the just war theory. As I think that the theory is too permissive, and that a virtuous leader would recognize the evil of war and would be more reluctant to have his state go to war, a war that is not a just war is an unlikely candidate as an example of a choice that accords with virtue ethics. Another kind of example I cannot use are wars chosen by leaders of doubtful virtue. As leaders who are clearly virtuous are rare, many examples of war must be ruled out from consideration here. I could perhaps use the difficulty of finding examples as proof that virtuous leaders would not fight enemies they could co-exist with. However, I do think the American Civil War and Lincoln's decision to fight to reconstitute the United States is an example that I could use here.

President Abraham Lincoln is considered as an exemplary president for his leadership and moral clarity. Apart from leading the Union in a successful war and proclaiming the end of slavery for African–Americans, he was known as "Honest Abe" for his virtue of honesty. The American Civil War from 1860 to 1864 is usually considered a good war in standard histories of the United States. Certainly, the slave-owners in the Confederacy were defending an evil system when they chose to assert "state rights" and broke away from the Northern states. But what was Lincoln choosing when, as president, he declared war on the Confederate states? The war could be viewed as a form of humanitarian intervention – a virtuous leader could not ignore the plight of the slaves on southern plantations. However, slavery had been around for the entire 84 years of American independence, so why did Lincoln choose at this point to use force to end the evil institution? Moreover, slavery might well have been slowly coming to an end on its own, as had been the case in the North, without military intervention.

The secession of the Southern states need not have posed any threat to those living in the North if war had not broken out. It is true that the first shots were fired by the Confederates seeking to remove Union soldiers from Fort Sumter in South Carolina. But this could have been avoided if the Union had turned over the US Army bases on Confederate territory and withdrew their units. The Union soldiers were under threat because the North had chosen to station them there.

So to the question of whether co-existence between the Union and the Confederacy was possible, the answer is that it was. Was Lincoln's choice still the correct one for a virtuous political leader to make? The choice he made was to begin a war that would send hundreds of thousands of young men to the battlefield to die or suffer grave injuries in a war in which a number of powerful new weapons were used for the first time. It was reported that Europeans who had endured centuries of European wars were horrified by the reports of what took place in battles during the American Civil War. This was a war that exemplified many of the things that constituted my case that war should be recognized as a great evil by a virtuous leader. But the evil of allowing the

Confederates to continue with slavery unchallenged is also a great one. Though the concept is anachronistic to use in this example, there may well be a case for a war of humanitarian intervention here.[17] The fact is that in 1860, Lincoln did not choose war as a means to end the evil of slavery. He chose war on the principle that the secession was illegal and he believed it was his duty as president to preserve the Union. He was displaying certain virtues in making the choice – fidelity in upholding his oath of office, and justice in punishing what he deemed to be the violation of the Constitution. He would have weighed his desire to act according to these virtues against his aversion to causing the killings that take place in war. Did he make the correct moral choice? Would a virtuous person in his place make the choice that Lincoln did?

I would argue that there were a number of things that Lincoln did not know or did not appreciate. He clearly did not expect the war to last as long as it did (due partly to the incompetence of several of the generals he appointed) and to be as brutal as it was. He also could not have known the outcome of the war – how even with the forced end of slavery, African–Americans would continue to suffer from poverty and discrimination for another hundred years, and that the evils of slavery would continue in the form of Jim Crow laws and the denial of civil rights to former slaves. Thus, the Civil War was much more evil than Lincoln had expected, and victory in the war did not end the evils that he had fought the war to eradicate. It seems to me that with hindsight, a virtuous leader who had to choose between co-existing with the Confederacy and fighting to preserve the Union would be correct to prefer the first alternative. For any leader who fully recognized the evil nature of war, Lincoln's decision was mistaken, given the facts, though it was understandable how in the circumstances, he made the choice he did.

So far, I have rejected two counter-examples that seem to show actual virtuous leaders choosing differently between co-existence and war from how I presented them as choosing in theory. I turn now to the philosophical view that there is a deficiency in virtue if the leader chooses not to fight an external enemy. In Aristotle's ethics, courage is presented as the virtue of being willing to fight for the *polis* against its enemies. In *Nicomachean Ethics* III.6, the courageous man is one who is properly unafraid in the face of a noble death, and the noblest death occurs in warfare. Those who are unwilling to risk their lives in combat cannot possess the virtue of courage.

Instead of faulting Aristotle's account of courage, we should recognize that his account is an intuitive one for an ancient Greek. Given that the Greeks at the time believed that life in the *polis* enabled them to lead civilized human lives and the main threat to the city-state came from barbaric outsiders, it was inconceivable for a courageous citizen to refuse to take up arms to defend the city-state. They were faced with the threat of aggressive invaders who would massacre and pillage cities that fell into their hands. But today, unlike in ancient Greek society, we can choose not to fight against aggressive enemies without failing to be courageous. We live in more complicated times in which a definition of courage simply in terms of willingness to engage in combat is bound to be problematic. First, unlike the idealized citizen-soldiers of the *polis*, the ones who fight in today's modern armies are not necessarily virtuous. Even if they fight on behalf of a good cause, their personal reason for fighting may be base rather than noble. And combatants cannot be assumed to be "fearless in the face of death," if the means with which they fight is relatively risk-free, relying on numerical or technological superiority. Second, those who are unwilling to fight may have moral reasons not to fight if, for instance, they think a war to be unnecessary or unjust or they are pacifists or they are virtuous people who have a strong aversion to killing people in war. Even in ancient Greece, wars were fought that were not defensive but expansionist and one could surely oppose such wars without being a coward. Most wars today are of questionable justice, and it is simplistic to assume that those who will not fight in such wars so choose because they lack courage. There need be no deficiency in virtue in choosing not to fight.

There is another view of human virtue that presents a challenge to the philosophy of co-existence. This is the view that what virtue requires is relative to the role of a person, and the role of a political leader is different from the role of an individual. Someone who takes this view could agree with me that a virtuous individual would have a strong aversion to killing other people, which would lead him to try to co-exist with threats, even when doing so puts him at risk. But it may be asked whether it follows that a virtuous political leader would be correct to put as much weight on avoiding killing people when choosing how to deal with threats to his state and its citizens. Perhaps it is a virtue for him as a leader to be willing to fight and kill enemies.

In a sense, there is some truth to this suggestion. People in special roles with special responsibilities may be morally required to do things that private individuals are not required to do. For instance, religious leaders may be expected to be more self-sacrificing than ordinary people. Thus, it may be a deficiency of virtue if they fail to intervene to save innocent lives in situations where others are not expected to do so.[18] An example of this is found in the theologian Dietrich Bonhoeffer's choice to participate in a (failed) plot to kill Hitler. Ordinary people who have compassion for the victims of Nazism may be expected to do what they can to help the victims, but it need not be a deficiency in virtue if they do not go so far as to attempt to take Hitler's life. But as a religious leader, Bonhoeffer seemed to believe that his choice is what his moral beliefs required him to do.

Of course, choosing to fight a war would be a much more serious violation of individual virtue than choosing to kill one person. The question concerns what it is about the political leader's role and the good he aims at in that role that could possibly make his choice of war the morally correct choice. There is a discussion of this issue outside of virtue ethics where the problem is formulated in terms of "dirty hands."[19] An example of this problem is whether a public official would be justified, or even required, to torture a terrorist to get information on the location of a ticking bomb that would soon go off and result in the deaths of thousands of people. In relation to the ethics of war, an example is the supreme emergency exception to the requirement in just war theory not to intentionally target and kill noncombatants.[20]

For a virtue ethicist to ask whether a political leader can demonstrate virtue in doing things that it would be a vice for individuals to do is not simply a matter of asking whether there should be exceptions to a rule against killing people. It is, rather, the question of whether the good that the leader acts to achieve is different enough from the good that private individuals aim at in their actions so that the right actions for the leader include ones that are the wrong actions for individuals. Of course, the question is best answered by giving accounts of individual and social human goods and comparing them. I have explained that this is too large a task to carry out here. I propose to answer the question about dirty hands using the method I used earlier of focusing just on the desire not to kill human beings, which is a very strong desire in any virtuous person. I argued that when a virtuous person makes choices, the desire not to kill others is difficult to outweigh in his moral reasoning. How would this desire impact the moral reasoning of the political leader?

One of the factors in recent times that have enabled political leaders to choose war is that they can distance themselves from the consequences of their choices. Unlike ancient and medieval times when rulers led their armies from the front, political leaders today send armies into battle down a chain of command that does not require them or the higher-ranking military officers to carry out or witness the killings that take place in war. The casualty rate is, of course, known to them, but their choice of war is framed in terms that need not make reference to the actual killings that take place in war. It is part of my critique of just war theory that a focus on legalistic requirements disguises the evil nature of war. So any argument that the desire not to kill others is not relevant in the choice of war on the premise that what the leaders are choosing is not the same as acts of killing that are chosen by individuals is an argument that I reject. A virtuous leader concerned with not killing people, especially the innocent, should for that reason have a strong aversion to choosing to engage in war.

So, a choice of war is a choice to bring about killing on a massive scale, which is something that a virtuous leader would have a strong desire not to engage in. On the other hand, there is a much larger good at stake. The political leader is not just aiming at his own good, but also the good of every citizen. It seems, however, that if one's own good is not enough to make it right for an individual to choose to kill, then the good of many people is not usually enough to make it right for the leader to choose to kill many people. Another consideration that enters into the leader's choice is that it is not just the good of individuals that he aims at, but the common good of the community. As a leader, he must put more weight on the common good than must individuals. On Aristotle's view of humans as political animals, the lack of community prevents individuals from fully flourishing. However, there is a difference between the loss of the existing community and the loss of all communal life. I have pointed out the difference between the situation in ancient Greece in which the fall of the *polis* to its enemies would lead to death and enslavement, and the consequences of military defeat in the world today, where one regime is replaced by another but there is no collapse into barbaric and disorderly anarchism.[21] Furthermore, once we take into account that war has a morally corrupting effect, the choice of war may be more damaging to individual flourishing than is the choice not to fight with one's enemies. An individual who chooses to kill must deal with the damage to his character from the violation of his aversion to killing. But when a leader chooses war, he also chooses for others that they should kill enemy soldiers and noncombatants. In a war, even those who are not soldiers may come under attack and have to kill in self-defense. All these people who engage in killing or are forced to make moral choices involving killing would suffer damage to their moral character that adversely affects their ability to flourish as human beings.

Walzer is right to point to the difficulty for political leaders who must choose not only for themselves but for all the people in their community. A choice not to fight may be a failure to protect their lives. But Walzer's point cuts both ways. The human good is also affected by a choice to fight, given that war is likely to damage the moral character of each person in the community. In so doing, the values of the political community are also compromised. In my argument for co-existence with enemies, I pointed out that war and what soldiers do in war often contradict the values of a liberal democracy. The supreme emergency exception is premised on the importance of saving liberal democratic values from defeat by oppressive and ruthless enemies, but in the course of a war, the same values may be damaged or lost, whether one wins or loses. There may be a better chance of those values surviving when the leader does not choose to fight.[22]

Sometimes, it may still be right for the virtuous leader to choose war. This was what the Hitler example was used earlier to show. The philosophy of co-existence I have presented is not pacifist. But it would be a great sacrifice of one's potential for a good human life to make the choice to kill and the choice for others to kill. The political leader might be right in choosing war, but he would be in the situation (on a much larger scale) that Bonhoeffer was in when he made the individual choice to join in the plot to kill Hitler. Bonhoeffer knew that he was compromising his own values and damaging his own goodness. The leader choosing war is doing that to himself and to all of those who end up killing in the war. Contrary to the point that the "dirty hands" problem attempts to make, it should be more not less difficult for the virtuous leader to legitimately choose such a course.

7
Practical Implications and Challenges

In this chapter, the philosophy of co-existence faces the tests of practical application. In particular, can it do better than the just war theory in dealing with the kinds of violence common in today's world? Proponents of just war theory have attempted to amend just war theory to account for the challenges of humanitarian intervention, terrorism and weapons of mass destruction. New versions of just war theory have been proposed for unconventional wars that do not satisfy all the conditions found in earlier versions. I have argued that the failure of just war theory in dealing with these challenges is not due to the newness of unconventional warfare, so that mere revision of the requirements of just war will not be adequate. For just war theory is an unsatisfactory ethics of war, even for the wars that have been fought in most of human history. Thus, I have argued for abandonment of the just war theory and its replacement by the philosophy of co-existence.

It is incumbent upon me to now address the challenges of humanitarian intervention, terrorism, and weapons of mass destruction. For I intend to show that the philosophy of co-existence can provide better answers than any amended version of just war theory, not only for wars of the past but for the wars of the present day. I shall discuss how the philosophy of co-existence can be used to answer questions about whether and when war can be the right moral choice in response to each of the three challenges. These answers will be different from any proposed by defenders of just war theory, and I hope to show that they are morally more-appealing answers. The main difference is that in my approach, the choice of war must be recognized as a choice to unleash forces that would result in great evil, even for one's own side and for the people we seek to protect. Another difference is that, in my approach, the correctness of the choice to fight does not turn on satisfying a set of legalistic conditions. I have, however, also argued that my approach does not commit me to pacifism and that war can be the correct moral choice when faced with a very great evil such as that posed by Hitler and Nazism.

It may seem that genocide and terrorism that may include the use of weapons of mass destruction would both qualify as evils of a scale comparable to Nazi death camps. My purpose in this chapter is to examine how the philosophy of co-existence would deal with the three challenges. In providing my answers, I will also comment on the issue of how new international agreements and increased global cooperation affect the policies of states when they face threats that in the past would have been dealt with by going to war.

Humanitarian intervention

The issue of humanitarian intervention is not new, but has become a matter of serious concern toward the end of the twentieth century after the Cold War ended.[1] In the last decade of that century, the need for intervention with the oppressive internal policies of a nation-state arose in the starkest terms in Rwanda, Kosovo, and East Timor. One of the reasons for policies of genocide and ethnic cleansing in many states was the inability to unite different communities into a nation-state with its own identity. Many of these were newly independent states with post-colonial boundaries that did not reflect actual relations between communities. There are also states artificially bound together by political ideologies. With the end of the Cold War, the collapse of Soviet hegemony and the breakup of the Soviet Union, separatism became the goal of formerly suppressed minorities in Yugoslavia, Chechnya, and other places in Eastern Europe and Central Asia. Nationalistic aspirations that had been frozen during the decades of global rivalry between the United States and Soviet communism were unleashed once the Berlin Wall fell and the Iron Curtain lifted.

The end of the Cold War also made it possible for the Western democracies to press for the respect of human rights. No longer was the West immobilized from taking action against oppressive regimes on its side for fear of losing a client state, and against totalitarian communist governments, such as the Khmer Rouge in Cambodia, for fear of provoking a wider conflagration with the Chinese or the Soviets.[2] But there is a need to justify the use of military force to intervene in another state to protect some of its citizens. The basis of relations between states in international law and the UN Charter derives from the Westphalian system that made it illegitimate for one state to intervene in the internal affairs of another state. The just war theory in its modern versions only recognizes self-defense against aggression as a just cause for going to war.[3] A state may be violently oppressing some of its own people, but it would be the victim of aggression if another state were to send troops to protect those people.

There are a number of responses from just war theorists. One response is to hold that the just war theory, in fact, has traditionally approved of humanitarian interventions, since earlier versions included as just cause the punishment of states for their crimes.[4] I think this is a confused interpretation, as the crimes referred to are either offenses against other states or offenses against God. But a state that oppresses its people is not necessarily one that is engaged in aggression against its neighbors. And it is considered an outdated idea to think that states have the authority to punish others on behalf of a divinity, especially when the states do not share the same religion. Another attempt by some just war theorists to allow for humanitarian intervention is to cast internal oppression as threats to international peace. But there is no reason to think that human rights violations as serious as genocide in faraway and isolated places must pose a threat to the security of other states. Yet it would seem odd if intervention is justified for less-serious violations just because there is more impact on regional stability, but not for more serious violations in places without spillover effects.

A second strategy for just war theorists is to amend just war theory so that humanitarian intervention can be accommodated. Each of the requirements for *jus ad bellum* in just war theory can be reinterpreted to provide conditions that justify humanitarian intervention along the lines of the conditions that justify war in defense of the state against external aggression.[5] The problem with this approach is that once the conditions are laid down, it is not clear that they can be realistically satisfied. For example, would any state engaged in humanitarian intervention satisfy the "right intention" requirement? The government of a state that intervenes in places where it has no national interest will find it difficult to make a case to its people for the sacrifice of blood and treasure. But if the state has interests that it advances by intervening, is the intention still a humanitarian one? Other conditions that pose problems are those of legitimate authority (who has the right to intervene?), last resort (should sanctions be used instead?), proportionality (would the intervention be equally or more harmful than the atrocities?), and likelihood of success (since there are hardly any successes to show in the history of such interventions).

Another version of the reinterpretation strategy is found in the work of Michael Walzer and John Rawls, who both try to ground just war theory partly or wholly on human rights.[6] If it can be shown that the ultimate justification for going to war is the defense of human rights, then there would be a unified account of both wars of self-defense to protect a country's citizens from human rights violations from abroad and wars of humanitarian intervention to protect another country's citizens from human rights violations that do not involve an outside party.

Walzer holds that, although the presumption against intervention is strong and must be to protect a community's processes of self-determination, "non-intervention is not an absolute moral rule: sometimes, what is going on locally cannot be tolerated."[7] What can justify an intervention is the need to stop actions of a state against its own people that "shock the conscience of humankind." For Rawls, human rights violations that are "egregious" and "grave" need not be tolerated under the Law of Peoples. He argues for the right of liberal and decent peoples to forcibly intervene in such cases.[8]

The success of the human rights interpretation of just cause faces two difficulties. First, the interpretation causes problems for the traditional just war theory. If respect for human rights is the basis for just war, what happens to national sovereignty and to the rights of combatants in war? Consider the latter. An account that waives the combatant's right not to be killed when and only when he is aggressively fighting would uphold the equal vulnerability of combatants without distinguishing between those fighting justly and those fighting unjustly. But if protection of individual human rights is the ground for just war, should the troops that violate the rights of inhabitants when they invade be given equal moral standing when they defend themselves from the troops that seek to drive them back? The root problem, as Rex Martin points out,[9] is that the application of human rights to norms of international conduct is a relatively new development that emerged after the Second World War, in contrast to the conventions of the just war tradition that have developed over more than two thousand years. Points of incompatibility between human rights theory and traditional just war theory are to be expected.

Consider now the issue of national sovereignty. Do nations deserve protection from aggression only if they live up to standards of human rights? If those standards reflect a liberal individualistic morality, would that be an imposition on societies that do not share in such moral values? The problems are manifold. Few nations, if any, actually do live up to absolute standards of human rights such as those in the Universal Declaration of Human Rights.[10] Sovereignty would be rendered meaningless by the requirement that they uphold these standards. One could perhaps justify imposing human rights standards on the basis of global acceptance of such values since the Second World War. But this is a move that is again a challenge to just war theory, not a development of ideas that is already implied or assumed by the theory.

A second problem for the human rights interpretation is that it is inevitable that war also involves the violations of rights. It is not clear that the proper response to human rights violations is to intervene militarily. Even the idea that the intervention would result in a reduction in human rights violations compared to non-intervention takes too utilitarian an approach, which is inconsonant with the meaning of rights. If human rights are to be taken seriously, one cannot be quantifying rights and trading off some people's rights in the name of protecting human rights.

There are two main obstacles to the moral permissibility of humanitarian intervention. One is the need to respect sovereignty. The other is the problem of how violence can be justifiably used to promote peace.[11] The inclusion of humanitarian intervention as a just cause conflicts with contemporary just war theory which takes self-defense as the only clear case of a just cause, and with international law which is premised on the importance of national sovereignty. A military intervention in the name of stopping human rights violations must take into account the violations of rights that war inevitably involves, given the destruction of lives and property and the interference with a community's right to self-determination. Would the philosophy of co-existence endorse some cases of humanitarian intervention and would it avoid the two obstacles to humanitarian intervention with which just war theory has difficulty?

Recall that the philosophy of co-existence is an approach that is critical of the requirements for just war found in the just war tradition. Instead, the decision to resort to war should be made by asking whether a virtuous leader who fully recognizes the evil of war would choose war as a means to morally legitimate ends. I have argued that such a leader would not go to war in many cases where the conditions for just war are satisfied. But I have also suggested that war against Hitler would be a morally appropriate choice. Now, such a war could be seen as both a war of self-defense and a humanitarian intervention on behalf of the Jews who were being exterminated in concentration camps by the Nazis. My approach did not require me to specify which kind of cause justifies war in the case of Hitler. The question of whether a virtuous leader would choose the evil of war for purely humanitarian intervention is the question of whether, without external aggression, Hitler or some other regime could be doing enough evil in oppressing its citizens to make war to end the oppression a lesser evil.

The philosophy of co-existence is more restrictive than the just war theory because many acts of aggression do not amount to the kind of evil posed by Hitler's takeover of Europe during the Second World War. Similarly, many cases of internal oppression do not rise to the level that would make military intervention a lesser evil. So, here is one advantage my approach has over the attempts to adapt just war theory to include humanitarian intervention as a just cause: the latter approach is likely to make wars of humanitarian intervention too easy or frequent (given that, today, human rights violations are a lot more common than aggression against other states). However, it cannot be denied that some cases of internal oppression, such as what took place during the genocide in Rwanda, do constitute such great evil that military intervention can be the morally correct choice of a virtuous political leader. This means that some, but very few, cases of humanitarian intervention are morally acceptable in the philosophy of co-existence. Only in a case such as Hitler's can we be quite certain that, had he stopped his external aggression, it would still have been reasonable for America or Britain to have attacked Nazi Germany to stop the Holocaust.

The idea that there are human rights violations and internal oppression that should not be stopped by outside military forces may seem unacceptable to those who would like to see more help given to the victims. But as I have explained in Chapter 4 on war as an evil, military solutions are very often worse than the problems they are meant to solve. This fact has not been fully appreciated in discussions on the ethics of war, in particular in just war thinking. A reluctance to go to war for humanitarian reasons does not necessarily mean a lack of compassion for the victims or an unwillingness to help them. Other means should be attempted, such as economic pressure and the provision of humanitarian assistance. But war may not be justified even if all other means have turned out to be unsuccessful. It is not the first of the two obstacles in our earlier discussion – namely, national sovereignty – that is at issue. It is rather the evil of war even when it is used to protect lives and to end suffering, and in this, the philosophy of co-existence takes the second of the obstacles with greater seriousness than does the just war theory.

In addition to seeing humanitarian intervention as a legitimate moral choice only when the evil to be prevented is very great, the philosophy of co-existence would require that the evil of war be minimized by stopping war as quickly as possible and fighting the war in a way that reduces the evils that take place in war, especially the killing of civilians. I argued earlier that the kind of war that would have been fought against Hitler by a virtuous political leader would involve less evil than how the Second World War in Europe was fought, and that the war would stop once Hitler was forced out of occupied territories and no longer posed a grave threat of aggression. Humanitarian interventions should also be ended quickly. Although the oppression and human rights violations must be of such a scale that there is sufficient moral reason for the intervention, the longer that military actions continue, the greater the evil of the intervention itself. So the intervening force must aim to very quickly reduce the level of the human rights violations. Death camps must be closed and ethnic cleansing must be stopped, while evil perpetrators must be removed from power or deprived of their ability to carry out atrocities. Once this is achieved, there is insufficient reason for the military intervention to continue. There may still be lesser human rights violations and there may still be a lack of political stability. But I think that this could already be the point at which further intervention and the continued occupation of the country by outside forces could on balance be a greater evil. Other means, such as economic pressure, should be used to deal with the smaller-scale human rights violations that remain.

I draw support here from many real-world examples of failures in nation-building taking place under foreign occupation. My point is not just about the right to national self-determination and the pragmatic need for there to be a local and popular element in the process of national reconciliation for the practical success of the effort.[12] Rather, my approach is one that is sensitive to the realities of war and it is not driven by idealistic or legalistic abstractions about war, such as those reflected in just war thinking.[13]

Since the longer the intervention, the less morally legitimate it would be, the intervention should be done with sufficient force to achieve its objective of ending the serious human rights violations quickly and effectively. This is where the philosophy of co-existence has another advantage. When humanitarian intervention is justified in the context of a just war tradition in which national sovereignty is strongly valued, it is done in incremental steps so as to minimize the violation of sovereignty. When the initial force is insufficient to end the human rights violations, slightly greater force is used, and this goes on, with the result that the intervention process is protracted. On the approach

I have proposed here, military intervention should not be carried out unless the evil to be stopped is very great. But since it is very great, and given that a lengthy intervention is also a great evil, an intervention that is the correct moral choice should not be embarked upon hesitantly and in small steps. The military intervention should instead be on such a scale as to achieve a quick success, so that the foreign troops can be withdrawn and the evils of war minimized. The intervening force should not end up in a long occupation or participating in the political processes of the state, and it should leave once the evils it came to prevent have been stopped.

War on terrorism

The 9/11 attacks on the United States by the terrorist organization Al-Qaeda in 2001 led to President George W. Bush declaring a global war on terrorism. This war has seen US military forces sent to Afghanistan to depose the Taliban regime that hosted Al-Qaeda training camps, and to capture the leaders of Al-Qaeda who directed the 9/11 attacks from there. The Bush administration later broadened the war on terrorism by naming rogue states that belonged to "an axis of evil," and in 2003, the United States launched an invasion of Iraq to depose its leader Saddam Hussein, who was accused of sponsoring terrorism and developing weapons of mass destruction to threaten the United States and its Middle-Eastern ally, Israel.

The issue of how to deal with countries that threaten world peace with weapons of mass destruction will be dealt with later. The questions to ask here is how the just war theory assesses the military response to terrorism seen in Bush's war, and whether the philosophy of co-existence would propose something different. Before I answer these two questions, it is necessary to define and understand the concept of terrorism. What is terrorism? Can it be justified? Is a terrorist attack an act of war? Once we answer these questions, we can go on to ask whether an attack by terrorists provides just cause to go to war and against whom. If not, what is the morally right thing to do about terrorism?

I begin with a definition of terrorism that comes close to a precise description of the concept but remains a bit inadequate:

> Essentially, terrorism employs horrific violence against unsuspecting civilians, as well as combatants, in order to inspire fear and create panic, which in turn will advance the terrorists' political or religious agenda.[14]

This definition captures the terrorist *modus operandi* of harming a direct target to send a message to an indirect target regarding what must be done in order to avoid more direct harm to other targets.[15] The problem with this definition of terrorism is that it includes attacks on combatants. It would seem that the use of violence on combatants is part and parcel of any military action, and the above definition fails to distinguish between war waged by insurgents and attacks by terrorists. One reason for the confusion is that as insurgents are trying to overthrow a regime or to push out an occupying invader, they usually do not represent an established state or belong to organized military units with uniforms. But what truly marks out an attacker as a terrorist is that the attacks are indiscriminate in treating combatants and civilians as equally appropriate targets. And since terrorist groups are usually too weak to confront their enemy on the battlefield, terrorists find greater success in picking on vulnerable civilians as soft targets. Moreover, attacks on civilians tend to generate greater fear, as well as the publicity desired by terrorists for spreading their message.[16]

This description of terrorists as "fighting dirty" in picking on civilian targets and not playing by the rules of combat between civilized peoples would seem to strip them of any moral legitimacy. But it is possible to argue in their defense that terrorists fight the way they do out of necessity and, if they have a just cause for fighting an enemy that is terribly oppressive, terrorism could be allowed as a way of leveling the playing field in an asymmetric war. It could further be pointed out that not only does the killing of civilians also result from conventional fighting in war, but that such killings are carried out on a much larger scale and in greater numbers by armies in battle with each other.[17] It is also a fact that wars have always involved spreading terror and intimidating the enemy. Terrorists may not necessarily follow the rules that armies follow in combat – but does this alone make them morally worse than the soldiers who fight in armies? I have already given reasons why war should be considered a great intrinsic evil, and perhaps terrorists can do no worse than soldiers in war. Nevertheless, any equivalence between the killing of civilians by terrorists and by soldiers in conventional warfare does not morally absolve the terrorists. Clearly, the 9/11 attacks and other terrorist acts of bombing, hijacking, poisoning, and kidnapping that have taken place against civilian targets in recent times are morally repulsive acts that deserve global condemnation and demand that action is taken by world leaders to stop the terrorists. But what should the leaders do?

After 9/11, the United States chose to use its military might against the terrorists of Al-Qaeda. In declaring itself to be at war, it was implicitly responding to the terrorist attacks as acts of war. Unfortunately, this grants to the terrorists a status that they may not deserve. Going to war against terrorism ultimately presented the Bush administration with a dilemma concerning how suspected terrorists in the custody of the United States should be treated. If the United States and Al-Qaeda were at war, then captured members on either side should have the status of prisoners of war. The Bush administration instead chose to detain them as "illegal enemy combatants," without granting to all of them the rights of POWs under the Geneva Convention, such as access to the Red Cross. Use of torture to extract information and plans to put them on trial before military tribunals also did not accord with international law applying to enemy combatants captured in the battlefield. The desire to try members of Al-Qaeda, especially those linked to the attacks of 9/11, for complicity in mass murder is a reflection of an ambivalence or lack of clarity on the part of American leaders concerning whether the attacks were criminal acts or acts of war.

Unlike the 9/11 attacks, there are other examples of terrorism carried out by the state and also examples of state-sponsored terrorism. State terrorism is practiced by authoritarian regimes to intimidate their opponents, using secret police and extra-judicial processes. Regimes that have done this include leaders of the former Soviet Union, the Chinese Communist Party, Argentina's military junta in the 1970s and '80s, and Saddam Hussein in Iraq. In reality, the practice of state terrorism goes back a long way in history, to the methods used to suppress opposition in imperial Rome, for instance. Such repressive practices toward the citizens of a country show the rulers to have no moral legitimacy and, in our times, have led to calls for outside intervention. Having earlier discussed humanitarian intervention, I set cases of state terrorism aside. What I must discuss now are terrorist acts directed across international borders.

Terrorist acts could be used by a state as a tactic to gain an advantage in wartime. Toward the end of the Second World War, the United States firebombed Tokyo and then dropped atomic bombs on Hiroshima and Nagasaki. The purpose of intentionally killing hundreds of thousands of Japanese civilians in an indiscriminate manner was to induce the Japanese government to accept the terms of an unconditional surrender. As described, the bombings fit the definition of terrorism given earlier. The use of terrorist tactics in fighting wars between states clearly violates the requirements of just war theory.[18] They are also among the most evil acts that can be carried out, so that no virtuous political leader would use such means.[19] When faced with an enemy willing to engage in terrorism, states face a difficult choice: should they continue fighting within the rules or should they fight *quid pro quo*? If the former, they are tying their hands against an enemy that does not fight fair. If the latter, morality is pushed aside by expediency and the desire for revenge. This seems to have happened during the Second World War, when the precision bombing of military targets escalated into area bombing of cities by both the Allies and the Germans.[20]

Another way in which states use terrorist tactics outside the state against its enemies is by sponsoring terrorist acts without going to war. This might be carried out by a state agency, as in the case of Libya's bombing in 1988 of a Pan Am airliner over Lockerbie in Scotland. State-sponsored terrorism could also be carried out by groups that are separate from the state. Such groups could be provided with facilities and funds by the state but operate independently. Terrorist groups may be harbored by a neighboring state to launch attacks across the border. For example, Kashmiri freedom fighters have crossed the border from Pakistan to attack India. The state that harbors them would often deny responsibility for what these groups do. Such acts of terrorism pose problems for the state that is the victim of attacks. Is there a just cause to attack the state from whose territory the terrorist acts originated? Or would a cross-border attack on the terrorist bases constitute an act of aggression against the neighboring state on whose territory they are located? One thing to consider is whether the state that harbors the terrorists has any control over what they do or any ability to stop the attacks. That is, is the state allied with the terrorists or is it a neutral bystander? The traditional meaning of neutrality holds that "a neutral state must not permit either its subjects or a belligerent to make any such use of its territory as amounts to taking part in an operation of war."[21] If the state is neutral, it may be legitimate to attack the terrorist bases as an act of self-defense, but not to attack the state to depose its rulers or harm those of its people whose only connection with the terrorists is that they live in the same country.

Bush's war on terrorism began with an attack on Afghanistan that could arguably satisfy the requirement for just cause under the just war theory. The Taliban regime did not meet the requirements for neutrality, as they had provided support to Osama bin Laden and his terrorist units in the form of bases and training camps. They also obstructed attempts to have bin Laden handed over for trial by an international or American tribunal. The difficulty in justifying the US attack on Afghanistan in response to 9/11 concerns other principles of *jus ad bellum*, as well as *jus in bello*, which I will now examine.

Americans were outraged by the loss of innocent lives and the scale and suddenness of the 9/11 attacks that they likened to the Pearl Harbor attack of 1941. Many, including politicians and opinion-makers in the media, voiced a desire for revenge to be carried out by using the force of US military might. In other words, they wanted the United States to "kick some butt." Some Americans took it personally and signed up to serve in the military just for that reason. If the United States went into Afghanistan with the intention to take vengeful actions using military force, then the principle of right intention may have been violated.

If the United States was acting in self-defense against the Al-Qaeda terrorists who carried out the attack of 9/11 as part of a larger-scale war against Americans, there arises the question of how appropriate or effective is the overthrow of the Taliban and the occupation of Afghanistan as a means of protecting Americans from further terrorist attacks. There were some short-term gains: Al-Qaeda training camps were closed down and the group's leadership had to flee its hideouts under US bombardment. Al-Qaeda may, thus, have been rendered less effective in planning terrorism. The US show of force may also have discouraged some terrorists and forced some countries to suspend their cooperation with terrorist groups. Viewed, however, from the longer perspective required by the likelihood of success requirement of *jus ad bellum*, the overall benefit of the military means of fighting terrorism is called into question, especially after the United States spread the war on terrorism to Iraq. For many years after the invasion, Osama bin Laden's capture seemed remote, and Al-Qaeda had evolved into and inspired an international network of terrorist cells, mostly based in Western countries that were able to carry out more terrorist attacks in Madrid and London. Moreover, the US occupation of Afghanistan and Iraq radicalized Muslims into opposition instead of cooperation in the war on terrorism and presented Al-Qaeda with propaganda that bolstered its recruitment of fighters.

Not only did the use of military force to combat terrorism prove less than effective, but it also did not seem to have been the last resort. If the goal was to keep its citizens safe from further terrorist attacks, the US could have focused its efforts on protecting the homeland and fostering international cooperation in intelligence and police work to deny Al-Qaeda and other terrorist groups the resources and opportunities needed for further acts of terrorism.[22] Although some steps were taken to do these things, these were overshadowed by the military effort, which from the beginning was the primary focus of the US fight against terrorism, diverting resources away from homeland security and also instigating and inspiring terrorists who responded to what was perceived to be American hostility toward Muslim people and states.

In the case of Afghanistan, US military action might satisfy the just cause condition but did not satisfy other conditions for *jus ad bellum*. In the case of Iraq, there was no just cause in terms of the need to defend Americans against terrorist attacks for the United States to invade as part of the war on terrorism. American and British attempts to make the case for the invasion on the basis of Saddam Hussein's alleged links with Al-Qaeda relied on either dubious intelligence reports or outright fabrications that served the interests of the Bush administration.[23] The war on terrorism as carried out by the United States in the two arenas of military combat cannot be justified since the conditions of *jus ad bellum* are not fully met.

The case against the war on terrorism is further undermined by a consideration of the *jus in bello* conditions (and the *jus ad bellum* proportionality condition). As I explained in Chapter 2, proportionality in war is a concept that is difficult to make sense of or to apply. But there is good reason to think that the military response to 9/11 could not be proportionate to the goal of preventing further terrorist attacks on the United States and other Western nations targeted by Al-Qaeda. The 9/11 attacks took about 3,000 lives in America. Just months after the United States began its military campaign in Afghanistan, estimates of Afghan civilian dead numbered in the thousands.[24] Ten years later, in 2011, American forces were still in Afghanistan in the longest war in US history, while the number of Afghan dead had increased multiple times. When the war on terrorism was expanded to Iraq in 2003, the number of Iraqi deaths connected to the US invasion and to the violent insurgency and civil war that subsequently started against the invaders and the American-supported government was even higher than in Afghanistan. The number of Iraqi civilians killed during the initial weeks of the invasion that led to the overthrow of Saddam Hussein numbered close to ten thousand.[25] By July 2006, three years later, with the end of the war nowhere in sight, a respectable estimate indicated that "there have been 654,965 (392,979–942,636) excess Iraqi deaths as a consequence of the war, which corresponds to 2.5% of the population in the study area. Of post-invasion deaths, 601,027 (426,369–793,663) were due to violence, the most common cause being gunfire."[26]

The way in which the war on terrorism has been carried out could not satisfy the *jus in bello* requirements of proportionality and discrimination.[27] The terrorists that are the combatants to be targeted in this war do not represent a state, are not in uniform, and do not fight openly on the battlefield. To get at them by military means requires that the US forces attack them in places where civilians are found who have not been linked with the cause that the terrorists fight for. Ground operations against the terrorists would be vulnerable to ambushes and would be costly in terms of US casualties. It would require long-term occupations and severe disruptions to the lives of people in the area to prevent the terrorists from resurfacing.[28] As a result, the occupying force would become unpopular and sympathy for the terrorists would increase.[29] The United States has tried, instead, to reduce both its exposure to attack and the resentment of locals by using high-tech methods to kill the terrorists, in particular by deploying unmanned drones and launching missile attacks to carry out targeted killings. The legality of such attacks has been questioned, since the rules of warfare forbid singling out individual enemies for assassination.[30] It is also doubtful that the principle of proportionality would be satisfied when fighting in a way that does not expose the soldiers who are attacking the enemy by remote control to any of the usual risks of battle.[31]

Even worse, American high-tech warfare using precision weapons did not succeed in preventing the killing of innocent civilians in fairly large numbers. For one thing, the greater accuracy of these weapons was compromised by failures in military intelligence in target identification that led, on many occasions, to the killing of the wrong people. For another, the precision weapons fostered a greater willingness by commanders to launch attacks in highly populated areas. Even if fewer civilians were killed in each attack, the larger number of such attacks had resulted in more civilian deaths overall. It may be argued that the civilians killed were not intentionally targeted. But the doctrine of double effect also requires proportionality. The success of taking out some terrorists is more than offset by the propaganda advantage and greater resolve of the enemy that resulted from the loss of civilian life and the resentment that was caused by the apparent cowardice of Americans and seeming disregard for innocent lives when they used such weapons. So in responding in this way to terrorism, the United States looked like a bullying superpower that placed much greater value on the lives of Americans (both civilians at home and members of its armed forces) than on the lives of noncombatants in Iraq and Afghanistan that were wiped out in the course of the global war on terrorism.

Given the difficulties in justifying the war on terrorism as a just war, it is not surprising that many who defend the US military actions in

Afghanistan and Iraq have chosen to cast the war as a new kind of war, to which traditional just war precepts and the conventions of international law no longer apply. In my view, such a move is tantamount to moving the goalposts. I have already challenged the "new war" thesis in the last chapter. In any case, proponents of the war on terrorism have not presented an alternative ethics of war to the just war theory. The view that the US must set aside established international law to achieve its goals seems to rest on realism, not on a new ethics of war that replaces the just war theory.[32]

Where does the philosophy of co-existence stand on the war on terrorism? A number of writers have pointed out that there are two contrasting paradigms for dealing with terrorists.[33] One is the paradigm of war and the other is the paradigm of law enforcement. In the philosophy of co-existence, war is a great evil that should not be used as a means unless the enemy is threatening actions that are exceptionally evil and which could not be prevented without war. On this basis, one can correctly reason that war against Hitler was indeed the choice of a lesser evil. But I do not think that the threat posed by terrorism is comparable to that posed by Hitler. I do not dispute that Osama bin Laden, like Hitler, had megalomaniacal ambitions and a total disregard for innocent lives. But he did not have the resources to overwhelm his enemies or to kill massively large numbers of people again and again. Although many people cannot help magnifying the existential threat and danger of terrorism,[34] it cannot be acceptable to unleash war for the purpose of dealing with Al-Qaeda and protecting citizens of Western countries from terrorist attacks. Those who advocate the global war on terrorism in response to the 9/11 attacks do not seem to appreciate the fundamental truth which was the subject of Chapter 4, namely the nature of war as one of the greatest intrinsic evils.

Of course, it does not follow from the rejection of the war paradigm that nothing needs to be done to reduce or eliminate the threat posed by terrorists. The law enforcement paradigm shows what may be done. The best examples of law enforcement in liberal democracies are fully respectful and protective of innocent lives. If possible, crime is dealt with by apprehending the lawbreakers and putting them on trial. Otherwise, criminal elements that are on the loose must be kept away from potential victims. Obviously, some criminals are very hard to capture. For instance, they may be sheltered by organized crime rings that have the ability to enforce a code of silence in certain communities. In such cases, police work includes investigating their finances, getting the cooperation of insiders to provide information and evidence, and winning the confidence of communities who are distrustful of the authorities. If successful, the criminals end up isolated and deprived of resources and opportunities to commit their crimes.

Good law enforcement also includes identifying the causes of crime and acting to remove them. If poverty, illiteracy, unemployment, discrimination, and the breakdown of family and social support contribute to the recruitment of criminals into gangs and crime syndicates, then the state must address these social problems in carrying out its duty to fight crime.

The applications for the problem of terrorism are quite obvious. The terrorists who kill innocent people are responsible for committing atrocious crimes. There may or may not be a political pretext for their actions, but by using the methods of law enforcement, the threat they pose can be reduced if they can be isolated and deprived of the resources and support that they need to carry out their attacks. In addition, it is necessary to address genuine injustices that have encouraged some people to join the terrorists and carry out attacks on the West. All these responses might strike some people as hopelessly inadequate. Terrorists who shelter in remote parts of the world in countries without effective governments, such as Afghanistan, Somalia and Yemen, are difficult to locate and capture. The idea of equating terrorism with criminal acts may seem to trivialize the former. Moreover, to call for an examination of the root causes of terrorism, and for the correction of global injustices that flow from US policies, may seem to be excusing or justifying terrorism. I will now explain in more detail what is involved in the approach to terrorism that I am suggesting and, hopefully, I can defuse many of these concerns.

First of all, we should recognize that we could not eliminate every one of the terrorists, whether we attempt to do so by war or by law enforcement. Domestic law enforcement has not eliminated every criminal, but its success is measured in terms of reducing crime to a level where citizens feel safe enough. Similarly, the law enforcement paradigm for dealing with terrorism should aim to reduce the likelihood, frequency, and impact of terrorist attacks to the degree that citizens no longer live in fear. The crucial point is that this goal can be achieved without declaring war on other states. In fact, US military actions in the war on terrorism are thought to have motivated more terrorist attacks and boosted the recruitment of terrorists. So, if the objective of the war is to eliminate the terrorists, the war on terrorism is unlikely to achieve its goal any better than using the methods of law enforcement. The fact that there have been few major attacks in the decade since 9/11 can be attributed more to the steps taken to boost homeland security, given that Al-Qaeda was still active on the border between Afghanistan and Pakistan for many years after US-led military forces entered into Afghanistan. Moreover, the war on terrorism has brought evils that would have been avoided if law enforcement had been used.

Another thing to note is that any successes in capturing terrorists would come slowly and cannot be achieved overnight. Gathering information, gaining cooperation and trust from other countries, and making it more difficult for terrorists to strike against open societies is an attenuated process that needs to be carried out painstakingly and patiently. There are no shortcuts to fighting terrorism in an ethical way, and suspending moral limits by going to war (and thereby violating just war theory or throwing it out) has not actually brought success any more quickly. Changing US policies and persuading citizens of other countries, especially Muslims, to view America more positively are goals that will obviously take a long time to achieve. But we should recognize that the military actions that were carried out as a response to 9/11, such as drone attacks that killed civilians, and the torture of prisoners in Abu Ghraib in Iraq and other US detention centers lacking legal protections, have only reinforced the negative image of the United States and gifted anti-American terrorist groups a number of propaganda successes.[35]

In dealing with domestic criminals, we have to ask whether some people are born to be criminals or turn to crime as a result of their environment. I think there is more truth to the latter, but it cannot be denied that there are sociopaths and "nut cases" in every society – people who would harm others and who do not care about moral considerations. No society is crime free but some do have less crime than others. To reduce crime, it is more effective for the state to ensure that apart from the sociopaths, all the other citizens would not turn to crime out of desperation, humiliation, or envy. This can be achieved by governments that work to ensure that citizens have access to education, shelter, jobs, and healthcare. As for the sociopaths, the state must provide security for its citizens and protect them from becoming victims of crime. But if the majority of citizens are law-abiding, it is necessary to balance the need for security with the need to respect the rights of individual citizens from oppressive policing by the state. Without surrendering basic civil liberties, the threat of crime can be greatly reduced but not eliminated.

An objection to the law enforcement paradigm for dealing with terrorists is that there is no international authority to do the policing. I think that this point would have validity if we were discussing the need to oversee the relationship between states on the model of the relationship between individuals within a state. If states were to engage in aggression against other states or use terrorism as a form of war, then the case would fall under the ethics of war as we have discussed earlier. But it is not criminal states but criminals within a state that pose the problem of terrorism by non-state groups, and each state is responsible for dealing with the individuals who operate there. It is a mistake to respond to the terrorist threat posed by groups such as Al-Qaeda as if the United States has been attacked by another state.[36] What the United States must do is to seek cooperation from states where the terrorists are found. The problem is that some states are either unwilling or unable to get rid of the terrorists hiding among their people. The challenge for the United States in enforcing the law against terrorists is to reduce the number of such states and isolate the remaining ones. Some changes in US and Western policies could be very useful in getting more cooperation from states where terrorists are located. To make these changes is not a concession to terrorism. In the first place, if the policies are unjust, they ought to be changed.[37] Furthermore, if changing the policies would mean that other states can be more successful in meeting the needs of their people, it is a good thing both in itself as well as in reducing the number of people who are driven to crime and, at the extreme, to carry out acts of terrorism.

My argument is premised on most people in the world not being among the "nut cases" who would do very bad things no matter what their environment is. As in the domestic scenario, the aim of law enforcement would be achieved not by eliminating terrorism altogether but reducing it to the level that only the "nut cases" do it. I recognize that there are those who would disagree with me on the causes of terrorism. They think, instead, that there are lots of people in the Muslim world who hate Westerners no matter what their policies are. Therefore, terrorism cannot be reduced to the acts of a few "nut cases" because Islam is in fundamental conflict with Western civilization.[38] If this is correct, then changes in US policies to foster more economic development, job opportunities, education, and social justice in Third World countries (and to establish a viable Palestinian state[39]) would not diminish the threat of terrorism posed by Al-Qaeda and supported by leaders and citizens of Muslim countries. The Huntington thesis of the clash of civilizations has been much discussed and I cannot refute it here.[40] I do think that fundamentalist Islam in the extreme and violent form motivating many anti-American terrorists will have much less appeal once the economic and political conditions in Muslim countries in the

Middle East are altered in the direction of greater justice and opportunity. In my view, those Muslims who wage religious war on the West and will continue to do so regardless of the economic and political environment of countries in the Muslim world[41] are like the sociopaths who commit crime in our society. They cannot be eliminated, but they are a small minority compared to those who turn to crime or terrorism as a result of social conditions.[42] If this is so, appropriate changes to American policies abroad, combined with other methods of law enforcement, would greatly reduce the threat of global terrorism without resort to war and would be a much more preferable option than war, with all the evils entailed by war. If law enforcement were successful, there would be fewer recruits to carry out terrorist acts, reduced funding, and very few states willing to provide sanctuaries for the terrorists to hide. We can live with that, just as we can live with a low level of crime in domestic society.

Weapons of mass destruction

The introduction of more powerful and destructive weapons has always been part of warfare. Historically significant developments include the use of gunpowder and firearms, machine-guns, tanks, ironclad warships, submarines, and fighter and bomber aircraft. The armed forces that developed and introduced the new weapons usually gained a significant but temporary advantage in the battlefield until the weapons became available for use by all sides. Changes in the technology of warfare are usually taken account of in the principles of *jus in bello*. However, weapons of mass destruction (WMDs) pose a special challenge, in that their use in war inherently violates the principles of proportionality and discrimination.[43] Their destructive power cannot be contained or controlled to do harm only in ways that are proportionate or discriminate. Another characteristic of many WMDs is the ability to deploy them very quickly from a great distance in a way that makes it difficult to defend against by intercepting the weapons or shielding the targets. In that case, changes may also be required in the principles of *jus ad bellum* when WMDs make preventive war necessary and leave little else to resort to short of war.

WMDs are a mixed bag that includes nuclear weapons as well as chemical and biological weapons. Nuclear weapons seem to be in a separate class, since they require cutting-edge scientific expertise and can only be produced and maintained at great expense. For most of the second half of the twentieth century, only a handful of countries, notably the two global superpowers of the United States and the USSR, had nuclear weapons, whereas there were many smaller countries that had chemical and biological weapons. Another thing different about nuclear weapons was that after 1945, when the Americans dropped two atomic bombs on Japan, no nuclear weapons have been used in war (as opposed to testing), whereas chemical and biological weapons have often been used, for instance by the Iraqis in their war against Iran in the 1980s. However, the situation is rapidly changing as India, Pakistan, and Israel joined the nuclear club toward the end of the twentieth century, and in the first decade of the new century, they have been joined by North Korea, an extremely impoverished but militarized society. The danger of the use of nuclear weapons in war increases as more countries acquire them, despite international efforts to limit nuclear proliferation. When small countries get hold of these weapons, they suddenly acquire a capability that enhances their military power several-fold. Based on the size of their populations and economies, they normally are unable to take on many foes in conventional warfare or fight protracted wars. But with nuclear weapons, the weakness of their conventional armies no longer limits their ability to challenge even a superpower. And their inability to prevail in conventional battles may make the resort to nuclear warfare more probable.[44] In addition, some of the new nuclear powers are in parts of the world where there are historical animosities and political instabilities that mean their leaders would have more incentives and fewer qualms about the use of nuclear weapons on their enemies.

Thus, however ethicists of war may have responded to new weaponry in the past, WMDs and nuclear weapons in particular pose a special challenge. If the use of WMDs violates the principles of *jus in bello*, is it always wrong for any country to *possess* these weapons? International agreements have been reached to outlaw chemical and biological warfare. Stockpiles of such weapons have been designated for eventual destruction and there is almost universal agreement that they should never again be used in war.[45] With nuclear weapons, attempts to limit their spread have relied on the Nuclear Non-Proliferation Treaty, which permitted peaceful uses of nuclear power to generate electricity by any country, as long as nuclear fuel is not diverted to the production of weapons. This agreement has not been effective because some countries, namely Israel and India, did not sign up to the agreement and acquired weapons without punishment. Also, the failure of the main nuclear powers to reduce their stockpiles has led to accusations of hypocrisy and double standards that have undermined the global consensus on non-proliferation. Instead, the possibility of eventually eliminating nuclear weapons hinges on arms reduction talks between the countries that possess the majority of nuclear warheads, namely the United States and today's Russia, which was formerly the main part of the Soviet Union.

The large numbers of nuclear weapons that these two countries possess in the present day are the legacy of the arms race that occurred during the Cold War. After the United States used atomic bombs to force Japan to surrender in 1945, the Soviet Union quickly developed a military nuclear capability to achieve parity with the United States. Each side saw it as necessary to match and outdo what the other side had. Each side pursued more powerful nuclear weapons, such as the hydrogen fusion bomb, and produced ever larger numbers of warheads, more than needed to destroy all major population centers in the other's territory and, in fact, more than needed to bring catastrophic destruction to the whole planet. Western military strategists and thinkers argued that, notwithstanding the moral revulsion against the use of nuclear weapons on Soviet cities whose populations were largely civilian, the nuclear policies of the Western powers were justified by the necessity of deterring the first use of nuclear weapons by the Soviets aimed at subjugating the American-led "free world."

What exactly is the deterrence argument, and does such a strategy satisfy the requirements of just war theory? The argument goes like this: If a hostile power has nuclear weapons that could be used against your cities to force your country into submission (as the United States had done with Japan), how could you prevent the enemy from succeeding, except by threatening an immediate retaliation with similar devastating consequences? The Soviets had to know that the launch of a nuclear missile against any American target would be detected before the missile reached its target, and the American response would consist of immediate retaliatory nuclear strikes against Soviet cities. Philosophers have tried to make sense of how it could be morally right to threaten to do something that is morally wrong.[46] The threat could not be a mere charade with no real intention to carry out the threat, as there would be no deterrent effect unless the retaliatory strike was guaranteed. So, in the face of an enemy armed with nuclear weapons who could be restrained only by the undesirable effects of mutual assured destruction, the threat to do what is morally wrong must be made with full sincerity and seriousness for the very necessary purpose of deterrence. And it is thought that the failure to make such a threat would be a dereliction of the duty of political leaders to protect citizens and to prevent the evils of a nuclear catastrophe or military subjugation to communism.

It remains that the just war principles of proportionality and discrimination are violated (or threatened to be violated). In fact, threats of nuclear retaliation are essentially terrorist threats as they are meant to influence the enemy's policies by creating fear among its population.[47] In addition, there are problems satisfying *jus ad bellum*, given that just war theory had traditionally proclaimed that peace should be an end of just war and part of the right intention in going to war. As Coady writes, "the climate of dominating fear is not a long-term recipe for the creation of genuine peace."[48] Michael Walzer has discussed exceptions to the principle of discrimination under conditions of "supreme emergency," in which a state is faced with military defeat that would threaten "everything decent in our lives" or lead to "a world where entire peoples are enslaved or massacred."[49] But whatever its merits, the supreme emergency exemption cannot possibly be used to justify nuclear deterrence as a strategy. As Henry Shue points out, "supreme emergency excuses violations of the principle of noncombatant immunity when danger is imminent and violations have usefulness and proportionality."[50] But a strategy of destroying enemy cities with nuclear weapons in retaliation for a nuclear attack by the enemy is simply "an-extermination-for-an-extermination" and "not the unavoidably only available response in the face of imminent danger."[51] As it is the national policies chosen that determine whether the threat of nuclear attack by the other side is imminent, each side in the nuclear standoff has the choice of trying to escape from the balance of terror. Moreover, the idea of supreme emergency cannot in reality be applied in the form of a "permanent" condition (Walzer's phrase) to legitimize the continued targeting of enemy civilians for nuclear annihilation year after year. Even in the Second World War, when Churchill evoked the notion of supreme emergency to justify Allied actions such as the mining of Norwegian waters (that provoked the Germans to invade neutral Norway) and the massive bombing of German cities, the time at which there was a genuine threat of devastating defeat by the Nazis passed too quickly to justify the killing of civilians that resulted.

Walzer, in fact, concedes that nuclear weapons originally developed to deter Nazi Germany and then deployed in large numbers to deter Stalinist Russia "are not being used for any comparable purpose right now."[52] He thinks, however, that disengaging from the system of nuclear deterrence is a complicated business, because "we are less afraid when there is mutual deterrence than we would be without it."[53] The question he turns to is how to deal with the risk of undeterred attack, a risk that he links with the problem of nuclear proliferation. This is partly the question of whether there is just cause to use military force to prevent other states from acquiring and using nuclear weapons. A related problem is that of "loose nukes" in the hands of rogue states and terrorist groups, and connected to this is the issue of preventive war as espoused in the Bush doctrine that I will be discussing in the next section. In the remainder of this section, I will focus on how the need to prevent the use of nuclear weapons by enemy states is fulfilled according to the philosophy of co-existence. Does my approach to the ethics of war contain a proposal for prevention that does not require deterrence or war?

The philosophy of co-existence is premised on the possibility of keeping enemies at bay without going to war to wipe them out. This is because to wage war would be to bring about a very great evil that should be avoided if it is possible to choose other measures that would be sufficient to protect one's country and its people from harm by one's enemies. The problem with enemies that possess nuclear weapons is that there seem to be few options that could be effective. It is no longer a matter of posting border guards to keep the enemies out. If we are going to make sure that our enemies do not use their nuclear weapons to either threaten us into submission or destroy us, we cannot simply rely on deploying conventional forces to build up the nation's defenses. Does this mean that the only possibility for co-existence short of war is deterrence, a policy that requires that we not only possess nuclear weapons, but also are prepared to use them?

In favor of deterrence is the fact that the Cold War ended without nuclear conflict. The United States and the Soviet Union did co-exist without wiping each other out with their nuclear arsenal. However, the Cold War lasted for decades, during which time numerous conventional proxy wars were fought by client states of the two superpowers. In addition, the United States and other like-minded countries were reluctant to engage in humanitarian intervention to defend human rights during the Cold War, as I mentioned earlier. The nuclear stalemate also caused generations of Americans and Russians to live in fear not just of deliberate attacks but also of inadvertent nuclear exchanges.[54] And the legacy of the Cold War continues, with the problem of nuclear proliferation and the danger of unsecured nuclear armaments falling into the hands of terrorist groups. (As previously mentioned, this topic will be discussed in the next section.)

Counting against deterrence as a form of co-existence is that for it to work, the leader of the country must sincerely intend to bring about a massive retaliatory strike in immediate response to the detection of a ballistic missile launch by the enemy. It is clear that a virtuous political leader could not so intend. For once deterrence has failed, the retaliatory strike constitutes an act of gratuitous and vengeful evil inflicted on mostly innocent people. Furthermore, the decision to retaliate must be made without full certainty about the accuracy of the report of an enemy first-strike. There will always be a possibility of mistakes, either in identifying the incoming missile or in interpreting it as a deliberate attack requiring a full-scale response. Such considerations should weigh heavily in deciding whether it is appropriate to order the killing of millions of innocent people. Yet there may be very little time for such a momentous decision to be made.[55]

There is a dilemma here that can be resolved only by finding another way to deter an enemy armed with nuclear weapons. Some considerations may help here. First, nuclear deterrence was not the only thing that prevented nuclear war during the period of Cold War rivalry. In fact, there were occasions, such as the 1962 Cuban Missile Crisis, in which nuclear war could have started, even with nuclear deterrence in place. Historians have shown that what made the difference was that US President John F. Kennedy made wise practical decisions that averted war and his choices were reciprocated by Soviet leader Nikita Khrushchev.[56] Second, most countries in the world did not and still do not possess nuclear weapons, including countries that were at war with the United States and the Soviet Union and countries that were and are hostile to them. What seems to be the case is that the superpowers found their nuclear capabilities to be of little utility for the kinds of war they actually fought during the Cold War period, while many smaller countries did not see the need to possess nuclear weapons to co-exist with the superpowers.

Could the United States have had a non-nuclear policy that could be effective in deterring the Soviets from attacking with its nuclear weapons? The example of non-nuclear regional powers indicates that there was such a possibility. Even if such a policy were less effective than nuclear deterrence, it should be preferred, for a number of reasons. First, the nuclear deterrence policy requires that the United States have leaders who intend to kill large numbers of innocent people. Such leaders would not be virtuous people. Second, safety from nuclear attack comes at an immense cost in terms of the citizens' moral well-being. Civilians live in fear, while the military trains men and women operating nuclear weapons to have no inhibitions in carrying out orders to begin a massive genocidal attack on enemy civilians.[57] Third, it is not clear how much more effective deterrence is in preventing nuclear war, given that it is not a fail-safe system. Besides the risk of accidental launches, the strategy rests on a presumption that the other side would make rational decisions based on the desire not to bring catastrophic harm to their own people. But dependence on the rationality of one's enemies in war has turned out in many instances to be misplaced and to have resulted in regrettable consequences.

There is more than one scenario to consider here. If a country does not have nuclear weapons, what can it do to deal with another country that does possess them? If a country already has nuclear weapons, how can it move away from a policy of deterrence toward a policy of nuclear disarmament? Consider the first scenario. A country without nuclear weapons need not be facing threats from nuclear powers all by itself. Its allies could include nuclear and non-nuclear powers. Dependence on the protection of a nuclear power is relying on deterrence provided by the readiness of the nuclear power to retaliate on its behalf. It is not a solution to the problem of how to prevent nuclear attack or intimidation without resorting to deterrence. Could an alliance of non-nuclear states be effective in preventing a nuclear-armed enemy from using its weapons? And what could be done to make such prevention far more effective?

As already noted, the relative restraint shown by superpowers during the Cold War was not entirely due to deterrence and the "balance of terror." Global institutions such as the United Nations and regional organizations were established after the Second World War to provide space for talks to settle differences between nations and to foster cooperation in trade and defense. This provides smaller nations with greater leverage and establishes international norms of behavior. Powerful nations find that it is in their interests, in terms of effectiveness and costs, to try to achieve their political goals by working within the system of international law. Global opinion has an influence on the behavior of all nations, and that is why the possession of nuclear weapons has not given much of an advantage to the superpowers in dealings with less-powerful non-nuclear states. If a nuclear power were to threaten another state with a nuclear attack unless it gets its way, its behavior would be viewed as criminal and beyond the pale, and it would have to pay a very heavy price in terms of its standing in the world. Nuclear powers are (and have been) more likely to instead violate the sovereignty of non-nuclear states with the use of conventional forces. The gist of the argument I am making here is that the world today is very different from the world in the 1940s. There was nothing Japan could do to stop the United States from using nuclear weapons. And if Hitler had acquired nuclear weapons, he would not have hesitated to use them. But, despite the United States having acquired a lot more nuclear weapons in its arsenal after 1945, it has not used them again. Neither has the Soviet Union nor China. My point is that it would be a mistake to attribute these facts entirely to deterrence.

Another fact about the world today that explains why non-nuclear states have less to fear from nuclear-armed states is that leaders who are the evil equivalent of Hitler are extremely rare. (Some would argue that past leaders of North Korea came close.) I would concede that it remains possible that a Hitler-like leader could surface now or in the future, and that such a leader could possess nuclear weapons. I have said that a virtuous political leader would choose to go to war against Hitler's Nazi regime, even while she recognizes the great evil of war itself. Nuclear war would be a much greater evil, so a virtuous leader should try harder to avoid a war in which nuclear weapons are used and to find a way to co-exist with the enemy, *even though without nuclear weapons, the right choice would be to fight a war rather than to co-exist because of the evil of the regime.*[58] But if the evil of submission is too high a price to pay to avoid war, then deterrence may be the best choice in these extreme circumstances. Thus, the United States was right to develop an atomic bomb, in case Hitler got one. (It was the use of the bomb against Japan after Germany was defeated that could not be justified, as this was a case of a nuclear-armed state using nuclear weapons on a state that did not possess them in order to force it to grant its political demands. This is something the international community today would find unacceptable and the United States would have faced repercussions if it had done a similar thing in wars it has fought since.) Because nuclear war is so evil, and threatening a nuclear attack as required for a deterrence policy is also greatly evil, the philosophy of co-existence treats deterrence the same way as it treats war: Deterrence and war would only be chosen by a virtuous political leader in very extreme circumstances that are not satisfied in many cases where deterrence or war could be justified by just war theory.[59] Once again, this view is not equivalent to pacifism, because it allows that there are (rare cases of) worse evils than war or deterrence – even as it maintains that just war theory is overly permissive in justifying the choice of war or deterrence.

I turn now to the second scenario of a country that already possesses nuclear weapons. Would it then be locked into a deterrence policy, or should it choose to disarm? Consider the situation in 1945. It was perfectly reasonable for other states to fear the United States, which had shown its willingness to use nuclear weapons against an enemy that did not possess them. The international organizations and legal tools for restraining the actions of more powerful nations did not yet exist. Any country that viewed the United States as a threat and which had the resources to acquire nuclear weapons would be prudent to do so. The Soviet Union was in such a situation and when it developed its own nuclear arsenal, the Cold War and nuclear deterrence began.[60] Given both the evil of deterrence itself and the danger of an attack by a nuclear-armed enemy that can be prevented by deterrence, is it right for the United States to continue with the policy of deterrence? If it were to disarm its nuclear arsenal, would it bring about a world with even worse evil?

Recall that in the philosophy of co-existence, though a virtuous leader would go to war against Hitler, the war that such a leader would fight would be less evil in the way it is prosecuted and the war would end earlier once Hitler was no longer capable of carrying out those evil actions that made his domination of Europe a worse evil than war. Likewise, a country that is engaged in a nuclear deterrence policy should end that policy as quickly as possible. Forty years of war would be too much of war, even against the evil of Hitler. Similarly, 40 years of nuclear deterrence would be too much of deterrence, whatever the justifications for the policy to begin with. What made sense at the beginning of the Cold War before international institutions and global opinion helped to protect less-powerful nations from aggression by more powerful nations did not continue to make sense 10, 20, or more years later. A virtuous leader would seek ways to replace deterrence with a state of co-existence that did not require threats of nuclear holocaust. Now, this would be easier to achieve if all the nuclear powers were led by people who reasoned in the way I have proposed that virtuous leaders would choose. But if the leader of the Cold War enemy did not think in this way, should the virtuous leader of a nuclear power still choose to disarm?

Agreements to mutually limit the growth of each country's nuclear arsenal were reached at various times during the Cold War, as a result of negotiations. A virtuous leader would have pushed for greater and faster disarmament on a mutual basis. This may seem to play into the hands of the enemy. Knowing the desire of the virtuous leader to get rid of nuclear weapons, the enemy's leader may use that knowledge to pursue a balance of power in its favor and to gain concessions to its advantage. But the fact that global opinion has come to matter even for superpowers may have an impact here. The leader who sets a goal of a world free of nuclear weapons and is willing to take the first steps toward that goal presents a challenge to the non-virtuous leader. If the latter shows obstinacy and resists disarmament, the leader risks being treated as a pariah and made to forego many of the benefits of international cooperation. The fact is that both the United States and the Soviet Union wanted to be viewed as a moral example to the world and to be respected as well as feared. Hitler may not have cared for global public opinion but Soviet leaders, by and large, did.[61] So, I do not think that it would be an unmitigated disaster for a virtuous leader to push hard for faster nuclear disarmament and seek their eventual obsolescence. Even more to the point, the fact that this is not being done after the collapse of the Soviet Union and the end of the Cold War is an absolute failure of any leader so far to live up to the standard that is set in the philosophy of co-existence.[62]

Of course, leaders of the United States point to new threats that have surfaced after the Cold War. Besides the threat of terrorism, which I discussed earlier, there is the threat of nuclear attack as a result of the proliferation of nuclear weapons in smaller states and terrorist groups. The question is whether such post-Cold War threats justify continuation of the policy of deterrence and the possession of nuclear weapons by the United States and other nuclear powers. And how should the United States deal with nuclear proliferation and the smaller states that are in the process of acquiring nuclear weapons? I will now examine the doctrine of preventive war, which is the Bush administration policy for dealing with such threats in the post-9/11 era.

The Bush doctrine of preventive war

I have so far looked at the issues of humanitarian intervention, terrorism, and weapons of mass destruction separately. In September 2002, a year after the terrorist attack of 9/11, the Bush administration issued a National Security Strategy (NSS) of the United States that used the combination of these three issues as a justification for preventive war.[63] What came to be known as the "Bush doctrine" argued that the United States had the right to go to war in self-defense against so-called rogue states that possessed weapons of mass destruction and that were sponsors of terrorism before any attack was launched against the United States. The logic behind the doctrine makes sense at a certain level.[64] Rogue states had authoritarian rulers who violated the human rights of their own citizens. If they possessed weapons of mass destruction, such rulers would not hesitate to use them, given that they had no respect for human rights. Nor could they be deterred from using them by the Cold War strategy of mutual assured destruction, since they could provide the WMDs to terrorist groups to carry out their attacks on other states, instead of launching WMDs from their own territories. And, given that terrorist groups have murdered innocent civilians across international borders, WMDs would magnify the threat that they pose.

The Bush doctrine was used to provide a just cause for the 2003 invasion of Iraq. Saddam Hussein's regime supposedly satisfied all the criteria for a preventive attack by the United States. Since he took power in 1979, he had imposed a reign of oppression against his own people and he had even used chemical weapons to carry out mass murder against those who opposed his rule. What the Bush administration needed to show in 2002 was that he still possessed stockpiles of chemical weapons after a decade of UN sanctions and weapons inspections that took effect after Iraq was defeated in the 1991 Gulf War. In addition, the Bush administration made the case that Saddam Hussein was in the process of acquiring uranium and reconstituting his nuclear program. To complete the case for preventive war, it was alleged that the Iraqi ruler had links with the Al-Qaeda terrorists who had carried out the 9/11 attacks and continued to provide assistance to this and other anti-American terrorist groups. There was, in fact, little evidence for both Saddam Hussein's nuclear program and his links to Al-Qaeda, and critics have accused the Bush administration of fabricating the case for the invasion.[65] But whether or not the Bush doctrine was misapplied in Iraq, the case for preventive war has been the subject of debate for ethicists of war. Traditional just war doctrine was formulated by thinkers, such as Gentili, who favored preventive war. But international law has been based on the American Webster doctrine that made a very limited case for pre-emptive strikes on the basis only of an imminent attack. Michael Walzer has argued for pre-emptive attacks in the face of a "sufficient threat" that is not necessarily imminent, but he draws the line against preventive war.[66]

In this chapter, I have argued that very few humanitarian interventions should be carried out and that non-state groups that carry out terrorism should be pursued through law enforcement. I have also argued that nuclear deterrence is a policy that is justified only against very evil and dangerous regimes, comparable to Hitler's Nazis, with nuclear weapons and which did not care about global opinion and international cooperation. So unlike some just war theorists, I have not found a broadening of the ethical case for war is needed to face the challenges of humanitarian intervention, terrorism, and weapons of mass destruction. The Bush doctrine basically combines the three challenges into one to claim that if they are co-present, then there is a new case in favor of war of the preventive kind. Apart from responding to the Bush doctrine, I also have reason to consider here the kind of case presented by Iraq (supposedly), Iran (possibly), and North Korea (actually). This has to do with the issue of how to respond to the problem of nuclear proliferation and whether it can be justified to attack a transitioning non-nuclear state to prevent it from acquiring nuclear weapons or to destroy the weapons it has acquired. This issue had been left unexamined in the previous section on weapons of mass destruction.

The discussion of preventive war has been carried out from both consequentialist and rights-based perspectives. The point has been made that preventive war is not unique, because justified defensive wars are also preventive. The victim of aggression can only defend against the continuation of harm caused by an attack in progress or the possibility of future harms.[67] The issue is how far in advance a state could act in order to prevent the future harms. If the harms are speculative and there is uncertainty about an attack in the future, then it seems less justified to strike first, whereas if the state had already suffered aggression or is about to, it could be more certain that it needed to respond militarily. The consequentialist argument reflected in the Bush doctrine for preventive war claims that imminence of attack is not required to justify action against an enemy that possesses nuclear weapons, provided that the preventive action is necessary and proportionate.[68] Since a nuclear strike would be devastating, the defending country would be acting proportionately in attacking first to prevent the nuclear strike. And if it could be shown that there was no less harmful way to avert the nuclear attack in the future, the preventive war would indeed be necessary. The necessity could be established with the argument that once a state had achieved nuclear capability and dispersed the weapons, it would be almost impossible to stop it from launching a nuclear attack.[69]

There are consequentialist objections against preventive war raised by critics of the Bush doctrine. One concern is that a change in international norms of war to permit preventive war would result in a less-secure world, filled with mutual suspicions.[70] Now consequentialists may respond that the dangers of preventive war depend on what kind of precedent is being set in the invasion of Iraq. The invasion could be seen as an exception to the norm against preventive war without changing the rule against preventive war,[71] or multilateral institutions could be set up to discourage abuse of preventive war, which would ensure that any permitted precedent is limited to good ones, while bad precedents are punished.[72] But a more serious difficulty undermining the use of consequentialism to justify preventive war is the difficulty of determining which scenarios apply to the future as consequences of an act of preventive war. This is a serious epistemological problem that is a fundamental weakness to consequentialist reasoning about preventive war. Not only do we not know whether a preventive war would undermine international security, but we also do not know if the war would be proportionate or necessary. For there is uncertainty about whether there is no other way to prevent a future nuclear strike or if such a strike would occur without preventive action. It is the need for certainty, after all, that makes a pre-emptive strike against an imminent attack seem more justified than a preventive war that takes place, "even if uncertainty remains as to the time and place of the enemy's attack."[73] The lack of a resolution to the epistemological problem leads to the impasse problem: "the existence of equally plausible rule-consequentialist arguments for countervailing conclusions."[74]

Given the indeterminacy regarding the acceptability of preventive war when using consequentialist thinking, there has been much discussion of whether the right to self-defense could include the right to launch a preventive war. Although for individual self-defense, preventive action in the form of violence seems unjustified since other means of defending against threats in the future are available, such as getting the help of law enforcement,[75] it is thought that states may have no other choice. There is no international police entity to protect states from aggression by other states, and the harms caused by aggression are on a much larger scale than the harm when an individual person is attacked. On the other hand, preventive war is objectionable because it violates the rights of those who are killed. A war of self-defense is premised on the persons against whom defensive force is exerted being liable to be harmed in this way. When aggression is under way, the aggressors are liable because of what they have done. Even in pre-emptive strikes, self-defense can be justified by the preparations of the other side and the threats that they make. But in a preventive war, "one attacks and kills those who have not yet committed an act of wrongful aggression against you."[76] Is it at all possible to determine that unless they are attacked and killed now, they will do so in the future?

We have seen the epistemological problems in speculating about what other people or states may do in the future and whether it is necessary to attack them now rather than delaying while pursuing other ways to thwart a possible attack. Although it is true that innocent people are killed in all wars,[77] in a just war, the innocent people are killed in the course of waging war on those who have done something to provide a just cause for war. Without actual aggression, every person attacked in a preventive war is innocent. In order to make the case that preventive war can be just, some theorists have argued that the leaders involved in a conspiracy to engage in aggression in the future have done enough to justify attacking them in advance to prevent them from carrying out their plans. It has been pointed out that conspirators are usually a small group until their plans are carried out, but the targets of attack in a preventive war are soldiers who are not aware of such plans. In response, those who favor preventive war argue that by signing up for military service, soldiers are aware that they will have to fight when ordered to do so, even if the wars are unjust acts of aggression.[78] I think this is too broad an account of liability to be attacked in preventive war. If this account is correct, then any soldier is liable to attack at any time, even if they are presently under the command of leaders who have no aggressive intentions. Moreover, even the broad account of liability does not justify the killing of the noncombatants that will take place once a preventive war is started. Such killings are difficult enough to justify in any war, but preventive war is a flimsy reason for the killings. Given that the Bush doctrine is concerned to prevent future attacks with WMDs, the preventive war could involve a high degree of violence and still be considered proportionate so civilian deaths may occur in greater numbers.

Ultimately, the acceptance of preventive war by just war theorists such as Luban amounts to a watering down of the moral restrictions on war for realist reasons.[79] But there is no consensus, and other views include those in favor of preventive war only with the right institutions (Buchanan), those who recognize a right to preventive war in theory but reject it in practice due to epistemological difficulties (McMahan), and those who think that it is wrong to engage in preventive war (Rodin). How can the dilemma posed by preventive war be resolved, given that various just war theorists have proposed reasons to both support and oppose it? I turn now to discuss how the philosophy of co-existence applies to preventive war.

The three dangers that combine to justify preventive war in the Bush doctrine are each necessary to justify preventive war. The case for preventive war is made on the basis of the nature of rogue states that oppress citizens, possess WMDs, and support terrorism. But if each danger can be dealt with without recourse to preventive war, then, unless the sum is more than the parts, there is no new reason for preventive war when they are presented together in making the case for war. I have suggested that a virtuous political leader might rightly choose to carry out military humanitarian interventions in extreme cases, comparable to Hitler's genocide against the Jews, but ordinary oppressions are usually not such great evils that the evil of war when another state intervenes would be the better moral choice. So, if Saddam Hussein had been engaged in Nazi-like genocide, a war to stop his atrocities would have been justified, and this would have been so whether or not he had WMDs or supported terrorism. But since the oppression of his regime did not seem to make the choice of humanitarian intervention right, we must ask how the added considerations of WMDs and terrorism change this. Each of the latter factors support a military attack on Iraq only if they are sufficient on their own to do so, not because they somehow justify a humanitarian intervention that was not justified before. Similarly, if the allegations that he supported terrorism carried out by Al-Qaeda and other anti-US terrorist groups are not enough to make it right to attack Iraq, given the evils that the war on terror itself entails, we must ask how the addition of the other two factors in the Bush doctrine changes that. And when we consider whether Iraq's possession or development of WMDs in itself provides a good enough reason for choosing the evil of war in order to neutralize the threat that these weapons pose, would a negative answer be reversed by factoring in the domestic oppression and the regime's support for terrorism?

In examining the case for invading Iraq and removing Saddam Hussein as part of the global war on terror declared by the Bush administration, I rejected the claim that terrorism by non-state groups should be dealt with by going to war with states. Instead, I proposed combating terrorists as criminals to be dealt with by police work that included seeking cooperation from states in which terrorists are active and isolating those states that do not cooperate. Terrorist acts are evil but could a terrorist group pose as much of a threat as a state like Nazi Germany could? Could terrorists carry out mass genocide and systematic extermination of innocent people in large numbers? If not, and if there are means available on the law enforcement paradigm that could reduce the threat of terrorism to a level where only the "nut cases" do it (as the goal is for domestic law enforcement), then there is no good reason for invading Iraq even if there were Al-Qaeda terrorists there. So far, acts of terrorism by non-state groups, including the 9/11 attacks, do not rise to the level of danger that was posed by the Nazis in the Second World War.

The WMD factor may become relevant here. If Saddam Hussein's regime was running a nuclear program aimed at providing him with an ability to launch nuclear attacks on his enemies, there are two ways he could be a threat sufficient to make the case for preventive war against Iraq. He could use nuclear weapons on his enemies, such as Israel, or he could provide them to terrorist groups to use against their enemies, such as the United States. I will examine the latter possibility first. Now, the likelihood of a state handing over nuclear weapons to a terrorist group is actually very small – too small to constitute an evil that must be dealt with through a war which is itself certain to lead to multiple and extreme evils. The reason is that states cannot control the terrorist groups and the WMDs can be used against the state that provides the weapons. Terrorists are more likely to obtain WMDs when states that possess them experience political upheavals. But the danger of terrorists possessing WMDs assumes that terrorists would seek such weapons and use them. Such a scenario might be fodder for a made-for-Hollywood action thriller, but is this likely enough to justify preventive war?

Consider the WMDs that have the greatest destructive power, namely nuclear weapons. It might seem obvious that no state could rely on the tools of law enforcement to contain the threat posed by terrorists who have the ability to strike with nuclear weapons. But consider what is required to maintain, transport, deploy, and launch nuclear attacks against an enemy. Terrorist groups are usually small and operate covertly.[80] Otherwise, they would be detected and rooted out. To carry out a terrorist nuclear attack, however, requires the coordinated work of a large group of personnel and a time frame for action that would expose the terrorists to the law enforcers searching for them. In fact, nuclear warheads and the launchers to fire them could not disappear in a crowd the way that terrorists armed with light weapons could. Given that terrorists can be highly effective in their attacks on the cheap and in small groups, as illustrated by the 9/11 attacks, it would seem that the use of nuclear weapons is unlikely to be an attractive option for terrorists. Moreover, their political goals are usually those of publicizing their grievances, winning the sympathy of public opinion, and exposing the brutality of the regimes that they are attacking. Nuclear weapons would enhance their ability to kill and destroy, but are more likely to undermine the terrorists' real objectives.

So, I can basically rule out the possible use of WMDs by terrorist groups as a reason for preventive war. I turn now to the possibility of a regime like Saddam Hussein's getting hold of nuclear weapons and using them against its enemies. I have examined what the United States should have done in the Cold War instead of engaging in a policy of nuclear deterrence, but I left aside the question of how to deal with smaller countries that seek to acquire nuclear weapons. This is the problem of nuclear proliferation. Recall that I considered nuclear deterrence to be almost as great an evil as war, and I suggested that the United

States should have moved away from a policy of deterrence during the Cold War with the Soviet Union because the existence of international organizations and the cooperation between non-nuclear states made it counter-productive, and, hence, unlikely that the Soviet Union would attack the United States with nuclear weapons. What supported my view is that the superpowers did not use their nuclear weapons in the wars that they did fight against non-nuclear states. Both superpowers seemed to have built up their nuclear arsenal solely for the purpose of deterring the other from a nuclear first-strike. Given the evil of deterrence, a virtuous leader should work hard to reduce the nuclear stockpile of each country through negotiations. But the end of the Cold War and the risk of nuclear proliferation in smaller countries present a new challenge. Having examined all the other dangers that the Bush doctrine made use of to justify preventive war, the disarming of nuclear weapons in smaller states such as Iran and North Korea may be the sole valid point in the doctrine. Or is it valid at all?

Critics make the point that the objection to nuclear proliferation is hypocritical in that the major world powers continue to build up and enhance their nuclear arsenal while denying non-nuclear states the right to acquire such weapons. This is indeed a legitimate criticism. As I argued earlier, the policy of nuclear deterrence should have been replaced by agreements to mutually disarm, aimed at eventually eradicating nuclear weapons altogether. But the efforts to halt nuclear proliferation reflect legitimate concerns about what smaller states with authoritarian rulers in insecure parts of the world would do once they got hold of nuclear weapons. Are these countries more likely to use them? If so, can they be deterred or should they be attacked to either disarm them or stop their nuclear programs? Preventive war is presented as the last and only resort by some who see no other way to prevent the use of nuclear weapons by states that refuse to abide by the Nuclear Non-Proliferation Treaty.

The idea that smaller countries are more likely to use nuclear weapons in war has some plausibility. One reason for thinking this is that these countries do not have the conventional forces that would enable them to win battles easily or the resources to grind out a long war. As I said earlier, WMDs enable such states to fight on another plane where they could have parity with or superiority over enemies with stronger conventional forces. Smaller countries also find defeat more costly and recovery from defeat more difficult. They are more likely to view the likelihood of losing a war as a "supreme emergency," which permits them to make exceptions to the *jus in bello* principles. In any case, if these countries are ruled by autocrats who do not respect human rights, the ethics of war would not constrain them in their desperation.

Deterrence may not work with undemocratic rulers who do not care about the well-being of their people and who do not rule with public support. North Korea and Iran have both been acquiring nuclear weapons in the face of economic sanctions that have harmed their own citizens. The leaders of such countries may even be willing to subject their own people to retaliatory nuclear strikes. What about the framework of international law, peacekeeping, and global security maintained by multilateral institutions? Would this be a way to make the use of nuclear weapons by smaller states highly unlikely, in the way that it worked with the superpowers? One reason to think that international pressure will not work is that many autocratic states already flout widely accepted standards of behavior in how they treat their own people. On the other hand, a despot who abuses the citizens of a country may be more cautious about harming non-citizens. The despot is shielded to a degree in carrying out internal oppression as foreign countries may not wish to intervene, but would be inviting such intervention if it attacked foreigners. Tyrants keep their hold on power through a security apparatus that includes their military forces and they risk weakening their troops by fighting foreign wars. It is true that tyrants may threaten neighboring countries or even superpowers in order to rally support at home. But that does not mean they actually want to fight or think they can prevail in war. A similar point can be made about the desire of such rulers to acquire nuclear weapons. The possession of nuclear weapons strengthens their hold on power by providing a source of national pride. The weapons may also be useful as a bargaining chip in negotiations to secure concessions from the international community if the state is facing economic sanctions due to its internal oppression. North Korea and Iran both seem to be playing such games with the outside world at the turn of the new century.

Under what conditions are small countries likely to use their nuclear weapons? There are two possibilities: when they attack another country, and when they are attacked. The first possibility would apply if the state with the nuclear weapons has a policy of territorial expansion or of settling scores with enemies. Are there states with ambitions of empire-building in the world today? What makes this unlikely is that the imperialism of earlier periods of history had occurred in a world where countries were not restrained by international law and a system of global security that protected recognized national borders. It is true that there are still disputed borders where skirmishes take place once in a while, as in the example of the Kashmiri border between India and Pakistan. Once again though, nuclear weapons may be acquired for the purpose of strengthening one side's prestige and position in negotiations. But it is hard to see the sense in using the weapons to annihilate the enemy over a border dispute. A nuclear attack on an enemy makes a little bit more sense if there is a history of animosity between two states. Note, however, that smaller states are capable of building up a small arsenal of nuclear weapons, but the use of these weapons will leave them with very few or nothing while they face the punitive actions that the international community would immediately impose on them, which may include military attacks. In other words, a small country that dares to launch a nuclear strike must be ready to take on almost the entire world, and it would not have the means to succeed in doing that. This puts pressure on the country to restrain itself.

The possibility remains that some country could use nuclear weapons in war. Take a mid-size country with plentiful resources. Once such a country goes nuclear, it could over a period of time build up a decent-sized nuclear arsenal. The country could start with using the nuclear weapons to strengthen its hand in negotiations but eventually, it may feel strong enough to use them against its enemies without fearing the retaliation from the international community, since it retains enough nuclear weapons to make it dangerous for other countries to strike at it. This buys it time to replace the weapons it has used and to stockpile more nuclear weapons. Eventually, it might have the ability to wage nuclear war not just to settle scores or to gain the upper hand in a border dispute, but to dominate other countries in its region.

My example may well describe a country very similar to Nazi Germany as it grew in power in the 1930s, with the only difference being the introduction of nuclear weapons into the mix. And in this scenario, the only option is for other countries to arm themselves with nuclear weapons to deter attack by the expansionist nuclear state. It should be noted how exceptional the circumstances described in this example are, just as Nazi Germany may well have been quite unique in history. But even with the safeguards provided by international institutions today, it is not impossible that we may one day have to deal with a version of Nazi Germany armed with nuclear weapons. What I can say here is similar to what I used the philosophy of co-existence to say about war. Only in the extreme situation of a Hitler-like threat would a virtuous political leader go to war, given that war is itself a great evil. I have said that nuclear deterrence is almost as evil as war. But if I cannot rule out war as an ethical choice, I cannot rule out deterrence but only in the face of a Hitler-like threat armed with nuclear weapons. I also said earlier that many threats that may provide sufficient reason for war under the just war theory do not constitute an evil equal or close to Hitler's evil. A similar point applies to deterrence. It is an evil policy and is usually unnecessary to deal with nuclear-armed states that do not pose a Hitler-like threat to the world community.

I mentioned a second possibility of smaller countries using nuclear weapons, namely when they are threatened and fear defeat by their enemies. As stated earlier, smaller countries do not have strong conventional armies and face defeat quickly when attacked. They may acquire nuclear weapons in order to deter attack. If this is the case, then a doctrine of preventive war is counter-productive. The fear of attack encourages smaller countries to violate the Nuclear Non-proliferation Treaty, and an actual attack may lead to the use of nuclear weapons that were meant to deter. This point reinforces the criticisms we looked at when we examined the Bush doctrine. The world is safer by relying on the system of global security built on international cooperation and respect for borders, whereas the legitimization of preventive war has the effect of sowing distrust so that nations see each other as potential threats. If any nation is unable to protect itself with conventional means of fighting, it is logical to acquire a nuclear arsenal to deter enemies who may wage war on them in the name of prevention.

Preventive war against smaller states that either possess or are acquiring nuclear weapons was the last possible justification for the Bush doctrine. I have now shown that the justification should be rejected. Nuclear proliferation is itself fueled by the threats made by bigger powers.[81] It is true that some nations would seek to possess nuclear weapons for reasons of prestige and as bargaining chips in negotiation. This does not constitute a good enough reason to go to war with them. But if international institutions that foster respect for the rule of law and protection of borders of all states, big and small, are strengthened, many of the insecure nations may feel less of a need to acquire nuclear weapons. After all, they are costly and unlikely to actually be used (as the superpowers learned, to their chagrin). The only scenario where the possession of nuclear weapons would pose a risk of their use is when they are in the hands of a Hitler-like regime. Even then, there is justification only for a policy of deterrence, not preventive war. There is, however, a conundrum here. Nuclear weapons cannot be built overnight to face a nuclear-armed enemy who is willing to use nuclear weapons. This means that some countries would have to be entrusted with keeping some nuclear weapons not for use or deterrence but in case a nuclear-armed Hitler-like regime emerges. This possibility cannot be ruled out, since the technology for building nuclear weapons cannot be un-invented. But if some countries continue to hold nuclear weapons, even though they do not threaten anyone, other countries may feel the need to have their own. And who are the countries who get to hold these weapons? Can they be trusted? Will their rulers become Hitler-like? But whatever we think of this conundrum, the solution cannot be a doctrine of preventive war.

The killing of Osama bin Laden

As I write this chapter of the book, events in the world took an unexpected turn. Ten years after 9/11, American forces located Osama bin Laden, the Al-Qaeda leader, in a mansion near a Pakistani city and a team of US Navy SEALs succeeded in carrying out a commando-style raid in which Osama bin Laden was killed. The American soldiers crossed the border from Afghanistan into Pakistan in helicopters without informing or getting permission from the Pakistani authorities.[82] They then took bin Laden's body and documents and other material and left Pakistan in a matter of hours. Bin Laden's body was buried at sea from an American aircraft carrier. The raid was seen as a great success and a courageous decision by President Barack Obama, and the death of bin Laden was celebrated by joyful Americans. There was some debate among commentators about the legality of the raid under international law. How should an ethicist who applies the philosophy of co-existence evaluate the American action?

Clearly, the raid into Pakistan is much more preferable to a military invasion of Pakistan. Thus, it did not have the drawbacks of the invasion of Afghanistan in 2001 when the country was attacked in order to apprehend or kill Osama bin Laden. However, the raid did not fit in with my earlier recommendation that terrorism be dealt with by law enforcement rather than military force. Is there a reason for the military raid that could make it the right choice by a virtuous political leader? I will attempt to provide such a reason here by considering the raid to be a form of military preventive action of a kind that does not have the drawbacks and problems I have attributed to preventive war.

One of the insurmountable difficulties in trying to justify preventive war is that its necessity cannot be determined with certainty. Added to that is the killing of large numbers of innocent people in war, which in the case of preventive war, includes not just noncombatants but troops that are not involved in any conspiracy by their leaders to carry out aggression some time in the future. Thus, neither consequentialist nor rights-based reasons could provide unambiguous support for preventive war. In the case of Osama bin Laden, there is little doubt that as long as he lived, he was plotting terrorist attacks against Westerners, particularly Americans, as well as Muslims that he viewed as corrupt, impious, and collaborators with the West. He had a long track record of terrorist crimes and never wavered in his resolve to repeat such attacks. These included the 9/11 attack that murdered almost 3,000 people and the attacks on American embassies in East Africa that took a few hundred lives. He had also inspired other extremists to carry out terrorist attacks in Bali, Madrid, and London.

As a principle conspirator in mass murder, Osama bin Laden was the most wanted person in the world. Domestic mass murderers pale in comparison to this man, in terms of wicked intentions and actions. The terrorist plots that he carried out or inspired killed men, women, and children alike, of any race or religion, including Arabs and Muslims. If it had been in the power of domestic or international law enforcement to do so, he would have been apprehended, put on trial, and punished for his crimes if he was found guilty. Since he continued to elude capture by hiding in areas of the world torn by war or civil strife, and where governments are weak or corrupt, the chances of arresting and extraditing him were non-existent. A second option for law enforcement when a criminal on the loose cannot be captured is to isolate him and deprive him of opportunities to commit his crimes. To some extent, that had been done with Osama bin Laden for more than ten years. He had been driven out of his safe haven in Afghanistan and subjected to a global manhunt.[83] However, numerous terrorist plots continued to be hatched, though not on the scale of 9/11, and the United States had been fortunate that these had not been successfully carried out.[84] The longer Osama bin Laden remained on the loose, the greater the chances that he would be able to launch or inspire another attack on a scale close to the 9/11 attack.

So, unlike the case for preventive war against Iraq that was highly speculative and based on dubious intelligence, there was no doubt about the seriousness of the threat that Osama bin Laden posed. Details that have been disclosed about the raid in Pakistan that killed him tell us that the United States suspected his location in late 2010. This was the first time there was reliable intelligence on Osama bin Laden's whereabouts since the end of 2001 when he escaped from the mountains of Tora Bora in Afghanistan. The previous time his location was known was in 1997, when the CIA provided President Bill Clinton with the opportunity to strike at him. What this sequence shows is that there were very few opportunities to get Osama bin Laden. It might have been another ten years before he was located again, and his next attack could have come sooner than that. Thus, the United States had a very good case that any military action to capture or kill bin Laden at his compound in Pakistan was truly preventive and urgent. The failure to do so could be very costly in terms of innocent lives lost. Moreover, in the meantime, the security and counter-terrorist measures that the United States and its Western allies have taken have had the effect of eroding democracy and undermining the values of civilized society. Even if there have been no successful terrorist attacks, the constant need for precautions against terrorism has had a very ugly and corrupting effect on the lives of hundreds of millions of people.

It would have been too risky to ask the Pakistani authorities to arrest Osama bin Laden, because the Pakistani forces were known to have been infiltrated by Al-Qaeda.[85] For US law enforcement to get to Osama bin Laden, they would have had to ask permission to send their men over, which would have risked alerting bin Laden. Thus, the only option was a military raid by forces trained for such purposes. In this case, the United States planned a very precise and limited military action, not a full-scale incursion or invasion. This plan was not just tactically judicious but had moral benefits. The raid avoided the deaths of civilians and of Pakistani troops that would have occurred with a larger military engagement. Moreover, it could end in a matter of hours. Thus, the evils of war could be mostly avoided by the kind of raid that the United States carried out. Nevertheless, there were some moral dangers. One is the possibility that Osama bin Laden was not there. It was reported that the United States was not a hundred percent certain that this was bin Laden's location. During the invasion of Iraq, more than 50 leaderships strikes were attempted by the United States to take out Saddam Hussein or high-ranking members of the Baath party or the Iraqi military. Not a single attack got the intended target, and in every one of these attacks, innocent people were killed by the dozens. [86] The second moral danger is of the raid not going according to plan.[87] In fact, the United States lost a helicopter that spun out of control and hit a wall. Fortunately, they had prepared for contingencies and achieved their goal, despite the mishap. But if more things had gone wrong, US forces might have had to engage in firefights with Pakistani forces, in which innocent people could have lost their lives. In choosing to carry out the raid, these are considerations relevant to the moral evaluation by a virtuous political leader.

I have tried to show that the consequentialist and rights-based objections to preventive war did not necessarily apply to the case of a preventive attack on a very specific target that was clearly necessary and was planned to avoid escalation into full-scale war. Thus, the raid that killed Osama bin Laden could be justified in a way that preventive war could not. The philosophy of co-existence stresses protecting citizens without going to war and only choosing deterrence or war in the face of a very evil threat comparable with that posed by the Nazis in the Second World War. Now the evil of Osama bin Laden and his terrorist attacks did not constitute evil on the scale of the Nazis. That is why Bush's global war on terror was not morally legitimate. What the raid that killed bin Laden illustrates is the possibility of going beyond law enforcement to fight terrorism by military means, but doing so without launching a preventive war. It should, however, be noted that the circumstances required to make a preventive attack of that kind the right choice are very rare.[88] But just as war, deterrence, and humanitarian intervention have been shown to be the right choice in exceptional circumstances (though not often in cases that satisfy just war criteria), a limited military strike against a very specific target to prevent the evil of terrorism may be the choice of a virtuous political leader aware of the intrinsic evils of war.

8
Is War Ever Justified?

I have now presented the philosophy of co-existence as an alternative to just war theory, and I have also applied the philosophy of co-existence to some recent ethical challenges to the morality of war. In concluding this book, I will try again to explain where the new ethics of war that I have laid out stands in comparison with pacifism and just war theory. For I recognize that there are pacifists who see my arguments in this book as support for their view that war is never justified. And there are just war theorists who will see me as justifying war, but with more restrictive conditions. In responding to such interpretations, I will also be able to show the reader how the philosophy of co-existence combines the good points of both pacifism and just war theory, while avoiding their problems.

The way I will make my case in this chapter is to examine an issue in just war theory that has engendered some recent controversy. Michael Walzer argued for an exception to the *jus in bello* principle of discrimination when a state is faced with imminent defeat at the hands of an enemy who would subject its people to "enslavement or extermination."[1] Using the example of Britain facing the evil of Nazi Germany alone before the entry of the United States into the Second World War, Walzer uses the phrase "supreme emergency" that he borrows from British Prime Minister Winston Churchill to justify the intentional bombing of German cities by the British to demoralize the enemy. I will argue that although just war theory is wrong, the concept of supreme emergency provides a useful way to understand how I view war. I will show the concept to be something that the philosophy of co-existence can borrow from Walzer's just war theory, and I will use it to explain why my view is not a pacifist one.

The supreme emergency exemption in just war theory

Walzer's idea that some rules of war can be overridden in extreme circumstances has been subject to analysis and criticism. Traditionally, the principles of just war are supposed to be absolute. The moral basis of the theory was either theological or deontological. If it is the former, the command of God that forbids the murder of innocent people does not allow for exceptions. If it is the latter, the principles are dictates of reason that are to be applied universally and that require respect for persons, meaning that an innocent human being's right to life cannot be violated to serve the purposes of other people. But Walzer thinks that, although utilitarian calculation is inappropriate for deciding whether people can be harmed, the extreme circumstances of a supreme emergency make for a special case:

> When our deepest values are radically at risk, the constraints lose their grip, and a certain kind of utilitarianism reimposes itself. I call this the utilitarianism of extremity, and I set it against a rights normality.[2]

Walzer recognizes that the concept of a supreme emergency is vague and open to abuse. Although an extreme measure such as deliberating attacking civilians in war should be used only when the danger is "of an unusual and horrifying kind," it is common for leaders to "say that their backs are to the wall whenever military defeat seems imminent."[3] Walzer's only example of a supreme emergency is that of Nazi Germany's threat to Britain, and only for the duration of the war before the United States joined the fight.[4] To justify the supreme emergency exemption, he argues that although individuals may uphold their moral principles by risking or sacrificing themselves rather than killing innocent people to save their own lives, a political leader cannot impose on their citizens such risks.[5] Rather, they have a duty to protect them from the extreme harms that they are in danger of suffering when the nation faces defeat by an evil enemy.

Walzer is attempting to find a balance between a purely utilitarian view that would permit the killing of innocent people, as long as doing so is necessary to achieve greater benefits, and an absolutist view of the rule against intentionally killing innocent people that cannot be violated, no matter what the consequences. The account he gives is one that he admits to be paradoxical. The intentional killing of the innocent remains wrong but it is right that leaders do so in a supreme emergency:

> A morally strong leader is someone who understands why it is wrong to kill the innocent and refuses to do so, refuses again and again, until the heavens are about to fall. And then he becomes a moral criminal (like Albert Camus's "just assassin") who knows that he can't do what he has to do – and finally does.[6]

To Walzer, this is a case of the "dirty hands" problem for political leaders,[7] in which political leaders must do wrong to do right.

The paradoxical nature of the claim in the quote above has led to a number of replies and the choice between these depends on one's prior commitment to a moral theory. A utilitarian or a realist would not view the killing of innocents in war as exceptional, but, rather, as something that is permitted whenever it is more beneficial or in one side's interests to do so. A traditional just war theorist would deny that the circumstances that Walzer describes as a supreme emergency are sufficient to permit the violation of the rules of war. A pacifist would see the wrongness of killing innocents as a case of the wrongness of all killing and of war in general. In none of these views is there room for making a special case for supreme emergencies. Given the paradoxical nature of Walzer's position, would it not be better to stick to a principled approach with no exceptions? Yet none of these other views seem to take seriously the moral dilemma that seems real for the political leader faced with defeat by a Hitler-like enemy.

I would suggest that what's missing from the above list of theoretical positions is that of virtue ethics as I have used it in the philosophy of co-existence. Before I turn to how I view supreme emergencies, I should mention one other view that comes closer to mine than any of the others. Brian Orend suggests that "from the moral point of view, a supreme emergency is a moral tragedy," in which "each viable option you face involves a severe moral violation" and "there is no way to turn and still be morally justified."[8] What this means is that, unlike Walzer, Orend does not think it is ever justified to deliberately kill innocent people. It is wrong for a political leader to do so in a supreme emergency, even if doing so is the lesser evil. In choosing to do so, the leader's justification is prudential, not moral. And since the circumstances are such that the leader would do what is morally wrong no matter what she chooses, she may be excused or bear lesser blame for her choice. But since what she does is not justified, the paradoxical view of "doing right in doing wrong" in Walzer's account is avoided.

Supreme emergency as a condition for war

In the philosophy of co-existence that I have presented in this book, war is considered one of the greatest evils for humankind. Yet, even though it seems to follow that one should avoid war at all costs, the position that I take is not that of absolute pacifism. Like pacifists, I do think that war should normally be avoided by co-existing with enemies while one is taking steps short of war to protect one's nation from attack. I do not accept that the state should wage war to destroy all enemies in order to remove the threats that they pose, as the Romans did in their time.[9] The choice of war to achieve such an aim is one that ignores the evil nature of war itself. I have cataloged the evil characteristics of war in my chapter on war as an evil. But I also argued that, in very rare cases, there are enemies that constitute such evils in the threat they pose that a state cannot co-exist with them, and that a virtuous political leader would, after giving due consideration to the evils that would be unleashed in war, be right to choose to go to war against such enemies. My example of an enemy so evil that co-existence with it is morally unacceptable is that of Hitler's Nazi regime. Thus war, which is normally not the right choice for a virtuous political leader, could be the right choice against a Hitler-like enemy carrying out massive aggression or genocide on the scale of the Holocaust.

It should be clear now that the circumstances in which war can rightly be chosen by a virtuous political leader are precisely those that Walzer considers supreme emergencies. The reason I am not a pacifist is that I do believe that there are such circumstances, and that I consider the pacifists to be unrealistic, either in thinking that there is nothing (ever) worse than war or in setting a moral standard of total non-violence that is inappropriate for human beings who have to care about families, friends, and community. But while I recognize the significance of the circumstances that constitute a supreme emergency, I use the concept differently from Walzer.

A supreme emergency provides a threshold, but for what? For a just war theorist such as Walzer, war is permissible on both sides of the threshold. Before the threshold is reached, all the requirements of just war theory, including the principle of discrimination, must be followed. Beyond the threshold, the political leader is justified in violating the principle of discrimination. On one side, we are supposed to have war ameliorated by the rules of war; on the other side, we have war with no holds barred. In the philosophy of co-existence, war should not be chosen at all until the threshold is reached. And even when the threshold is reached and war is chosen, the war should be fought in such a way that the evils of war are minimized. This means that civilian deaths should be avoided to the greatest extent feasible and that war should never take the form of "no holds barred." For instance, I said earlier that a war against Hitler fought by a virtuous political leader would be less evil than the actual war that was fought. One reason for this is that such a leader would not engage in the bombing campaign against German cities that Churchill endorsed.

Thus, it turns out, on my view, that wars should be fought only in supreme emergencies and never otherwise. Now, the question may be asked why a supreme emergency should bring a virtuous leader to choose what he would not normally choose (just as the question was asked of Walzer why it can be justified to kill civilians in a supreme emergency when it is normally wrong to do so). It would be a mistake to think that the threshold is the point at which utilitarian calculations show that the sum of evils in war is less than the sum of evils to be prevented by going to war. Such a complex calculation is beyond the capacity of anyone to make. The decision-making process of a virtuous political leader is not the application of a calculus of goods and evils. In virtue ethics, a person of good character has a capacity developed through experience of making the right judgments in choosing what to do. There are hard cases where the evils of war and the evils to be prevented are so close as to make the choice difficult, and only a person with immense practical wisdom can discern the right thing to do. But the case of Hitler's evil is not a hard case. I think that it is obvious to most people, whatever their favored moral theory, that Hitler needed to be stopped – by war if necessary.[10] It is the clarity of this case that leads me to use it to differentiate my view from a pacifism that cannot permit war in any event, even to stop Hitler. The absolute pacifist fails to take seriously the evil that is Nazism. But the just war theorist errs on the other side of the threshold in failing to take seriously enough the evil of war. So on that side of the threshold, I disagree with the just war theorist.

The just war theorist permits a "sanitized" war to be fought when there is no supreme emergency. But the just war is a myth, in that no actual war satisfying the conditions for just war has ever been fought nor is there likely to ever be one.[11] Because just war is a myth, those who recognize this tend toward pacifism. Since I share this criticism of just war, I need to explain my resistance to pacifism, and I have done that in the last paragraph and in other parts of this book. What I wish to say to the just war theorist, on the other hand, is that war in reality is evil not just because the rules of war are violated, but is evil even when they are followed. For a full accounting of the evils of war, as set out in Chapter 4, go well beyond the kinds that are supposedly minimized by applying the conditions of just war. Thus, the philosophy of co-existence would, instead, restrict war only to the circumstances that count as supreme emergencies. Most of the wars countenanced by just war theory are ones that take place before the threshold of supreme emergency is reached. When these wars are chosen, the just war requirements can be satisfied in legalistic fashion, but they still fail to give full and proper weight to the evils of war. In contrast, the philosophy of co-existence restricts war to supreme emergencies.

A further disagreement I have with Walzer's use of supreme emergency concerns what can be done in cases where the threshold is reached. Walzer endorses the killing of noncombatants, such as what took place in the Second World War when the British carried out numerous air raids on German cities. The clear danger of this, as Walzer himself noted, is that, once begun, the Allied air raids continued even after the United States entered the war and as late as 1945, when Germany was on the brink of defeat.[12] In the philosophy of co-existence, the virtuous political leader, aware of the evils of war, would fight the war in a way that minimized its evils, while doing enough to achieve the goal of preventing the evil against which the war is fought. It would be a war with moral limits though the limits are not necessarily identical with those that are contained in just war theory. It would also be a war that would be ended when the evil of the enemy had been reduced to a level that could be co-existed with. The killing of innocent people is one of the great evils of war. In permitting war in supreme emergencies, the political leader is choosing to do evil deliberately, since he knows that the killing of noncombatants is, alongside other evils, part and parcel of war.[13] But a lot more innocent people will be killed in war if attempts are not made to avoid killing them, and more so if civilians are made the deliberate targets of attack. For Walzer, deliberate attacks on non-combatants are permitted in supreme emergencies. In the philosophy of co-existence, a virtuous leader could choose war in a supreme emergency but would not choose to deliberately kill innocent people.

Now Walzer might object that by limiting what can be done in a supreme emergency and ruling out attacks on noncombatants, I have misunderstood the meaning of a supreme emergency. As he describes it, a political leader resorts to the killing of enemy noncombatants in a supreme emergency in order to prevent imminent defeat by an evil enemy such as Hitler. If the leader did not do that, his nation would be defeated and the evils of enslavement or massacre would be realized. So, the concept of supreme emergency that I use to mark the point at which war could rightly be chosen cannot be the same concept as Walzer's. I think that in one sense, I am not using supreme emergency to mark the same circumstances as Walzer, but in another sense, I am. If a supreme emergency occurs only when nothing except killing enemy noncombatants would avert defeat at the hands of a very evil enemy, then it is a different concept from mine. But such a concept would make it harder for Walzer to say the things he says in his discussion of supreme emergency. For one thing, it may not be the case that Britain's circumstances in fighting alone against Nazi Germany were those in which deliberately bombing German cities was necessary, or that these actions made the world less evil. It might have been the case that Britain would not have been defeated by the Nazis even if the British did not bomb German cities, and it might have also been the case that the bombing raids made no difference for Britain's survival.[14] And it would follow from this that the bombings made the Second World War more evil, as it added greatly to the civilian death toll, without any military benefit. So if Walzer's concept of supreme emergency necessitates the intentional killing of noncombatants to avoid defeat, it is a different concept from mine. But then, he cannot make use of the Hitler example to illustrate supreme emergencies, since it would fall on the side of the threshold where the principle of discrimination applies. And if the Hitler example is not applicable, does he have any other example to use, given that he does not, in fact, provide any others? If not, the absence of a real-world example would be rather telling. What it would mean is that the violation of the principle of discrimination can be justified only in hypothetical examples of extreme circumstances that have not occurred in the history of warfare![15]

If, on the other hand, Walzer thinks that the Hitler example illustrates his concept of supreme emergency very well, then it does not follow that the political leader of a nation faced with a supreme emergency must resort to the killing of enemy noncombatants, or else allow his nation to suffer the evil consequences of defeat. But then I am fully entitled to make use of Walzer's concept to mark the point at which a nation can rightly go to war but not fight a war without moral limits, and I am safe from the objection that I have used a different concept of supreme emergency.

Let me now consider whether my view is paradoxical in the way that Walzer's view is. In saying that a virtuous leader could choose war in the face of a worse evil than war, I am not justifying the choice of war. I think that the leader who chooses war would be choosing to do very evil actions, even if it would be morally worse to not fight a Hitler-like enemy. My view on this comes close to that of Orend, which I presented earlier. There is no paradox in saying that the leader who chooses war with all the evil that it entails is choosing to carry out wrongful acts. It is not the case that he is doing right by doing wrong.[16] What this means is that the leader may have to pay for his choice of war. (There remains a paradox of a different kind, in that a virtuous leader is one who would make the kind of choice that involves sacrificing his moral goodness to do what is needed in the face of a dilemma of choosing between evils. This paradox does not reflect a flaw in virtue ethics. What causes this paradox is that perfect goodness may not always be possible in the real world of finite human beings.) Even if he is excused by others who appreciate the tragic choice the leader faces, he cannot escape the corruption of his character and the psychological burden he bears from doing evil.[17] Having made the choice of war, he may not be suited to continue as the leader after the war is over, as he is no longer the virtuous leader that he once was.

There is one other thing different in my view of supreme emergency. Compared to Walzer, who follows the just war theory in thinking about war as self-defense against aggression, the kind of emergencies that a virtuous leader might deal with by choosing war includes genocide and massive violations of human rights by a leader against his own people. As I have shown, the evil of an extremely oppressive regime might be so serious as to make it the right choice for another state to intervene to stop the evil. The points I made about war in supreme emergencies apply also to humanitarian interventions.

Let me stress that I see supreme emergencies as very rare. I have already said that there are few cases that compare with the evil of Hitler's aggressive and brutal military expansionism and the Nazi program to exterminate millions of Jews in Europe. There may also be a few other cases of regimes that are not as evil, but sufficiently evil to make it right to choose war as the lesser evil.[18] But, given that I have characterized war as one of the greatest intrinsic evils, it is not surprising that war can only be justified in the rare cases where the enemy's evil is close to that of Hitler's. It is not that there are not many evil regimes around. It is just that they are not close enough to the evil that Hitler's regime represents. If we do not pay attention to how evil they are compared to war, and simply go to war on the basis of their evil, there would be too many wars. What just war theory enables leaders to do is to look at a particular evil deed that an enemy has done, such as building up their military forces and threatening their neighbors or suppressing their own people, and use that as a basis for satisfying the conditions for going to war. What the philosophy of co-existence requires leaders to do is to think about how they should avoid introducing more evil in the world in choosing to go to war when the situation is not that of a supreme emergency.

This will not satisfy the pacifist. Having alleged that the just war theory relies on a myth about sanitized war that makes it too easy to go to war, I may now, in turn, be accused of indulging in a different but equally dangerous myth – the myth of supreme emergencies. Are there really worse evils than war? The pacifist thinks that it is less evil to not resist Hitler by military means. She points to the fact that leaders keen on war are always going to exaggerate the evil of their enemies to justify their war-mongering and to rally their people. Maybe there is, in reality, no regime that can be so evil that it is less evil to fight against them. By falling for the myth that some regimes are so evil that nations must fight them in the face of a supreme emergency, it might be thought that I am opening the door to the abuse of the concept to justify wars that should not be fought.

Since I use virtue ethics, not utilitarianism, as my approach to the ethics of war, I do not assume that we can quantify and compare evils. This deprives me of the most direct way of refuting the pacifist. My answer involves making two points. First, it is more controversial to say that we are better off letting Hitler have his way than to say that we are better off fighting him and the Nazis. Not only does this place the burden of proof on the pacifist, but the fact that the greater evil of Hitler's regime is generally recognized by people regardless of their moral beliefs (with the exception of pacifist beliefs) provides all the proof we need that it is not a mistake to think so.[19] What reason do we have for thinking that a vast majority of people is mistaken about Hitler's evil, and what explanation can we give for an error on this scale? I do not see any.

My second point is to refute a further argument the pacifist may be making in denying supreme emergencies. She may be saying that it is always, in principle, possible to deal with any evil, even that of Hitler's regime, without going to war. It is not that we are mistaken about Hitler before and during the Second World War. It is rather that the multilateral institutions we now have would have succeeded in dealing with Hitler had they been in place at the time. And now that we do have such institutions, it is a mistake to rely on the Hitler example to guide our thinking about war. There is some truth to the idea that the

institutions set up after the Second World War to improve global security and cooperation have made the world safer today than it used to be.
That partly explains why since 1945, Western European countries, for
instance, have been able to reduce the size of their armed forces and
some of their people would even like to completely disarm.[20] It also
explains why so many small countries in the world, including Costa
Rica which has no army, have remained unmolested, despite their
inability to mount a full defense on their own should they be attacked.
As I mentioned in the last chapter, these countries may not even fear
attack by nuclear-armed superpowers. There is also a further truth in
the idea that political leaders who seek war often pretend that the world
is as insecure as it was hundreds or thousands of years ago, when there
were no international law and peacekeeping, and no organizations
to provide regional and global security.[21] So I grant that not only are
supreme emergencies rare but they are getting more rare, and that is a
good thing. And if it were possible that the global security apparatus
was so successful that we never had to worry about a Hitler-like evil
again, then it would be logical for the philosophy of co-existence to
converge with pacifism.

However, the international institutions that keep the peace nowadays
have done so with intermittent success and many failures. There is no
basis for extrapolating to the day when they achieve a hundred percent
success. And as contingent facts of history, the international cooperation we see today could well dissolve tomorrow. There is no inevitable
path toward greater security and peace. There is no reason to discard
the concept of supreme emergency from our theory, simply based on
hope and optimism. This is the basic flaw of the form of pacifism that I
oppose. Absolute pacifists are unrealistic and overly idealistic. The philosophy of co-existence, in accepting the possibility and even the reality
of supreme emergencies, is less rooted in myth than is pacifism. Not
only are the pacifists thinking about a utopian future, but they might
also be fantasizing about how Hitler could have been stopped without
war. It is not obvious that any international institution or global security organization could have done enough to reduce the evil of Hitler's
regime and to make war with Hitler the greater evil. And if they could
not have succeeded with Hitler, they might not succeed with a Hitler-
like regime that could arise in the future.

So, in conclusion, I would agree that in the present day, supreme
emergencies are rare and may be getting more rare, but they are real
possibilities that any ethics of war must take into account. The philosophy of co-existence does come close to pacifism. But in recognizing that

there have been, and might again be, supreme emergencies, my theory allows for the rightness of going to war against Hitler-like enemies now and in the future. In this, it is a more realistic and practical ethics of war than is absolute pacifism. Yet it is not the same supreme emergency thesis that I hold as that found in Walzer's just war theory. War in supreme emergency is not a "no holds barred" war, and deliberate attacks on noncombatants are not morally acceptable. And, in the majority of cases that are not supreme emergencies, the philosophy of co-existence does not hold war to be an acceptable choice at all. There is no room for the sanitized wars that just war theorists permit when it is not a supreme emergency scenario.

Providing guidance on war

I turn, finally, to the one thing that probably makes the philosophy of co-existence hard to accept. It has a characteristic that has been considered a fault of virtue ethics when it comes to providing practical guidance in decision-making: the lack of a clear procedure that could be followed by anyone to arrive at the right answers when making moral choices, especially difficult ones. For this reason, virtue ethics has not had much appeal among applied ethicists, for instance those doing medical ethics. We want an ethics of war to show us how to make the world better. But if our ethics of war does not show us how to choose correctly, what advice might we give to political and military leaders to improve their behavior?

Here, just war theory seems to have an apparent advantage. (Pacifists do not need a decision-procedure, since they consider all use of force to be wrong. They do not have to decide whether and how to fight a war.) The just war criteria provide a set of necessary conditions for justice in going to war and another set for justice in fighting a war. I have argued that these conditions are, in fact, deficient. They are vague in application and they do not capture or give sufficient weight to all that matters in moral choices about war. So, in truth, when asked for advice, just war theorists only provide ambiguous answers or wrong answers. But can we do better? At least the just war theorist ameliorates the evil of war. The worry is that if we discard just war theory, we have nothing to replace it with, except pacifism (an unrealistic moral theory) and realism (no morality in war at all).

Is the philosophy of co-existence suited to replace just war theory as an ethics of war? I have been presenting its strengths as I explained my theory in this book. Here, I shall say something in response to its alleged

184 Beyond Just War: A Virtue Ethics Approach

weakness. The practical contribution of the philosophy of co-existence is that it holds a virtuous political leader to be the criterion for correct moral choices about war.[22] The problems with this statement are that first, we might not agree or be able to identify who is a virtuous leader, and second, what the virtuous leader does might not always be right. The solution to these problems seems to require that we have a prior way of deciding what the right thing to do is. If we do, then we can identify the virtuous leader as the one who usually does the right thing, and we can recognize when she fails to do the right thing. Since virtue ethics does not provide a criterion for right action that is independent of the concept of a virtuous person, it seems unable to avoid the above problems when challenged to provide practical guidance.

But this objection to the philosophy of co-existence flies in the face of the practical application of my theory to the problems of humanitarian intervention, terrorism, weapons of mass destruction, and preventive war discussed in Chapter 7. My answers on these issues may not be fully determinate and may leave room for hard cases. But I would argue that other moral theories that provide precision and dismiss the possibility of dilemmas are theories that fail to do justice to the complexity of real world moral problems. Their determinate decision procedures succeed at the cost of ignoring morally relevant considerations that complicate the choices we make in real life. My criticisms of just war theory illustrate this point. Besides the fact that the conditions for just war are a lot more vague and imprecise than those who use the theory have been willing to admit, the satisfaction of these conditions does not fully or properly take into account the evils of war and what war does to people on all sides. Taking these evils into account (in a non-utilitarian way) introduces complexities that make moral decisions about war into very hard cases. It is far better for a moral theory to allow for hard cases than to deny or oversimplify them.[23]

But even the less than determinate answers I have given may invite the suspicion that I have smuggled in some assumptions about right action that enable me to make practical recommendations. This suspicion is bolstered by the fact that I did not try to provide an account of what a virtuous person's character is like. I have not done so because such an account is part of a complete theory of virtue ethics that many moral philosophers have explored and answered in different ways. To fully discuss theoretical issues in this book would go beyond its scope and take up too much space. What could be considered an assumption here is that I have discussed what a virtuous political leader would do by making use of the idea that *a virtuous person has a strong disposition not to engage in the killing of human beings.* This is one thing about the character of a virtuous person that I felt could be stated without having a full account of what a good person is. This claim about the virtuous disposition has provided me with a direct way to say something about moral choices in war that did not require me to resolve theoretical issues in virtue ethics. The status of the claim rests on an appeal to intuition. I think that intuitive support can be found by comparing two people.[24] Give the first person *P*, but not the second person *Q*, a strong disposition not to engage in the killing of human beings. Then give *Q* any other disposition that are candidates for virtue, and deprive *P* of that disposition. Keep every other state of character possessed by *P* and *Q* the same. My intuition is that whatever the disposition that *Q* has and *P* lacks, we would still judge *P* to have at least as good a character as *Q* and, in many cases, a better character. If readers share my intuition, there is reason for them to agree with me that the disposition not to engage in the killing of human beings is central to virtuous character and that it is legitimate for me to assume that the virtuous political leader would have this disposition.

There is a further practical recommendation that can be drawn from the philosophy of co-existence. This concerns the kind of leader that we should have. Because the virtue ethics approach of the philosophy of co-existence is one that does not appeal to general rules to decide what to do, it is crucial that the people who make the decisions have the right character. Decisions must be made about whether war is less evil than the evil that it prevents, whether it is not more evil to intervene in another country to save its people from oppression, and whether the evil of deterrence should be chosen to deal with a nuclear-armed enemy. The right decision is the one that a political leader with practical wisdom would make. If the leader is virtuous, then she can be relied upon to make the correct decisions about war. In practice, this means that leaders should be chosen based on their character and experience, not on what they promise to do.

In the United States, respondents in opinion polls claim that the moral character of a candidate for political office is important in choosing for whom to vote. But this is often confused with two other things, namely a candidate's religious beliefs and likeability. Philosophers have long pointed out that although some moral theories see religion as a basis for morality, there is no necessary connection, and the concepts of religion and morality are quite different. And it is not really any reflection or sign of a person's moral character whether they would be fun to have a drink with or to party with. Sometimes, a person's character is not known until they are tested. But in virtue ethics, a good person acquires the ability to judge well by having the experience of making the right choices and through exposure to the kinds of situation where moral judgment is called for. Unfortunately, such factors have often been disregarded by voters in democracies. It is also not a good thing that politicians get elected because they promise to do certain things that reflect what the people want. The majority of people may not have the practical wisdom to decide on the right thing to do, and their leaders are supposed to have superior expertise and knowledge to make the decisions when they are in office. It makes little sense for candidates to promise in advance that they will defend the country in a certain way if elected. But if they have good character, we can count on them to make the right decisions later.

The fact that the democratic process of choosing leaders in the United States does not ensure that the ones elected are of virtuous character might help to explain why the country has many a times made the wrong decisions on war. The simplistic notion that democracies are less likely to either go to war by choice or violate the rules of war has been contradicted time and again in American history – the wars in Vietnam and Iraq being two of the more recent examples. The response of just war theorists has been either to call for more training in the rules of war for military leaders, or to point to special or new circumstances that require an adjustment to their theories to accommodate them. Besides all the points I have made in arguing for a shift in paradigm away from the tradition of just war thinking in this book, I can add this one. The philosophy of co-existence can explain how we have not been getting it right on the ethics of war and it can provide practical recommendations on how we can do better. Far from the virtue ethics approach lacking practical use, I have provided an account of how to apply the approach to the difficult subject of war. The philosophy of co-existence is a new ethics of war that has not before been applied to the problems of war. We will have to see if it really does a good job when it is put into practice. But it is yet another myth to think that the just war theory is more practical because it provides rules and conditions for just war. Its application across more than two thousand years of history shows it to be severely deficient in theory and in practice. Those who adhere to the theory because it seemed to be the only ethics of war that avoided the extremes of realism and pacifism should think again now that there is a new ethics of war in the form of the philosophy of co-existence that I have presented in this book.

Notes

Introduction: The State of Ethics of War

1. It was released in the form of the National Security Strategy (NSS) of the U.S. in September 2002.
2. I will discuss the ethics of the GWOT and the killing of Osama bin Laden by U.S. Navy SEALs during a raid in Pakistan in 2011 in Chapter 7 of this book.
3. For example, Mary Kaldor's thesis of "new wars" had influenced Paul Gilbert in his *New Terror, New Wars* (Washington, D.C.: Georgetown University Press, 2003). I examine the thesis in Chapter 6.
4. Among those taking a more traditionalist approach are George Weigel, James Turner Johnson and Joseph Boyle.
5. Andrew Fiala, *The Just War Myth: The Moral Illusions of War* (Lanham: Rowman & Littlefield, 2008).
6. *Philosophy* 78 (2003), p. 317.
7. *Humanity: A Moral History of the Twentieth Century* (New Haven: Yale University Press, 1999), p. 103.
8. Given the universalistic claims of theories in the just war tradition, any changes to just war theory are not taken as evidence for relativism but as improvements made in the light of additional moral knowledge.
9. Michael Walzer, *Just and Unjust Wars* (New York: Basic Books, 1977), chapter 16. There will be more discussion of supreme emergency in Chapter 8 of this book.

1 The Moral Problem of War

1. Well-known books on just war theory include A. J. Coates, *The Ethics of War* (Manchester: Manchester University Press, 1997), James Turner Johnson, *Morality and Contemporary Warfare* (New Haven: Yale University Press, 1999), and Michael Walzer, *Just and Unjust Wars* (New York: Basic Books, 1977).
2. The most relevant works on war of Marcus Tullius Cicero are *De Officiis* [On Duties] and *De Re Publica* [On the Commonwealth].
3. The Romans did not in practice follow such moral strictures in war, but they did have a college of priests called the fetials (*fetiales*) that functioned to oversee treaties and declarations of war in order to ensure the justice and legality of Roman wars in the pre-Imperial era.
4. Seneca wrote *De Clementia* [On Mercy] and dedicated it to Nero.
5. The Romans were reported to have had the notion that they gained their huge empire entirely on the basis of defensive wars.
6. He actually took the trouble to write an account of the Gallic Wars, in which he offered justifications for his military campaigns in order to satisfy a Roman Senate that took pride in Rome's observance of rules of war that were rooted in universal laws of nature. See Julius Caesar, *The Gallic War* (Cambridge, Mass.: Harvard University Press, 1952).

7. Roland H. Bainton, *Christian Attitudes toward War and Peace* (New York: Abingdon Press, 1960), p. 71.
8. Frederick H. Russell, *The Just War in the Middle Ages* (Cambridge: Cambridge University Press, 1975), p. 17.
9. Augustine, *The City of God*, Book 19, chapter 12.
10. R. Hartigan, "Saint Augustine on War and Killing: The Problem of the Innocent," *Journal of the History of Ideas* 27 (1966), p. 201.
11. Russell, *The Just War in the Middle Ages*, p. 26.
12. See ibid., pp. 57 ff., for a discussion of Gratian's Causa 23.
13. Aquinas's discussion of killing in self-defense in *Summa Theologica* II-II, q. 64, art. 7, resp., is thought to be the first statement of the doctrine of double effect in natural law ethics. Whether or not the attribution is correct, this doctrine evolved into an important part of the just war account of non-combatant immunity.
14. Russell, *The Just War in the Middle Ages*, p. 275.
15. As noted earlier, the concept of last resort and the use of arbitration was part of the Roman institution of fetials. Suarez is responsible not for inventing the concept but for bringing it back into prominence in just war thinking.
16. *On the Law of War*, Book I, chapter 14.
17. This differs from modern laws of war that presume the moral equality of combatants on both sides, holding them responsible for their conduct in war but not for the justice of the war.
18. However, from the point of view of external justice, the killing of prisoners may be carried out even though it was a violation of natural law. There is a tension here between Grotius's appeal to natural law and his foreshadowing of some modern ideas of jurisprudence.
19. Hobbes, in his *Leviathan*, famously portrayed the state of nature (before society is formed) as a state of war in which every human being has the right to do whatever he deems necessary for his self-preservation.
20. *On War*, Book I, chapter 1, Section 24.
21. Besides his *Morality and Contemporary Warfare* mentioned in Note 1, Johnson has numerous other writings on just war, including *Just War Tradition and the Restraint of War* (Princeton: Princeton University Press, 1981).
22. James Turner Johnson, *The War to Oust Saddam Hussein: Just War and the New Face of Conflict* (Lanham: Rowman & Littlefield, 2005), pp. 36–7.
23. George Weigel, "The Just War Tradition and the World after September 11," *Logos: A Journal of Catholic Thought and Culture* 5 (2002), pp. 22–6, made similar criticisms of the Catholic bishops.
24. As this book was being prepared for publication, I read Michael L. Gross, *Moral Dilemmas of Modern War* (New York: Cambridge University Press, 2010), who argues that laws and conventions of war must be adapted into new norms to meet the changing demands of asymmetric conflict.

2   Just War Reconsidered

1. In Chapter 1, I described the principles that featured in the history of just war theories that together form a common tradition of moral thinking about war in Western philosophy and moral theology.

2. David Rodin, *War and Self-Defense* (Oxford: Clarendon Press, 2002).
3. For another, Rodin continues to engage in discussions of the principles of just war theory in many of his other writings.
4. Besides the fact that it is sufficient for me to reject any one or more of the necessary conditions for *jus ad bellum*, I do not take on the right intention principle here because something like it is found in the idea of choosing to act from the right desires that is central to the virtue ethics approach that I shall present later.
5. The Principle of Discrimination requires that there be some way to decide who counts as a noncombatant, and different proposals have been presented about how this can be done in a way that supports the moral distinction between combatants and noncombatants. I use here the "chain of agency" criterion from Jeffrie Murphy, "The Killing of the Innocent" in *War, Morality, and the Military Profession*, ed. Malham M. Wakin (Boulder: Westview Press, 1979) p. 346. The meaning of innocence in war as it applies to noncombatants has been usefully discussed by Thomas Nagel, "War and Massacre," *Philosophy and Public Affairs* 1 (1972), pp. 123–44.
6. *Summa Theologica* II-II, q. 64, art. 7, resp.
7. Many recent articles on the doctrine are found in *The Doctrine of Double Effect*, ed. P. A. Woodward (Notre Dame: University of Notre Dame Press, 2001). I have discussed many of these interpretations in "Intention and Responsibility in Double Effect Cases," *Ethical Theory and Moral Practice* 3 (2000), pp. 405–34.
8. G. E. M. Anscombe, "War and Murder" in *The Collected Philosophical Papers of G.E.M. Anscombe, Vol. 3* (Minneapolis: University of Minnesota Press, 1981), pp. 51–61.
9. My paper, "Intention and Responsibility in Double Effect Cases," op. cit., describes many of the main problems for the DDE and suggests that the DDE in the form that it is used nowadays does not work. (In fact, I am writing this book with the goal of replacing the deontological basis of just war theory with a virtue ethics account in a way that mirrors my earlier work on the DDE which sought to overthrow the view that it is a deontological constraint in favor of a virtue ethics version.)
10. This assumption is made here to discount the cases where failure to apply the principle of discrimination and other requirements of just war is due to ignorance or indiscipline. I make the assumption to show that, even in the best case, the principle of discrimination does not do what it is supposed to do as a *jus in bello* requirement. I do not deny that, in reality, the conventions that govern conduct in war have often failed to protect civilians because many countries do not care or soldiers deliberately choose to violate the rules.
11. See Tibbets obituary in *The New York Times* at www.nytimes.com/2007/11/01/obituaries/01cnd-tibbets.html.
12. I do not take on the task of evaluating Truman's decision. Though the fact that the atomic bombing was carried out as a terror bombing is not in dispute, historians disagree about the reasons for Truman's decision and many Americans think that it is justified by military necessity or utilitarian reasons. Michael Walzer, *Just and Unjust Wars* (New York: Basic Books, 1977), pp. 263–8, takes a critical view of the use of the atomic bomb on Japan.

13. Walzer, ibid., pp. 154–5, uses this example as reported by a British journalist in discussing the doctrine of double effect. It illustrates a choice that is all too common in modern warfare from Vietnam to Iraq.
14. It is now a commonplace in war for troops to open fire in densely populated areas of a town or city, or for missiles and bombs to be dropped on such areas. But attacking civilians was also part of the conduct of war in ancient or medieval siege warfare. My point is that the invention of the DDE makes little difference.
15. The reasoning that led him to prefer the course of action that involves killing civilians is prudential reasoning. My point here is that there is no conflict between prudential reasoning and the requirements of morality only if the agent already has a reason to do the morally right thing, as would be the case if he finds the killing of civilians morally repugnant and does not want to do it, and he values doing the morally right thing more than he values achieving his military objective.
16. G. E. M. Anscombe, "War and Murder," pp. 58–9.
17. Jonathan Bennett, "Morality and Consequences" in the *1980 Tanner Lectures on Human Values*, ed. S. McMurrin (Salt Lake City: University of Utah Press, 1981), pp. 45–116, points out that a terror bomber needs only to intend that the civilians seem dead in order to achieve his goal of demoralizing the enemy, so their actual deaths are unintended side-effects of the actions needed to make them seem dead.
18. In a modern army like that of the United States, the training that makes soldiers follow orders does not deprive them of the ability to think and choose. What it does is to get soldiers to identify with the values of the unit, so that they have no reason to oppose or disobey orders unless they think their superiors are violating those values. Thus, I am not saying that soldiers are being turned into mindless machines.
19. Kateri Carmola, "The Concept of Proportionality: Old Questions and New Ambiguities" in *Just War Theory: A Reappraisal*, ed. Mark Evans (New York: Palgrave Macmillan, 2005), p. 96, traces the idea of proportionality all the way back to Aristotle's account of justice.
20. Carl von Clausewitz, *On War*, chapter 1, section 3.
21. Carmola, "The Concept of Proportionality," documents statements by a prosecutor at the International Criminal Tribunal and by US Secretary of Defense, Donald Rumsfeld, expressing bewilderment about what the standard for proportionality is or should be.
22. I set aside the more recent introduction of *jus post bellum* as a third component of just war theory.
23. This statement of *in bello* proportionality and the previous statement of *ad bellum* proportionality follow those in Thomas Hurka, "Proportionality in the Morality of War," *Philosophy and Public Affairs* 33 (2005), pp. 35–6. Hurka points out that his *in bello* principle is reflected in the 1977 Additional Protocol I to the Geneva Convention.
24. This version is used by Paul Ramsey in *War and the Christian Conscience* (Durham, NC: Duke University Press, 1961).
25. This is the proportionality criterion in *The Challenge of Peace*, a pastoral letter issued by the American National Conference of Catholic Bishops in 1983.

26. John Rawls, *A Theory of Justice* (Cambridge, Mass.: Harvard University Press, 1971), p. 379.
27. Hurka, "Proportionality in the Morality of War," pp. 57–66, provides an excellent discussion of the question of comparing lives.
28. Walzer, *Just and Unjust Wars*, chapter 16. The supreme emergency exemption has been the subject of much discussion among recent just war theorists and I will comment in more detail in Chapter 8.
29. I will be discussing the United States's Global War on Terror in Chapter 7.
30. For critical discussion, see Jeff McMahan, "On the Moral Equality of Combatants," *Journal of Political Philosophy* 14 (2006), pp. 377–93.
31. Michael Ignatieff, "Annals of Diplomacy: Balkan Physics," *New Yorker* (May 10, 1999), p. 79. In fact, there were incidents where they mistook civilians for Serbian troops.
32. The estimates were made by independent groups as the US military did not count the number of Iraqi civilian dead. The PBS Frontline documentary on *The Invasion of Iraq* released in 2004 includes a website that examines the civilian casualty numbers at www.pbs.org/wgbh/pages/frontline/shows/invasion/.
33. Gary D. Brown, "Proportionality and Just War," *Journal of Military Ethics* 2 (2003), p. 181, criticizes James Turner Johnson for an incorrect reading of proportionality and asserts that "a weak formation of enemy troops is not protected from a stronger enemy force merely because of its impotence."
34. Hurka, op. cit., pp. 63–6, discusses this trade-off and concludes that "any act that kills significantly more civilians than it saves soldiers is morally impermissible."
35. *Just and Unjust Wars*, pp. 89 & 96.
36. *War and Self-Defense*, pp. 1–2. Rodin's book on national self-defense provides the basis of my critique of just cause in what follows.
37. Humanitarian intervention and pre-emption have very recently been discussed as just causes by just war theorists. I will examine these topics in Chapter 7. I will note here that many of those who advocate these two kinds of war also think that the appropriate agency to execute them is an international institution.
38. *War and Self-Defense*, p. 162.
39. Ibid., p. 127.
40. Ibid., p. 130. As Rodin explains it, if the citizens of State *A* were under attack by State *B*, State *C* may intervene to protect *A*'s citizens, who have the right of self-defense, but this is true even when State *A* and State *B* are the same, that is, in the case of humanitarian intervention.
41. Ibid., p. 154.
42. Ibid., p. 155.
43. Rodin is making use of Michael Walzer's view here.
44. I have noted earlier in this chapter the difficulty of deciding whether Rodin is revising the just war theory or replacing it with a view that does not fit into the tradition of just war thinking.
45. I will provide more arguments for my concept of war in Chapter 6 when I examine the attempts to distinguish "old wars" and "new wars" in recent discussions of terrorism and humanitarian interventions.
46. This issue came up in the prelude to the invasion of Iraq by the United States in 2003. While critics objected that the United States had not given enough

time for a peaceful resolution to the dispute about Iraqi WMDs that could have been pursued through UN weapons inspections, the Bush administration claimed that delay in using military force would only replicate the appeasement policies of British Prime Minister Chamberlain in the face of Hitler's aggression against its neighbors.

47. This is the view of traditionalists such as James Turner Johnson in *The War to Oust Saddam Hussein: Just War and the New Face of Conflict* (Lanham: Rowman & Littlefield, 2005), pp. 36–7, who views the principles of last resort, proportionality and likelihood of success as prudential criteria of *jus ad bellum* to be distinguished from the traditional deontological criteria provided by the principles of legitimate authority, just cause and right intention (and the aim of peace) that were in Augustine's just war theory.

48. John Howard Yoder, "When War is Unjust: Being Honest in Just-War Thinking" in *The Morality of War*, ed. Larry May, Eric Rovie & Steve Viner (Upper Saddle River, NJ: Pearson Prentice Hall, 2006), p. 158.

3   From Rights to Virtues

1. Readers familiar with both theories and who do not need a review of concepts will not miss anything of crucial importance by skipping to the next chapter.

2. Most of the ideas for Kant's ethics can be found in the *Groundwork of the Metaphysic of Morals*, although Kant scholars also draw from his *The Metaphysics of Morals* (that includes the *Doctrine of Right* and the *Doctrine of Virtue*), *Religion within the Limits of Reason Alone* and *Critique of Practical Reason* for a deeper account that also connects Kant's ethics with his other philosophical ideas.

3. A hypothetical imperative commands the agent to do an action if he has a certain end, whereas a categorical imperative commands the agent to do an action without reference to his ends. Thus, the agent can opt out of doing what a hypothetical imperative commands by giving up on certain ends, but he cannot escape his duty to do what a categorical imperative commands.

4. Earlier forms of just war theory that were formulated by Christian moral theologians reflect a natural law ethics and not a deontological ethics. But natural law principles are also absolutist.

5. Their right to life is not necessarily forfeited, but they may be suspended while they serve in combat.

6. For an account of noncombatant immunity of this kind, see Thomas Nagel, "War and Massacre," *Philosophy and Public Affairs* 1 (1972), pp. 123–44.

7. One criticism of pacifism is that it does not take this point seriously.

8. There has been much discussion about the right to kill an innocent threat or an innocent bystander in self-defense. See for instance, Judith Jarvis Thomson, "Self-Defense," *Philosophy and Public Affairs* 20 (1991), pp. 283–310. And I raise the question about how uncertainty regarding the threat may affect the right of self-defense in "Self-Defense and Possible Threats" (unpublished manuscript).

9. This is the subject of David Rodin's book, *War and Self-Defense* (Oxford: Clarendon Press, 2002), which I discussed and used in the last chapter.
10. This rights-based account of just war is found in David Luban, "Just War and Human Rights," *Philosophy and Public Affairs* 9 (1980), pp. 160–81. Luban uses the account to justify humanitarian interventions.
11. In the next chapter, such harm and suffering, if intolerable, are part and parcel of the definition of evil that I apply to war.
12. Critics such as Bernard Williams, *Morality: An Introduction to Ethics* (New York: Harper & Row, 1972), pp. 73–4, point out that many activities that are distinctive of humans compared to other species are not morally good, including the destructive activities of war, weapons design and environmental denigration.
13. Philippa Foot, *Natural Goodness* (Oxford: Oxford University Press, 2001).
14. Martha C. Nussbaum, "Non-Relative Virtues: An Aristotelian Approach" in *Midwest Studies in Philosophy*, Vol. 13, ed. Peter A. French, Theodore E. Uehling, Jr. & Howard K. Wettstein (Notre Dame: University of Notre Dame Press, 1988), pp. 32–53.

4   War as an Evil

1. For instance, the Italian jurist Alberico Gentili writes in *De Jure Belli* (1598) that "wars are just even though so many things which come from them are evil, because their final aim is good." The Spanish Jesuit priest Francisco Suarez writes in his Disputation XIII on War (c. 1610) that "war, absolutely speaking, is not intrinsically evil, nor is it forbidden to Christians". Contemporary just war theorist James Turner Johnson in *The War to Oust Saddam Hussein* (Lanham: Rowman & Littlefield, 2005), pp. 27–33, concurs with Michael Walzer's conception of just war and criticizes the Conference of Catholic Bishops for "cast[ing] the just war idea as beginning with a general presumption against war."
2. Claudia Card, *The Atrocity Paradigm: A Theory of Evil* (New York: Oxford University Press, 2002), p. 7.
3. In Chapter 3, I have connected the rights-based accounts of recent just war theories and international humanitarian law with a deontological ethics derived from Kant. In *Humanity: A Moral History of the Twentieth Century* (New Haven: Yale University Press, 1999), p. 103, Jonathan Glover laments the failure of philosophy to make a serious impact on the thinking of the wider community on matters related to the wars of the twentieth century.
4. Card, *The Atrocity Paradigm*, p. 3. John Kekes, *The Roots of Evil* (Ithaca: Cornell University Press, 2005), offers a similar definition of evil as serious excessive harm caused by the actions of agents with malevolent motivations who lack morally acceptable excuse for these actions.
5. Note that culpability for wrongdoing does not require that the agents who bear some responsibility for the harm desire the harm or know that they will cause harm or even be the ones who bring about the harm. Thus, in describing the evils of war later on, I focus more on the intolerable harms than on identifying the evil agency behind the harms. However, these evils

would not have happened without some agency, whatever the motives of the agents may be. Since wars are not natural disasters, there will be culpability even if it is difficult to pinpoint the persons who are culpable, given the complexity of war.

6. Here I diverge from Card's account on the basis of my own work on intention and desire. Card thinks that persistent evil intentions can make someone an evil person. I believe that intentions do not reflect on a person's character in the way that intrinsic desires do. The objects of intrinsic desires are the ends that are pursued for their own sake and thus the motive for which a person acts. Intentions concern means to the desired ends, which need not be desired. Intentions are subject to norms of rationality, not morality. This distinction between intention and desire plays a role in my account of how a good leader can choose war.

7. Kekes, *The Roots of Evil.*

8. *Eichmann in Jerusalem* (New York: Penguin, 1965).

9. Card, *The Atrocity Paradigm,* p. 15.

10. William Styron, *Sophie's Choice* (New York: Random House, 1979).

11. Card, *The Atrocity Paradigm,* p. 57.

12. Antony Beevor, *D-Day: The Battle for Normandy* (New York: Viking, 2009).

13. Card, *The Atrocity Paradigm,* p. 82.

14. The sequence of events leading to the First World War is detailed in Glover, *Humanity,* chapter 21.

15. Although the doctrine originated in the natural law ethics of Aquinas, its recent use has been in the form of a deontological constraint. Warren Quinn, "Actions, Intentions, and Consequences: The Doctrine of Double Effect" in *Morality and Action* (Cambridge: Cambridge University Press, 1993), pp. 175–97, attributes a Kantian rationale for the doctrine.

16. In early human history, before the use of standing armies to fulfill the political aspirations of powerful rulers, "war" often took the form of raiding parties aimed at seizing crops and supplies without permanently occupying territory and avoiding violent confrontations, if possible. Apparently, this was the case in early Greece prior to the rise of Athenian and Spartan hegemony. Doyne Dawson, *The Origins of Western Warfare: Militarism and Morality in the Ancient World* (Boulder: Westview Press, 1996) describes fighting as taking place in a small window in the summer before the harvest, with citizen-soldiers returning to their farms when raiders had been driven off. In Chapter 2, I stated that I did not consider such fighting as the kind that should come under the concept of "war." I will say more on the subject in Chapter 6.

17. Primo Levi, *The Drowned and the Saved* (New York: Vintage, 1989), pp. 36–69.

18. I explain in detail the lessons that can be learned about war, and the importance of Euripides as a moral thinker, in "How War Affects People: Lessons from Euripides," *Philosophy in the Contemporary World* 13 (2006), pp. 1–5. In that paper, I draw parallels with the 2003 US invasion of Iraq.

19. To take just one example, consider the following. During the First World War, soldiers were routinely sent out again and again in human waves from the trenches to assault the enemy, only to be mowed down mercilessly by enemy machine gun fire. Little territory or advantage was gained from

fighting in this way and after many months, the lines of the opposing sides hardly moved, despite the high casualty rate.
20. This was repeatedly stated by officials in the Bush administration. In speeches in the middle of 2002, both President George W. Bush and Vice-President Dick Cheney argued that the United States had to identify any threat and destroy it before it reaches US borders, and it had to "take the battle to the enemy."
21. Andrew Fiala, *The Just War Myth* (Lanham, Md.: Rowman & Littlefield, 2008).
22. Claudia Card has suggested to me that this is also how the ticking-bomb scenario is used to justify torture. The scenario requires conditions that are never satisfied in reality: that the person tortured can provide accurate information that will enable the bomb to be defused within a very short time and that torture is the only way to prevent a real and impending disaster. Although the scenario is unreal (existing only in the movies), it is discussed in the literature on torture as if it is a genuine possibility, creating a myth that some such scenarios do occur in real life so that some cases of torture are justified.
23. Compare how capital punishment has been administered by the judicial system. Despite the rules and safeguards, the bureaucratic way in which trials and sentencing has been carried out has enabled abuse and injustices. Studies of capital punishment in the United States and documented cases of exoneration have shown that lots of innocent people have been executed, and racism is pervasive in the use of the death penalty. See for instance Scott Phillips's study on racial disparities in capital punishment in the *Houston Law Review* (2008).
24. Carl von Clausewitz, *On War*, Book I, chapter 1; Michael Walzer, *Just and Unjust Wars* (New York: Basic Books, 1977), chapter 16.
25. Michael L. Gross, *Moral Dilemmas of Modern War* (New York: Cambridge University Press, 2010), disagrees because he takes the rules to depend on reciprocity and the violation of the rules by one side may prevent the other side from exercising its "right to a fighting chance." Gross also discusses my next point in this paragraph: precision weapons which are thought to ameliorate the risk of direct harm to civilians.

5 The Philosophy of Co-existence

1. I do not count it a war of choice if it is a supreme emergency where there is no alternative to war except total capitulation to an enemy with evil plans of genocide or enslavement of the people it defeats.
2. Carl von Clausewitz, *On War*, is the most well-known realist who wrote about war.
3. Absolute pacifism was the view of the early Christian Church. Many pacifists today are conditional pacifists, who object to all actual wars on the grounds that the conditions for just war are never satisfied.
4. For instance, the Romans returned to completely destroy Carthage in 146 BC after the latter had already been decisively defeated in 202 BC at the end of the Second Punic War, just in case Carthage became a threat again.

In the Third Punic War, most of the city's 500,000 people were slaughtered and the rest were sold into slavery after the city was burned and the ground sown with salt. This was but one example of the many preventive wars that the Romans fought on the pretext of possible hostilities against Rome.

5. Consider the criticisms in the 2008 American elections of Alaskan governor Sarah Palin for promoting wolf hunting in Alaska. I grant that some would dispute that attitudes toward the elimination of species have changed or that there is widespread agreement on the value of wildlife conservation. There are certainly those who would defend Palin and the hunting even of endangered species.

6. More information can be found at www.montereybayaquarium.org/cr/whiteshark.asp.

7. The use of force to deal with human threats is also seen in the practice of domestic law enforcement, though such force is more restrained, as I will discuss later.

8. In fact, there are those who go so far as to permit war in order to punish unjust leaders of other states not only for waging war, but also for crimes against their own people or sins against God.

9. The first response is how the United States sees its relation with Iran and North Korea in the first decade of the twenty-first century (and with Iraq under Saddam Hussein prior to the 2003 invasion). The second response is how the United States dealt with the Soviet Union during the Cold War. I will discuss nuclear proliferation and nuclear deterrence in Chapter 7.

10. Thomas Hobbes, *Leviathan*, chapter 13, believed that a state of war of every human against every other is a natural state before the formation of human society, due to competition between humans. Peace can be achieved only by way of a social contract with mutually agreed laws and restrictions on the use of violence.

11. As Michael Walzer, *Just and Unjust Wars* (New York: Basic Books, 1977), p. 59, points out: "Every conflict threatens the structure as a whole with collapse. Aggression challenges it directly and is much more dangerous than domestic crime, because there are no policemen."

12. My domestic analogy differs from Walzer's, which is about how states are like persons in having rights.

13. Thanks to Jeremy Wisnewski for suggesting that I mention this.

14. In Chapter 6, I say more about the importance of appealing, as we are doing in the ethics of war, to liberal democratic values in moral discussions of the use of violence by the state.

15. This is a well-known quote from Carl von Clausewitz, *On War*. Another realist, General William Tecumseh Sherman during the American Civil War simply declared that, "War is hell."

16. Former Vice-President Dick Cheney maintains that attacks were prevented and lives were saved by the "enhanced interrogation techniques" carried out by military intelligence and the CIA that were authorized by the Bush administration. Detractors have argued that these claims exaggerate the value of information that was extracted by torture and that the same information could have been obtained without coercion.

17. The "new war" thesis is discussed in Chapter 6 and the "War on Terror" in Chapter 7.

18. This objection to torture was presented by Claudia Card in her paper, "Ticking Bombs and Interrogations," presented at the Central Division APA Meeting in Chicago on April 28, 2006.

19. Thus, if the Bush administration had passed laws that enabled torture and wiretaps before carrying them out, public condemnation would not include the charge of creating an imperial presidency.

20. In other words, racial profiling is morally unacceptable and unjust in the eyes of many Americans.

21. Obviously, I have been assuming the moral legitimacy of liberal democratic values such as autonomy. In Chapter 6, I will undertake the task of defending my use of liberal democratic values in this argument. Here, I will just say that in making use of a domestic analogy, it makes no sense to draw lessons from a repressive regime to figure out how to respond to foreign enemies, since what such regimes do domestically is morally reprehensible. There is however room to dispute what the best liberal democratic values are.

22. In my paper, "How War Affects People: Lessons from Euripides," *Philosophy in the Contemporary World* 13 (Spring 2006), I compare the moral harm to the Greek warriors in the Trojan War with the American experience in Iraq.

23. In a paper, "Morality, Prudence, and the Limits of War Conventions," that I presented at the 2009 International Society for Military Ethics (ISME) Symposium, I argued that what the conventions of war create, once their conditions are satisfied, is the illusion of an entitlement to go to war and to take certain actions in war, including the killing of innocent people.

24. Thomas Nagel, "War and Massacre," *Philosophy and Public Affairs* 1 (1972), p. 139, whose definition has recently been endorsed by Jeff McMahan in "The Ethics of Killing in War," *Ethics* 114 (2004), p. 695.

25. In "Courage and Those Who Will Not Fight" (conference paper presented at Viterbo University, La Crosse, Wisconsin, on March 29, 2008 and available at www.viterbo.edu/ethics.aspx?id=33622), I pointed out that people in ancient Greece lived in greater danger than we do, as defeat would mean the massacre or enslavement of the entire population and the sacking of cities. Those who claim we now live in especially dangerous times and have no choice but to fight all enemies should be asked whether they would be safer in ancient times or the Middle Ages in Europe than they are now.

26. My view may seem to be pacifist, given that in every war, innocent people have been killed. But I do recognize the need to defend borders and that fighting cannot be avoided if negotiations fail. What I want to say is that since innocent lives are lost in war and the values of a liberal democracy are corrupted by war, war is an evil (in all the ways described earlier). As a means to protect the state and its people, war should not be a resort when there is some way to avert the threat from another state by non-violent means, even if the threat is not eliminated altogether and we have to live with some risk of attack in the future.

27. In "Ticking Bombs and Interrogations," Claudia Card concludes with the remark: "The question needs to be faced whether a nation that defends itself at the cost of torture is worth preserving." For me, the same question arises with regards to a nation that defends itself by fighting wars when

there are ways to co-exist with enemies without sending people out to kill and to die in war. Most Americans eventually realized that the war to oust Saddam Hussein was not worth the lives of the people killed. Yet at the time that President Obama took office, there were not many who thought similarly about intensifying the war in Afghanistan to get Osama bin Laden. Americans eventually grew weary of the war in Afghanistan as they did with the occupation of Iraq, but only after a huge human cost had been incurred with little to show for it.

28. Contrast this with Michael Walzer's version of just war theory in *Just and Unjust Wars*, pp. 255–63, where he uses the concept of a supreme emergency to permit terror bombing against Nazi Germany when Britain was on the verge of defeat before the United States entered the war. I will say more on supreme emergencies in Chapter 8.

29. In World War Two, the Allies sought to occupy Germany and remove Hitler's regime, not just to weaken Germany and force it out of occupied territories. Terror bombing of cities such as Dresden was carried out after the latter goals had already been achieved and, as Walzer noted, there was no supreme emergency.

30. In virtue ethics, the judgment of the practically wise (or *phronimos*) is not determined by a utilitarian calculation, nor is it a matter of following rules.

31. It may be objected that there are successful societies that brutalized humans, such as the Roman, Mongol, and Aztec empires. But these societies distinguish between citizens and the outsiders that they wage war on and abuse. They do not hold homicide in general to be acceptable. Moreover, few people today would suggest these societies as models for humanity to emulate.

32. I have argued in "Are There Extrinsic Desires?" *Nous* 38 (2004), pp. 326–50, that the concept of extrinsic desire is theoretically redundant and it should be replaced by the concept of intention. But this point does not affect what I am saying here.

33. In reality, there would be many more desires involved in moral reasoning, since a virtuous person would have many virtues of character. Other intrinsic desires that may be relevant are those that reflect the virtues of care and concern for loved ones, loyalty to her society, courage, and justice.

34. The Trolley Problem is the subject of many articles on killing and letting die, in particular Judith Thomson's "Killing, Letting Die, and the Trolley Problem" and "The Trolley Problem," both in *Rights, Restitution, and Risk*, ed. William Parent (Cambridge, Mass.: Harvard University Press, 1986). The scenario is that of a runaway trolley on course to kill five people on the track who could be saved only if the trolley was diverted to a side track, where only one person would be killed. The passenger on the trolley has to make the choice of either letting the five die by doing nothing or switching the trolley onto the side track, thereby saving five lives but killing one.

35. Bear in mind that this is a tragic choice and the virtuous agent would not see the killing as a pain-free or easy choice. Her failure to live by her desire not to kill will do some damage to the goodness of her life, even if it is the right choice in the circumstances.

36. I argue for this in "A Reappraisal of the Doctrine of Doing and Allowing" in *Action, Ethics, and Responsibility*, ed. Joseph Keim Campbell, Michael

O'Rourke & Harry S. Silverstein (Cambridge, Mass.: The MIT Press, 2010), pp. 25–45.

37. Since I am concerned with whether a virtuous political leader would choose to fight a war against Hitler and the Nazis, I leave out from this discussion the Pacific War against Imperial Japan.

38. Carl Lesnor, "The 'Good' War," *The Philosophical Forum* 36: 1 (Spring 2005), pp. 77–85, makes the point that in every war since the Second World War, the West has sought out Hitler clones to repeat the justification for the "Good" War.

39. The Bush doctrine of preventive war that the US administration applied in invading Iraq is discussed in Chapter 7.

40. On tragic choices, see Martha C. Nussbaum, *The Fragility of Goodness* (Cambridge: Cambridge University Press, 1986).

41. Bear in mind that the judgment about which is the lesser evil is not based on measurements and calculations, as there are too many incommensurable goods for comparisons to take place. That is why not just anyone, but a virtuous person, is needed to make the judgment correctly. For those who are skeptical about the possibility of using reason to make a non-comparative judgment, I have a response to them in "Reasoning without Comparing," *American Philosophical Quarterly* 47 (2010), pp. 153–64.

42. This is where a virtue ethicist differs from a Kantian deontologist. The latter would hold that moral goodness and the intrinsic worth of a person is unaffected by the consequences of her choice and determined only by what she wills or intends.

43. An example of the sacrifice involved in doing evil for a good purpose is the story of Christian theologian Dietrich Bonhoeffer, who believed killing to be a sin but participated in the (unsuccessful) plot to kill Hitler. He fully recognized that he could face God's judgment for his sin, but believed it was the right thing to do.

6   Theoretical Implications and Challenges

1. Mary Kaldor, *New and Old Wars* (Cambridge: Polity Press, 1999) which influenced Paul Gilbert's philosophical response to the post 9/11 war on terror in *New Terror, New Wars* (Washington, DC: Georgetown University Press, 2003).

2. *New and Old Wars*, p. 73.

3. Ibid., p. 22.

4. Kaldor had first-hand experience of the conflict to draw on as a result of her extensive travels in the region as one of the chairs of the Helsinki Citizens' Assembly. In the second edition of her book (2006), Kaldor added a chapter that attempts to identify the features of new wars in the American-led invasion and occupation of Iraq that began in 2003.

5. *A History of Warfare* (Toronto: Key Porter Books, 1993), chapter 1.

6. Arther Ferrill, *The Origins of War: From the Stone Age to Alexander the Great* (London: Thames and Hudson, 1985), p. 11.

7. In contrast, the early forms of Greek "warfare" were apparently fought by citizen-farmers who took up arms when citizens of a neighboring state

encroached and tried to take their crops or burn them. The fighting stopped when the intruders were defeated or had withdrawn back to their farms at harvest time. See Doyne Dawson, *The Origins of Western Warfare* (Boulder, Colo.: Westview Press, 1996), p. 50.

8. The best examples of the power of religious ideology were the poor and unarmed peasants who followed Peter the Hermit to their deaths at the hands of the Turks in the People's Crusade that preceded the First (official) Crusade, led by kings and knights.

9. *New and Old Wars*, p. 42.

10. Kaldor actually makes a similar point in the process of defending her New War Thesis in "Elaborating the 'New War' Thesis," in *Rethinking the Nature of War*, ed. Isabelle Duyvesteyn & Jan Angstrom (London: Frank Cass, 2005), pp. 212–13, where she writes, "[T]he legitimizing discourse is important in the way that it influences how wars are fought... [T]he construction of nationalist or religious ideologies is a form of political mobilization." Where we differ is on whether a new ideology thesis would entail a new war thesis. It would not, if my view is correct on what war essentially is.

11. This was true of the Romans, whose empire was limited by empty deserts and oceans, and whose people chose to have mercenaries do the fighting for them.

12. It is possible to use this line of reasoning to explain the spread of liberal democratic values around the world toward the end of the twentieth century, although there are other explanations, such as American economic and cultural success, and the process of globalization that is breaking down cultural barriers. Perhaps there is something to the claim that the pursuit of peace has the universality of a natural law in the way that Hobbes suggested in *Leviathan*.

13. More details on British rule in India can be found in Barbara D. Metcalf & Thomas R. Metcalf, *A Concise History of Modern India*, 2nd edn (New York: Cambridge University Press, 2006).

14. For an account of how India gained independence from Britain without fighting a war of independence, see Larry Collins & Dominique Lapierre, *Freedom at Midnight* (New York: Simon & Schuster, 1975).

15. Arthur Herman, *Gandhi and Churchill* (London: Arrow Books, 2009), p. 445.

16. Ibid., p. 446.

17. I will discuss in the next chapter whether virtuous leaders should choose humanitarian interventions of the military kind.

18. This is actually an application of a point that Aristotle makes (although he does not make it in terms of social roles). In the *Nicomachean Ethics*, Aristotle says that the right thing to do is a mean between excess and deficiency, but it is a mean relative to us. He gives the example of how a certain amount of food may be enough for an ordinary person but insufficient for Milo, the professional wrestler.

19. See Michael Stocker, "Dirty Hands and Ordinary Life," in *Plural and Conflicting Values* (Oxford: Clarendon Press, 1990), pp. 9–36. Michael Walzer originally discussed the problem in "Political Action: The Problem of Dirty Hands," *Philosophy and Public Affairs* 2 (1973), pp. 160–80.

20. Walzer, *Just and Unjust Wars*, chapter 16. Although he does not describe it as a problem of dirty hands, Walzer implies it when he writes:

Can soldiers and statesmen override the rights of innocent people for the sake of their own political community? ... They might sacrifice themselves in order to uphold the moral law, but they cannot sacrifice their countrymen. ... the sense of obligation and moral urgency they are likely to feel at such a time is so overwhelming that a different outcome is hard to imagine. (p. 254)

21. Recall also David Rodin's argument presented in Chapter 2 that the appeal to self-defense by the state cannot be based on some idea of the communal life that needs to be protected rather than the impact on individual lives. Defeat in war may mean the replacement of one form of communal life with another and this need not prevent individuals from getting the communal goods they need to flourish.

22. There have been many examples in history where the winners in war have gone on to adopt many of the ideas and values of those that they conquered. Take, for instance, the Mongols, who were absorbed into the cultures of the people in China and Persia.

7 Practical Implications and Challenges

1. C. A. J. Coady, "The Ethics of Armed Humanitarian Intervention," *US Institute of Peace Policy Paper* (July 2002), begins his paper with a quotation from US President William McKinley. Others go further back to the "white man's burden" in colonial policy during the centuries of Western imperialism. In the previous chapter, I mentioned how President Abraham Lincoln could have argued for humanitarian intervention in the American South to end the mistreatment and abuse of African–Americans under slavery.

2. A good account of how the West viewed humanitarian intervention before and after 1992 is found in Clifford Orwin, "Humanitarian Military Intervention: Wars for the End of History?" *Social Philosophy and Policy* (2006), pp. 196–217.

3. The United Nations Charter does not permit war without UN authorization, except in self-defense.

4. Robert W. Hoag, "Violent Civil Disobedience: Defending Human Rights, Rethinking Just War" in *Rethinking the Just War Tradition*, ed. Michael W. Brough, John W. Lango & Harry van der Linden (Albany: State University of New York Press, 2007), p. 233.

5. Examples of the restatement of just war theory are found in Coady, op. cit., and George R. Lucas, Jr, "From *Jus ad Bellum* to *Jus ad Pacem*: Re-thinking Just-War Criteria for the Use of Military Force for Humanitarian Ends," in *Ethics and Foreign Intervention*, ed. Deen K. Chatterjee & Don E. Scheid (Cambridge: Cambridge University Press, 2003), pp. 72–96.

6. Rex Martin, "Just Wars and Humanitarian Interventions," *Journal of Social Philosophy* 36 (2005), pp. 439–56. Also using human rights as the basis for just war is David Luban who attempts, in "Just War and Human Rights," *Philosophy and Public Affairs* 9 (1980), pp. 160–81, to justify a much wider scope for humanitarian intervention than Walzer and Rawls do, by placing little weight on state sovereignty and communal self-determination (which I think would not count as "amending" the standard just war theory).

7. Michael Walzer, "The Politics of Rescue" in *Arguing About War* (New Haven: Yale University Press, 2004), p. 69.
8. John Rawls, *The Law of Peoples* (Cambridge, Mass.: Harvard University Press, 1999), p. 81.
9. Martin, "Just Wars and Humanitarian Interventions," p. 445.
10. The widespread violation of human rights that takes place around the world, including in the United States, has been repeatedly documented in reports by Amnesty International and Human Rights Watch.
11. The two problems are stated in Gillian Brock, "Humanitarian Intervention: Closing the Gap between Theory and Practice," *Journal of Applied Philosophy* 23 (2006), p. 278.
12. See Coady on the sovereignty debate and the theory of aggression, presented in "The Ethics of Armed Humanitarian Intervention."
13. The contrast between theory and the many risks, dangers, and imperfections of real-world humanitarian interventions are discussed in Richard W. Miller, "Respectable Oppressors, Hypocritical Liberators: Morality, Intervention, and Reality" in *Ethics and Foreign Intervention*, pp. 215–50.
14. Louis P. Pojman, "The Moral Response to Terrorism and Cosmopolitanism" in *Terrorism and International Justice*, ed. James P. Sterba (New York: Oxford University Press, 2003), p. 140.
15. The distinction between a primary and secondary target is found in Carl Wellman, "On Terrorism Itself," *Journal of Value Inquiry* (1979), pp. 250–8. These targets may be the same or distinct persons or groups, that is to say, the persons attacked may or may not be the same persons as those to whom the message is being sent.
16. I should clarify that I do not maintain that insurgents cannot be terrorists. If they are careful to target enemy troops and do not intend to kill civilians, they are not terrorists, even if they kill civilians. But if they intend to kill soldiers and civilians alike, they are likely to pick on civilians who are more vulnerable. Insurgents tend to use terrorism when they face a vastly superior enemy and are ill equipped to fight against military forces. My criticism of Pojman's definition is that in labeling it terrorism when horrific violence that inspires fear and panic is inflicted on *combatants*, he allows for discriminate insurgents and even regular troops to count as terrorists when they attack combatants.
17. Terrorists could also appeal to the doctrine of double effect to justify the killings of civilians, as just war theorists have sought to do for noncombatant deaths in war. I have already argued in Chapter 2 against the use of the doctrine to support the principle of discrimination in just war theory.
18. Although I do not accept the moral distinctions made using the doctrine of double effect, the doctrine clearly cannot render the atomic bombings permissible, as the evil act of killing civilians was intentional. Interestingly, James Sterba, "Terrorism and International Justice" in *Terrorism and International Justice*, p. 213, writes that the demand for unconditional surrender is not even a morally legitimate goal in war.
19. In Walzer's *Just and Unjust Wars*, exceptions to the rules of just war to directly attack civilians during "supreme emergencies" are allowed. This is a controversial weakening of a central rule of *jus in bello*, with the effect of also permitting terrorist acts by revolutionary and secessionist groups that

have no other way of fighting against a much superior enemy, such as the Palestinians using suicide bombings on Israel.

20. While it is true that the narrative of the Second World War and other wars are often matters of historical controversy, there will be few examples to discuss if we limit ourselves to undisputed ones. In the case of area bombing of cities in the Second World War, I follow the narrative from Jonathan Glover, *Humanity: A Moral History of the Twentieth Century* (New Haven: Yale University Press, 1999), pp. 69–73.

21. John Westlake, *International Law, Part II: War*, 2nd edn (Cambridge: Cambridge University Press, 1913), quoted by Richard W. Miller, "Terrorism, War, and Empire" in *Terrorism and International Justice*, ed. James P. Sterba (New York: Oxford University Press, 2003), p. 187.

22. Daniele Archibugi & Iris Marion Young, "Envisioning a Global Rule of Law" in *Terrorism and International Justice*, ed. James P. Sterba (New York: Oxford University Press, 2003), p. 161, write that "a genuinely global cooperative law enforcement response would be more effective in identifying and apprehending culprits, as well as preventing future attacks...than has the war against Afghanistan."

23. Other justifications from the Bush administration, such as Saddam Hussein's possession of weapons of mass destruction (to be discussed later in this chapter) and his regime's violation of human rights, as well as the goal of democratizing Iraq, do not provide a case for the invasion as part of the war on terrorism. In any case, these causes also rest on claims and predictions that were exaggerated, dubious, or outright false.

24. Richard W. Miller, "Terrorism, War, and Empire," p. 189, provides the numbers and sources.

25. Sources for estimates of civilian deaths are cited in the PBS Frontline documentary on *The Invasion of Iraq* broadcast in 2004. The United States has not attempted to count Iraqi civilian deaths.

26. Gilbert Burnham, Riyadh Lafta, Shannon Doocy, & Les Roberts, "Mortality after the 2003 Invasion of Iraq: A Cross-Sectional Cluster Sample Survey," *The Lancet* (October 2006), pp. 1–8. It is troubling that the US and UK governments decided not to track civilian deaths resulting from the invasions of Afghanistan and Iraq. Without doing so, how could the government leaders judge the wars to be proportionate as responses to terrorist attacks against the West by Al-Qaeda?

27. Interestingly, Joseph Boyle, who defends the American response to terrorism on the basis of just war theory in "Just War Doctrine and the Military Response to Terrorism," *The Journal of Political Philosophy* 11 (2003), pp. 153–70, passes over the *jus in bello* requirements without much discussion.

28. One method of isolating an unconventional enemy fighting a guerilla war that was tried in Malaya by the British and in Vietnam by the Americans is to move civilians into camps.

29. Evidently, the US and multilateral forces are viewed unfavorably by the majority of Afghans and Iraqis.

30. Michael L. Gross, "Assassination and Targeted Killing: Law Enforcement, Execution or Self-Defense?" *Journal of Applied Philosophy* 23 (2006), pp. 323–35.

31. Kateri Carmola, "The Concept of Proportionality: Old Questions and New Ambiguities," in *Just War Theory: A Reappraisal*, ed. Mark Evans (New York: Palgrave Macmillan, 2005), p. 108.
32. Ironically, as pointed out by Karsten J. Struhl, "Is War a Morally Legitimate Response to Terrorism?" *The Philosophical Forum* 36 (2005), p. 134, if the existing constraints of just war theory are discarded in fighting against terrorism, the United States itself becomes vulnerable to justified attack as a sponsor of terrorism, since it granted asylum in 1991 to the Cuban terrorist responsible for bombing a Cuban airliner in 1976.
33. Archibugi & Young, "Envisioning a Global Rule of Law" and Gross, "Assassination and Targeted Killing". Michael Walzer, "After 9/11: Five Questions about Terrorism," in *Arguing about War* (New Haven: Yale University Press, 2004), pp. 136–41, seems to advocate war in combination with police work and diplomacy. But he does not address the problem of the contradictory status of terrorists in war as opposed to law enforcement. I limit myself here to the two paradigms, as it seems to me that any other methods would involve elements of each.
34. Thomas Pogge, "Making War on Terrorists – Reflections on Harming the Innocent," *The Journal of Political Philosophy* 16 (2008), p. 1, compared the threats of disease and traffic accidents with post-9/11 terrorism, in terms of lives lost, to show the discrepancy.
35. Pogge, "Making War on Terrorists," p. 3, states that "our media and politicians are helping the terrorists achieve exactly what they want: attention and public fear."
36. In the philosophy of co-existence, war may not be morally right, even if another state threatened the United States.
37. Boyle, "Just War Doctrine and the Military Response to Terrorism," p. 165, who, unlike me, uses a war paradigm, also requires that "unjust policies that provoke terrorist responses" be changed not as a concession to terrorism but to meet the just war requirement of right intention. Refusal of a state to change its unjust policies that are obstacles to peace prevents it from going to war with the intention of achieving the proper goal of a just and lasting peace.
38. This is the thesis put forward by Samuel Huntington in "The Clash of Civilizations," *Foreign Affairs* (1993). Walzer, "After 9/11," p. 132, also prefers a cultural and religious explanation of terrorism.
39. For the view that US policy on the Israeli–Palestinian conflict, reflecting the power of the Israel lobby in America, is not only unjust but undermines US interests in the war on terrorism, see John J. Mearsheimer & Stephen M. Walt, "The Israel Lobby and US Foreign Policy," *London Review of Books* (2006).
40. I discuss the Huntington thesis in a paper, "The Myth of Religious War," that I presented as an Ethics Center Lecture at California State University–Fresno on February 2, 2009, and at the Institute for Research in the Humanities at the University of Wisconsin–Madison on March 2, 2009.
41. In fact, they are ultra-conservatives who oppose modernization and opportunities for women, so the justice they seek is not the social justice that the United States can bring about in the Muslim world. The mistake in the Huntington thesis is to assume that the ultra-conservative view is typical of Islam.

42. In comparing Muslim extremists with sociopaths and "nut cases," I do not mean that they are mentally unstable. What I do mean is that they are resistant to disagreeable facts and rational discourse, and they react violently to imaginary or exaggerated injustices. But it is possible that some of these characteristics have a psychological basis. These points apply not just to Muslims, but also to violent extremists of every stripe, such as both right-wing and left-wing extremists in America who have carried out terrorist acts. The fact that war has not been considered an appropriate response to domestic terrorists in America bolsters my case against waging war to deal with Al-Qaeda and other Islamic terrorists.
43. As C. A. J. Coady points out in "Natural Law and Weapons of Mass Destruction" in *Ethics and Weapons of Mass Destruction*, ed. Sohail H. Hashmi & Steven P. Lee (Cambridge: Cambridge University Press, 2004), pp. 118–19, machine guns could be employed as weapons of mass destruction but are not in themselves geared for such use, whereas WMDs such as nuclear bombs are such that "their normal use will rain death and destruction on the just and unjust, on civilians and troops, on hospitals and military installations alike."
44. Nuclear weapons are to conventional warfare what, in J. K. Rowling's Harry Potter books, the Golden Snitch is to the game of Quidditch played by the students at Hogwarts. The capture of the Golden Snitch is equal to 15 goals and ends the game at once, offsetting a team's inability to score goals.
45. Unfortunately, some countries, including the United States, have not fully complied in destroying these weapons. On the other hand, international opinion has successfully restrained the use of these weapons. Even Saddam Hussein did not use his chemical weapons in the First Gulf War in 1991 when faced with utter and overwhelming defeat by the US-led coalition to free Kuwait from Iraqi occupation.
46. This is the Paradox of Deterrence. As Walzer, *Just and Unjust Wars*, puts it, "our familiar notions about *jus in bello* require us to condemn even the threat to use them" (p. 282).
47. In addition, the United States did not renounce the first use of nuclear weapons in the event of a Soviet invasion of Western Europe using conventional forces.
48. "Natural Law and Weapons of Mass Destruction," p. 122.
49. *Just and Unjust Wars*, pp. 253–4.
50. "Liberalism: The Impossibility of Justifying Weapons of Mass Destruction" in *Ethics and Weapons of Mass Destruction*, p. 156.
51. Ibid.
52. "A Liberal Perspective on Deterrence and Proliferation of Weapons of Mass Destruction" in *Ethics and Weapons of Mass Destruction*, p. 164.
53. Ibid., p. 165.
54. Shue, "Liberalism: The Impossibility of Justifying Weapons of Mass Destruction," p. 157, writes that "nuclear forces are catastrophic accidents waiting to happen."
55. One possibility is to have the deterrence system automated without having the leader form an intention or make a decision. But the risks of such a system going awry are even greater. Wise practical judgment is needed to evaluate the appropriateness of launching nuclear weapons.

56. A nice discussion of how nuclear war was averted in the Cuban Missile Crisis is found in Glover, *Humanity*, chapter 22.
57. Contrary to Walzer's view that deterrence works because it is easily doable (*Just and Unjust Wars*, p. 271).
58. Throughout history, many have voiced the hope that as war became more catastrophic, fewer wars would be fought. That has not happened. What the philosophy of co-existence shows is that it would require virtuous leaders who take the evil of war into consideration to avoid wars that have become too terrible.
59. Walzer, *Just and Unjust Wars*, pp. 278–83, does a superb job demolishing Paul Ramsey's use of the Doctrine of Double Effect and other tools of just war theory to justify nuclear deterrence by distinguishing threatening from acting. But Walzer carves out the supreme emergency exemption for justifying the targeting and killing of innocents in exceptional circumstances. My point here is to reiterate that the circumstances that constitute supreme emergencies are extremely rare, despite what many political leaders (such as Churchill) may think. I will compare my view of supreme emergency with Walzer's in Chapter 8.
60. The philosophy of co-existence does not really justify the Soviet acquisition of nuclear weapons, as the United States was not a Hitler-like evil regime (though it may be, from the Soviet point of view). But the absence of other safeguards and protections for non-nuclear states makes the Soviet decision to go nuclear a more ethical choice than it is for non-nuclear states that decide to go nuclear in today's world.
61. Soviet leader Stalin may be an exception, and Stalinism is viewed by Walzer, "A Liberal Perspective on Deterrence and Proliferation of Weapons of Mass Destruction," p. 163, as an evil comparable to Nazism.
62. In Chapter 8, I will make the point that the virtue ethics approach of the philosophy of co-existence depends not on rules to ensure leaders do the right thing, but on the virtuous character of leaders.
63. This document was available on the White House website during the Bush administration.
64. The logic of preventive war is laid out in David Luban, "Preventive War and Human Rights," in *Preemption*, ed. Henry Shue & David Rodin (Oxford: Oxford University Press, 2007), pp. 188–90, with one difference in that he distinguishes between rogue states that are merely despotic and those that threaten their neighbors, that is, threat states. Although there is a conceptual difference, I think the Bush doctrine uses a state's domestic oppression as evidence of its disregard for international standards and the rule of law, as shown in the case the Bush administration made against Saddam's regime to justify the invasion of Iraq.
65. The "fixing" of intelligence to support the Iraq invasion was made public by the release of the Downing Street Memorandum that was reprinted in Mark Danner, "The Secret Way to War," *New York Review of Books* (June 9, 2005), p. 71.
66. *Just and Unjust Wars*, chapter 5. The Webster doctrine of 1842 refers to the argument condemning the British by US Secretary of State Daniel Webster in the case of the sinking of an American steamship, the *Caroline*, in US territorial waters by the British in 1837. The British justification was that

the ship had been used, and probably would again be used, to support a Canadian rebellion against the British.

67. Jeff McMahan, "Preventive War and the Killing of the Innocent," in *The Ethics of War: Shared Problems in Different Traditions*, ed. Richard Sorabji & David Rodin (Aldershot: Ashgate, 2006), p. 172.

68. Necessity, proportionality, and imminence are required for the right of self-defense, as noted by David Rodin, "The Problem with Prevention," in *Preemption*, p. 160.

69. This last resort argument could be used to help justify the Israeli attack in 1981 on the Osirak nuclear reactor in Iraq, and would also have applied to a preventive war against Saddam Hussein's regime in 2003 had the US intelligence reports about his nuclear capability been true, a point made by Henry Shue, "What Would a Justified Preventive Military Attack Look Like?" in *Preemption*, p. 228.

70. See, for instance, UN Secretary-General Kofi Annan's address to the United Nations General Assembly on September 23, 2003. If one side is prepared to wage preventive war, the other side is justified in attacking first, making war a self-fulfilling prophecy and producing a downward spiral into violence.

71. Rodin considers this possibility in "The Problem with Prevention," p. 157.

72. A multilateral accountability regime is discussed in Allen Buchanan, "Justifying Preventive War" in *Preemption*, and in other papers cited there that Buchanan has co-authored with Robert O. Keohane.

73. National Security Council, The National Security Strategy of the United States of America 2002, chapter V, available at http://georgewbush-whitehouse.archives.gov/nsc/nss/2002/.

74. Rodin, "The Problem with Prevention," p. 149.

75. Jeff McMahan, "Preventive War and the Killing of the Innocent," disagrees and invents a number of examples where individuals are justified in preventive killing of threats they have no way of defending against later or getting help to stop the threat. I think his examples ignore the epistemological problem about knowing if the threat is genuine and whether it can be avoided by other means. In any case, he accepts that the case does not transfer to preventive war because "the burden of justification for preventive war will in practice be very difficult – though not impossible – to meet" (p. 188). Thus, his view is the opposite of the one under discussion here.

76. Rodin, "The Problem with Prevention," pp. 164–5.

77. Luban, "Preventive War and Human Rights," p. 180, asserts that "even in a war fought on behalf of basic human rights, soldiers will knowingly kill innocent human beings to protect the rights of others no more innocent," and that only utopian pacifism can avoid such killings.

78. I have followed the essays by Buchanan, Rodin, and Luban in *Preemption* in making the points in this debate. I think Rodin makes a telling point in his remark that "a soldier sitting in his barracks or going on exercise while his leadership, largely unbeknown to him, plots an aggressive war has not engaged in any use of force at all, let alone an objectively unjust one" (p. 169).

79. This is clearly the case with Luban's view in "Preventive War and Human Rights," pp. 180–3, that the morality of war differs from the morality of peacetime and that what would otherwise be murder could be allowed in war.

80. This is almost true by definition, because a group with large numbers would be able to fight more effectively in open combat against the military forces of the state that they oppose. Terrorism is the tactic of the weak and terrorist groups do not have a good record of achieving their political objectives.
81. Many commentators have suggested that both Iran and North Korea pursued their nuclear programs because American threats against their leaderships had fostered an extreme sense of insecurity.
82. The Americans suspected that there were Al-Qaeda sympathizers and infiltrators in Pakistan's military and intelligence communities, and they feared that alerting Pakistan to the raid would jeopardize their mission.
83. The lack of success in capturing Osama bin Laden in Afghanistan makes the American military presence there difficult to justify, as it has imposed on the Afghan people the evils of war on a long-term basis. Now that bin Laden is dead (and found to have been in Pakistan since 2005 or earlier), the war in Afghanistan looks even more wrong than it did before. At the time of writing, the United States is scheduled to begin withdrawal in 2011, but whether any withdrawal is symbolic or substantive is not clear.
84. For instance, the Shoe-bomber, the Underwear Bomber, and the bombs sent by airfreight.
85. There have been questions asked about the possibility that Osama bin Laden was actually being provided with sanctuary and protection by the government of Pakistan, since his compound was a short distance away from Pakistan's military academy (its version of West Point).
86. This was reported in the PBS Frontline documentary on *The Invasion of Iraq* mentioned in note 25 above.
87. Philosophers will recognize this as a version of the much-discussed problem of moral luck.
88. I do not think there is comparable justification for a broader policy of using drone strikes against suspected terrorist leaders around the world, as the United States has been doing under President Obama.

8   Is War Ever Justified?

1. Michael Walzer, *Just and Unjust Wars* (New York: Basic Books, 1977), p. 254.
2. Walzer, "Emergency Ethics" in *Arguing About War* (New Haven: Yale University Press, 2004), p. 40.
3. *Just and Unjust Wars*, pp. 252–3.
4. Walzer, *Just and Unjust Wars*, p. 261, points out that the continuation of the air raids on German cities between 1942 and 1945 could not be justified by appeal to supreme emergency.
5. *Just and Unjust Wars*, p. 252; "Emergency Ethics," pp. 41–2.
6. "Emergency Ethics," p. 45.
7. Walzer first discussed this problem in his essay, "Political Action: The Problem of Dirty Hands," *Philosophy and Public Affairs* 2 (1973), pp. 160–80. See my discussion of the problem in Chapter 6.
8. Brian Orend, "Is There a Supreme Emergency Exemption?" in *Just War Theory: A Reappraisal*, ed. Mark Evans (New York: Palgrave Macmillan, 2005), p. 148.

9. The annihilation of Carthage illustrated this policy of destroying all enemies. Roman policy, of course, did not remain the same throughout the history of the empire, as it evolved into a policy of border defense and containment of enemy threats in the later period of the empire. There were also enemies who were not eliminated but were forced to pay tribute and contribute soldiers to Rome.

10. Walzer, *Just and Unjust Wars*, p. 253, described Nazism as "an ultimate threat to everything decent in our lives" and "evil objectified in the world."

11. Andrew Fiala, *The Just War Myth: The Moral Illusions of War* (Lanham: Rowman & Littlefield, 2008).

12. *Just and Unjust Wars*, p. 261.

13. In "Intention and Responsibility in Double Effect Cases," *Ethical Theory and Moral Practice* 3 (2000), pp. 405–34, I reject the use of the doctrine of double effect to "pretend" that evil effects that are foreseen with certainty are unintended and permitted. If the leader knows that by choosing war, innocent people will be killed in large numbers, then he intends to and is fully responsible (and blameworthy) for bringing about this evil effect of war.

14. Martin L. Cook, "Michael Walzer's Concept of 'Supreme Emergency'," *Journal of Military Ethics* 6 (2007), p. 142, makes similar points about the problem of "contrary-to-fact speculation about how the world might have evolved without area bombing of German cities." Orend, "Is There a Supreme Emergency Exemption?" p. 141, mentions that Britain "had the advantage of geography."

15. Walzer, "Emergency Ethics," p. 33, notes that "hard cases make bad law" but entirely hypothetical hard cases would make worse law.

16. The leader's choice of war can be compared with theologian and philosopher Dietrich Bonhoeffer's choice to participate in the political assassination of Hitler, which reflecting his views in his *Ethics*, was a sin for which he bore personal guilt and responsibility, even though it was done to stop evil.

17. Tragic heroes in Greek tragedy illustrate the appropriateness of paying for doing evils, even when the lesser evil is chosen. For instance, Agamemnon paid a price for choosing to sacrifice his daughter Iphigenia so that the Greek fleet could sail off to fight the Trojans, as commanded by Zeus. Thus, I disagree with Daniel Statman, "Moral Tragedies, Supreme Emergencies and National-Defense," *Journal of Applied Philosophy* 23 (2006), p. 314, who criticizes Orend by saying: "The fact that all available options are morally wrong does not mean that they are *equally* wrong, and when they are not, then the agent *is* culpable for failing to choose the one that is less wrong" (emphasis in original). He fails to appreciate that in a tragic choice, one is wrong and culpable even when one chooses the lesser evil.

18. Note also, as previously mentioned, that in virtue ethics, the line between the right choice and that which is not right cannot be clearly and precisely drawn. It is easier to know that the choice of war is right when facing a Hitler-like regime, compared to facing one that is less evil.

19. Aristotle's methodology for doing virtue ethics is to use the appearances (*phainomena*), including what is commonly believed (*endoxa*), as the starting points and the basis for moral knowledge. See Martha C. Nussbaum, "Saving Aristotle's Appearances" in *The Fragility of Goodness* (Cambridge:

Cambridge University Press, 1986), who contrasts Aristotle with Plato who attempts to find a God's eye viewpoint for deciding on the truth.

20. Many American politicians have held an alternative explanation, namely that Western Europeans have benefited from American protection and the nuclear umbrella provided by the United States.

21. For instance, a superpower like the United States could pretend after 9/11 that it was in continual danger of devastating attack from small and mid-sized nations as well as non-state groups whose members number in the hundreds. This was used to justify a policy of "destroy or be destroyed" (in Bush's words, "fighting them there so that we don't have to fight them here") toward other states similar to the Romans' policy, despite the obvious difference that in the ancient world, defeat at the hands of enemies often meant the execution of all males and the enslavement of all women and children, and the only recourse lay in using all means possible to defeat the enemy militarily.

22. Recall that in virtue ethics, following Aristotle, the criterion for right action is that which would be chosen by a person of practical wisdom in such circumstances.

23. This is Aristotle's point in the *Nicomachean Ethics* about not looking for more precision than the subject matter allows.

24. I have previously used this method of comparison in my paper, "A Reappraisal of the Doctrine of Doing and Allowing," in *Action, Ethics, and Responsibility*, ed. Joseph Keim Campbell, Michael O'Rourke & Harry S. Silverstein (Cambridge, Mass.: The MIT Press, 2010), pp. 25–45.

Bibliography

Annan, Kofi, Address of the Secretary-General to the United Nations General Assembly on 23 September, 2003.

Anscombe, G. E. M., "War and Murder" in *The Collected Philosophical Papers of G.E.M. Anscombe, Vol. 3* (Minneapolis: University of Minnesota Press, 1981), pp. 51–61.

Aquinas, Thomas, *Summa Theologica*, trans. Fathers of the English Dominican Province (London: Burns, Oates & Washburne, 1920–42).

Archibugi, Daniele & Young, Iris Marion, "Envisioning a Global Rule of Law" in *Terrorism and International Justice*, ed. James P. Sterba (New York: Oxford University Press, 2003), pp. 158–70.

Arendt, Hannah, *Eichmann in Jerusalem* (New York: Penguin, 1965).

Aristotle, *Nicomachean Ethics*, trans. David Ross (New York: Oxford University Press, 1998).

Augustine, *The City of God*, trans. Henry Bettenson (Harmondsworth: Penguin, 1984).

Bainton, Roland H., *Christian Attitudes toward War and Peace* (New York: Abingdon Press, 1960).

Beevor, Antony, *D-Day: The Battle for Normandy* (New York: Viking, 2009).

Bennett, Jonathan, "Morality and Consequences" in the *1980 Tanner Lectures on Human Values*, ed. S. McMurrin (Salt Lake City: University of Utah Press, 1981), pp. 45–116.

Boyle, Joseph, "Just War Doctrine and the Military Response to Terrorism," *The Journal of Political Philosophy* 11 (2003), pp. 153–70.

Brock, Gillian, "Humanitarian Intervention: Closing the Gap between Theory and Practice," *Journal of Applied Philosophy* 23 (2006), pp. 277–91.

Brown, Gary D., "Proportionality and Just War," *Journal of Military Ethics* 2 (2003), pp. 171–85.

Buchanan, Allen, "Justifying Preventive War" in *Preemption*, ed. Henry Shue & David Rodin (Oxford: Oxford University Press, 2007), pp. 126–42.

Burnham, Gilbert; Lafta, Riyadh; Doocy, Shannon & Roberts, Les, "Mortality after the 2003 Invasion of Iraq: A Cross-Sectional Cluster Sample Survey," *The Lancet* (October 2006), pp. 1–8.

Caesar, Julius, *The Gallic War*, trans. H.J. Edwards (Cambridge, Mass.: Harvard University Press, 1952).

Card, Claudia, *The Atrocity Paradigm: A Theory of Evil* (New York: Oxford University Press, 2002).

—— "Ticking Bombs and Interrogations," presented at the Central Division APA Meeting in Chicago on 28 April, 2006.

Carmola, Kateri, "The Concept of Proportionality: Old Questions and New Ambiguities" in *Just War Theory: A Reappraisal*, ed. Mark Evans (New York: Palgrave Macmillan, 2005), pp. 93–113.

Chan, David K., "A Reappraisal of the Doctrine of Doing and Allowing" in *Action, Ethics, and Responsibility*, ed. Joseph Keim Campbell, Michael O'Rourke & Harry S. Silverstein (Cambridge, Mass.: The MIT Press, 2010), pp. 25–45.

—— "Are There Extrinsic Desires?" *Nous* 38 (2004), pp. 326–50.

—— "Courage and Those Who Will Not Fight," presented at Conference on Courage at Viterbo University, La Crosse, Wisconsin on March 29, 2008 and available at http://www.viterbo.edu/ethics.aspx?id=33622

—— "How War Affects People: Lessons from Euripides," *Philosophy in the Contemporary World* 13 (2006), pp. 1–5.

—— "Intention and Responsibility in Double Effect Cases," *Ethical Theory and Moral Practice* 3 (2000), pp. 405–34.

—— "Morality, Prudence, and the Limits of War Conventions," presented at the 2009 International Society for Military Ethics (ISME) Symposium.

—— "Reasoning without Comparing," *American Philosophical Quarterly* 47 (2010), pp. 153–64.

—— "Self-Defense and Possible Threats" (unpublished manuscript).

—— "The Myth of Religious War," Ethics Center Lecture presented at California State University – Fresno on 2 February, 2009.

Cicero, Marcus Tullius, *De Officiis*, ed. M.T. Griffin & E.M. Atkins (Cambridge: Cambridge University Press, 1991).

—— *De Re Publica*, ed. James E.G. Zetzel (New York: Cambridge University Press, 1999).

Clausewitz, Carl von, *On War*, trans. Michael Howard & Peter Paret (Princeton, NJ: Princeton University Press, 1976).

Coady, C.A.J., "Natural Law and Weapons of Mass Destruction" in *Ethics and Weapons of Mass Destruction*, ed. Sohail H. Hashmi & Steven P. Lee (Cambridge: Cambridge University Press, 2004), pp. 111–31.

—— "The Ethics of Armed Humanitarian Intervention," *US Institute of Peace Policy Paper* (July 2002).

Coates, A.J., *The Ethics of War* (Manchester: Manchester University Press, 1997).

Collins, Larry & Lapierre, Dominique, *Freedom at Midnight* (New York: Simon & Schuster, 1975).

Cook, Martin L., "Michael Walzer's Concept of 'Supreme Emergency'," *Journal of Military Ethics* 6 (2007), pp. 138–51.

Danner, Mark, "The Secret Way to War," *New York Review of Books* (9 June, 2005).

Dawson, Doyne, *The Origins of Western Warfare: Militarism and Morality in the Ancient World* (Boulder, Colo.: Westview Press, 1996).

Ferrill, Arther, *The Origins of War: From the Stone Age to Alexander the Great* (London: Thames and Hudson, 1985).

Fiala, Andrew, *The Just War Myth: The Moral Illusions of War* (Lanham: Rowman & Littlefield, 2008).

Foot, Philippa, *Natural Goodness* (Oxford: Oxford University Press, 2001).

Gentili, Alberico, *De Jure Belli Libri Tres*, trans. John C. Rolfe (Oxford: Clarendon Press, 1933).

Gilbert, Paul, *New Terror, New Wars* (Washington, DC: Georgetown University Press, 2003).

Glover, Jonathan, *Humanity: A Moral History of the Twentieth Century* (New Haven: Yale University Press, 1999).

Gross, Michael L., "Assassination and Targeted Killing: Law Enforcement, Execution or Self-Defense?" *Journal of Applied Philosophy* 23 (2006), pp. 323–35.
—— *Moral Dilemmas of Modern War* (New York: Cambridge University Press, 2010).
Grotius, Hugo, *On the Law of War and Peace*, trans. Francis W. Kelsey (Oxford: Clarendon Press, 1925).
Hartigan, R., "Saint Augustine on War and Killing: The Problem of the Innocent," *Journal of the History of Ideas* 27 (1966), pp. 195–204.
Herman, Arthur, *Gandhi and Churchill* (London: Arrow Books, 2009).
Hoag, Robert W., "Violent Civil Disobedience: Defending Human Rights, Rethinking Just War" in *Rethinking the Just War Tradition*, ed. Michael W. Brough, John W. Lango & Harry van der Linden (Albany: State University of New York Press, 2007), pp. 223–42.
Hobbes, Thomas, *Leviathan*, ed. Richard Tuck (New York: Cambridge University Press, 1991).
Huntington, Samuel, "The Clash of Civilizations?" *Foreign Affairs* 72: 3 (1993), pp. 22–49.
Hurka, Thomas, "Proportionality in the Morality of War," *Philosophy and Public Affairs* 33 (2005), pp. 34–66.
Ignatieff, Michael, "Annals of Diplomacy: Balkan Physics," *New Yorker* (10 May, 1999).
Johnson, James Turner, *Just War Tradition and the Restraint of War* (Princeton: Princeton University Press, 1981).
—— *Morality and Contemporary Warfare* (New Haven: Yale University Press, 1999).
—— *The War to Oust Saddam Hussein: Just War and the New Face of Conflict* (Lanham: Rowman & Littlefield, 2005).
Kaldor, Mary, *New and Old Wars* (Cambridge: Polity Press, 1999).
—— "Elaborating the 'New War' Thesis" in *Rethinking the Nature of War*, ed. Isabelle Duyvesteyn & Jan Angstrom (London: Frank Cass, 2005), pp. 210–24.
Kant, Immanuel, *Critique of Practical Reason*, trans. Lewis White Beck (Indianapolis: Bobbs-Merrill, 1956).
—— *Groundwork of the Metaphysic of Morals*, trans. H. J. Paton (New York: Harper & Row, 1964).
—— *The Metaphysics of Morals*, trans. Mary Gregor (Cambridge: Cambridge University Press, 1991).
—— *Religion within the Limits of Reason Alone*, trans. Theodore M. Greene & Hoyt H. Hudson (New York: Harper & Row, 1960).
Keegan, John, *A History of Warfare* (Toronto: Key Porter Books, 1993).
Kekes, John, *The Roots of Evil* (Ithaca: Cornell University Press, 2005).
Lesnor, Carl. "The 'Good' War," *The Philosophical Forum* 36: 1 (2005), pp. 77–85.
Levi, Primo, *The Drowned and the Saved* (New York: Vintage, 1989).
Luban, David, "Just War and Human Rights," *Philosophy and Public Affairs* 9 (1980), pp. 160–81.
—— "Preventive War and Human Rights" in *Preemption*, ed. Henry Shue & David Rodin (Oxford: Oxford University Press, 2007), pp. 171–201.
Lucas, George R. Jr., "From *jus ad bellum* to *jus ad pacem*: Re-thinking Just-war Criteria for the Use of Military Force for Humanitarian Ends" in *Ethics and Foreign Intervention*, ed. Deen K. Chatterjee & Don E. Scheid (Cambridge: Cambridge University Press, 2003), pp. 72–96.

Machiavelli, *Discourses on Livy*, trans. Julia Conaway Bondanella & Peter Bondanella (New York : Oxford University Press, 1997).

Martin, Rex, "Just Wars and Humanitarian Interventions," *Journal of Social Philosophy* 36 (2005), pp. 439–56.

McMahan, Jeff, "On the Moral Equality of Combatants," *Journal of Political Philosophy* 14 (2006), 377–93.

—— "Preventive War and the Killing of the Innocent" in *The Ethics of War: Shared Problems in Different Traditions*, ed. Richard Sorabji & David Rodin (Aldershot: Ashgate, 2006), pp. 169–90.

—— "The Ethics of Killing in War," *Ethics* 114 (2004), pp. 693–733.

Mearsheimer, John J. & Walt, Stephen M., "The Israel Lobby," *London Review of Books* 28: 6 (2006), pp. 3–12.

Metcalf, Barbara D. & Metcalf, Thomas R., *A Concise History of Modern India*, 2nd edn. (New York: Cambridge University Press, 2006).

Miller, Richard W., "Respectable Oppressors, Hypocritical Liberators: Morality, Intervention, and Reality" in *Ethics and Foreign Intervention*, ed. Deen K. Chatterjee & Don E. Scheid (Cambridge: Cambridge University Press, 2003), pp. 215–50.

—— "Terrorism, War, and Empire" in *Terrorism and International Justice*, ed. James P. Sterba (New York: Oxford University Press, 2003), pp. 186–205.

Murphy, Jeffrie G., "The Killing of the Innocent" in *War, Morality, and the Military Profession*, ed. Malham M. Wakin (Boulder: Westview Press, 1979), pp. 343–69.

Nagel, Thomas, "War and Massacre," *Philosophy and Public Affairs* 1 (1972), pp. 123–44.

National Conference of Catholic Bishops, *The Challenge of Peace* (1983).

Nussbaum, Martha C., "Non-Relative Virtues: An Aristotelian Approach" in *Midwest Studies in Philosophy*, Vol. 13, ed. Peter A. French, Theodore E. Uehling Jr., & Howard K. Wettstein (Notre Dame: University of Notre Dame Press, 1988), pp. 32–53.

—— *The Fragility of Goodness* (Cambridge: Cambridge University Press, 1986).

O'Hear, Anthony, "Editorial: The Just War," *Philosophy* 78 (2003), pp. 317–18.

Orend, Brian, "Is There a Supreme Emergency Exemption?" in *Just War Theory: A Reappraisal*, ed. Mark Evans (New York: Palgrave Macmillan, 2005), pp. 134–53.

Orwin, Clifford, "Humanitarian Military Intervention: Wars for the End of History?" *Social Philosophy and Policy* (2006), pp. 196–217.

Phillips, Scott, "Racial Disparities in the Capital of Capital Punishment," *Houston Law Review* 45 (2008).

Pogge, Thomas, "Making War on Terrorists – Reflections on Harming the Innocent," *The Journal of Political Philosophy* 16 (2008), pp. 1–25.

Pojman, Louis P., "The Moral Response to Terrorism and Cosmopolitanism" in *Terrorism and International Justice*, ed. James P. Sterba (New York: Oxford University Press, 2003), pp. 135–57.

Quinn, Warren, "Actions, Intentions, and Consequences: The Doctrine of Double Effect" in *Morality and Action*, ed. Philippa Foot (Cambridge: Cambridge University Press, 1993), pp. 175–97.

Ramsey, Paul, *War and the Christian Conscience* (Durham, NC: Duke University Press, 1961).

Rawls, John, *A Theory of Justice* (Cambridge, Mass.: Harvard University Press, 1971).
—— *The Law of Peoples* (Cambridge, Mass.: Harvard University Press, 1999).
Rodin, David, "The Problem with Prevention" in *Preemption*, ed. Henry Shue & David Rodin (Oxford: Oxford University Press, 2007), pp. 143–70.
—— *War and Self-Defense* (Oxford: Clarendon Press, 2002).
Russell, Frederick H., *The Just War in the Middle Ages* (Cambridge: Cambridge University Press, 1975).
Seneca, *"De Clementia"* in *Moral and Political Essays*, trans. John M. Cooper & J. F. Procopé (New York: Cambridge University Press, 1995).
Shue, Henry, "Liberalism: The Impossibility of Justifying Weapons of Mass Destruction" in *Ethics and Weapons of Mass Destruction*, ed. Sohail H. Hashmi & Steven P. Lee (Cambridge: Cambridge University Press, 2004), pp. 139–62.
—— "What Would a Justified Preventive Military Attack Look Like?" in *Preemption*, ed. Henry Shue & David Rodin (Oxford: Oxford University Press, 2007), pp. 222–46.
Statman, Daniel, "Moral Tragedies, Supreme Emergencies and National-Defense," *Journal of Applied Philosophy* 23 (2006), pp. 311–22.
Sterba, James, "Terrorism and International Justice" in *Terrorism and International Justice*, ed. James P. Sterba (New York: Oxford University Press, 2003), pp. 206–28.
Stocker, Michael, "Dirty Hands and Ordinary Life" in *Plural and Conflicting Values* (Oxford: Clarendon Press, 1990), pp. 9–36.
Struhl, Karsten J., "Is War a Morally Legitimate Response to Terrorism?" *The Philosophical Forum* 36 (2005), pp. 129–37.
Styron, William, *Sophie's Choice* (New York: Random House, 1979).
Thomson, Judith Jarvis, "Killing, Letting Die, and the Trolley Problem" in *Rights, Restitution, and Risk*, ed. William Parent (Cambridge, Mass.: Harvard University Press, 1986), pp. 78–93.
—— "Self-Defense," *Philosophy and Public Affairs* 20 (1991), pp. 283–310.
—— "The Trolley Problem" in *Rights, Restitution, and Risk*, ed. William Parent (Cambridge, Mass.: Harvard University Press, 1986), pp. 94–116.
Walzer, Michael, "A Liberal Perspective on Deterrence and Proliferation of Weapons of Mass Destruction" in *Ethics and Weapons of Mass Destruction*, ed. Sohail H. Hashmi & Steven P. Lee (Cambridge: Cambridge University Press, 2004), pp. 163–7.
—— "After 9/11: Five Questions about Terrorism" in *Arguing about War* (New Haven: Yale University Press, 2004), pp.130–42.
—— "Emergency Ethics" in *Arguing about War* (New Haven: Yale University Press, 2004), pp. 33–50.
—— *Just and Unjust Wars* (New York: Basic Books, 1977).
—— "Political Action: The Problem of Dirty Hands," *Philosophy and Public Affairs* 2 (1973), pp. 160–80.
—— "The Politics of Rescue" in *Arguing about War* (New Haven: Yale University Press, 2004), pp. 67–81.
Weigel, George, "The Just War Tradition and the World after September 11," *Logos: A Journal of Catholic Thought and Culture* 5 (2002), pp. 13–44.

Wellman, Carl, "On Terrorism Itself," *Journal of Value Inquiry* 13 (1979), pp. 250–8.

Westlake, John, *International Law, Part II: War*, 2nd edn (Cambridge: Cambridge University Press, 1913).

Williams, Bernard, *Morality: An Introduction to Ethics* (New York: Harper & Row, 1972).

Woodward, P.A. (ed.), *The Doctrine of Double Effect* (Notre Dame: University of Notre Dame Press, 2001).

Yoder, John Howard, "When War is Unjust: Being Honest in Just-War Thinking" in *The Morality of War*, ed. Larry May, Eric Rovie & Steve Viner (Upper Saddle River, NJ: Pearson Prentice Hall, 2006), pp. 153–9.

Index

absolutism, 59, 174, 192n4
Abu Ghraib, 147
Afghanistan, 1, 95, 138, 141, 143, 146,
    169–70, 208n83
    see also Taliban
Alexander the Great, 46
Al-Qaeda, 1, 28, 138, 140, 142–3, 159,
    171, 208n82
    see also bin Laden, Osama
Ambrose, 11
America, see United States of America
American Civil War (1860–64), 125–6
Amnesty International, 202n10
Annan, Kofi, 207n70
Anscombe, Gertrude Elizabeth
    Margaret, 36, 39, 189n8
Aquinas, Thomas, 14–15, 35,
    188n13
Archibugi, Daniele, 203n22
Arendt, Hannah, 70
Aristotle, 14, 62–4, 103–4, 113, 126,
    129, 190n19, 200n18, 209n19,
    210n22–3
asymmetric war, 188n24
atomic bombs, see nuclear weapons
Augustine, 11–13, 34, 47
Aztecs, 110, 198n31

Bainton, Roland H., 188n7
Balkan conflict, 28
    in Bosnia-Herzegovina, 78,
    114–15, 118
    in Kosovo, 44, 78, 132
    see also new wars
Beevor, Antony, 194n12
Bennett, Jonathan, 190n17
bin Laden, Osama, 1, 141, 145,
    208n83
    killing of, 169–72
bombing, 25, 77
    atomic, 25, 37, 38, 45, 72, 82, 140,
    150, 151, 189n12, 202n18; see also
    Hiroshima

of cities, 59, 141, 152, 173, 177–9,
    190n14, 198n29, 203n20,
    208n4
    strategic, 35–6
    suicide, 29, 203n19, 208n84
    terror, 35, 37, 101, 190n17,
    198n28–9
Bonhoeffer, Dietrich, 113, 128, 130,
    199n43, 209n16
Boyle, Joseph, 187n4, 203n27
Britain, 74, 80
    in India, 123, 200n14
    and Iraq, 203n26
    in World War Two, 107, 179
Brock, Gillian, 202n11
Brown, Gary D., 191n33
Buchanan, Allen, 162, 207n72
Burnham, Gilbert, 203n26
Bush, George W., 88, 138, 195n20,
    210n21
Bush administration, 29, 83, 138,
    140, 143, 158–9, 192n46, 197n19,
    203n23
Bush doctrine, 1, 158–60, 162–3,
    168, 206n64

Caen, see D-Day
Caesar, Julius, 10, 187n6
Cajetan, Thomas de Vio, 15
Calvin, John (Jean), 16
Card, Claudia, xiii, 70, 71, 72,
    194n6, 195n22, 197n18,
    197n27
Carmola, Kateri, 190n19, 204n31
Carthage, 195n4, 209n9
Chamberlain, Neville, 30, 109,
    192n46
character, 39, 64, 103–5, 113, 130,
    185–6, 194n6
    see also virtue(s)
chemical weapons, 91, 150, 159
Cheney, Dick, 195n20, 196n16
chivalry, 41, 44

CPSIA information can be obtained
at www.ICGtesting.com
Printed in the USA
BVHW04*1818200918
528090BV00007B/28/P